Bernie, Bill, and the Browns

The Last Great Era of Football in Cleveland

Vince McKee

Indianapolis, Indiana

Bernie, Bill, and the Browns:
The Last Great Era of Football in Cleveland

Published by Blue River Press
Indianapolis, Indiana
www.brpressbooks.com

Distributed by Cardinal Publishers Group
Tom Doherty Company, Inc.
www.cardinalpub.com

ISBN: 978-1-68157-011-2

Author: Vince McKee
Editor: Teresa Abney
Interior Design: Dave Reed
Cover Design: Phillip Velikan
Cover Photograph: AP Images #673314574433

Printed in the United States of America

Acknowledgements

I want to thank my parents Don and Maria McKee for always being there for me and encouraging me over the years. I know I have your full support at all times and it keeps me going. Thank you both for taking care of me when I was badly sick in the summer of 2015, and I promise next time I won't wait so long to go to the emergency room. Thank you for raising me the right way, to be respectful, to give to charity, and to always remember that with God anything is possible. No amount of money in the world can ever buy what we have and what you taught me and Donald growing up.

Thank you to the *Cleveland Plain Dealer* who brought me on as a high school beat reporter in the fall of 2015, and helped me reach a dream I worked a lifetime to achieve. Thank you to my brother Don and my sister Abbie. You two have always been in my corner and believed in me years ago when I was first getting started. To my little buddy Matt, I'm ready to wrestle you one more time for the World Wrestling Championship of the Galaxy!

I want to send a special thanks to Bill Belichick, for a phone call that changed my life and outlook on life in many ways. For a long time I needed that confidence, you gave it to me in one phone call and I thank you! Thank you to Jim Friguglietti for your continued guidance. Last but not least, I want to thank my lord and savior Jesus Christ, it is through your work that all is work is done.

Dedication

This book is dedicated to my wife Emily and my daughter Maggie. You remain my rock, my reason for breathing and the biggest reason to get out of bed in the morning to face a world full of challenges. I have no idea where I would be if it wasn't for you both. You give me the energy during the 2 a.m. writing sessions and the long road trips in which I do multiple book signings in one day. I love you both dearly and our family "snuggle" times are better than any amusement park in the world.

Contents

Chapter One

The New Era Begins

The story of the Orange and Brown dates back to 1946 when owner Mickey McBride formed the team and hired legendary coach Paul Brown, who won several championships. Thus began a dynasty that is still respected sixty plus years later. Under the reign of Paul Brown, the Cleveland franchise won the AAFC championship four times in 1946, 1947, 1948 and 1949. Their dominance upon entering the National Football League was just as good as they won the NFL Championship in 1950, 1954 and 1955. In the earliest days of professional football, the Cleveland Browns were the most coveted and respected franchise in existence.

The Cleveland Browns last won the NFL Championship in 1964 with a group of players drafted and trained by Paul Brown. Despite Brown not being there, his impact still loomed over the team, and was a huge reason they took home the title in 1964. They were coached by Blanton Collier but it seemed as though their dynasty built under Paul Brown would continue on with several more championships; however, it was the last world championship Cleveland has obtained in any major sport.

They returned to the NFL championship game three more times in the next four years. They lost all three times to the Green Bay Packers, Baltimore Colts, and Minnesota Vikings. By that point and time, the NFL winner was playing the AFL winner in a championship game known as the Super Bowl. They fell short of the championship game in 1971 and 1972 with losses to the Baltimore Colts and Miami Dolphins. They went the rest of the 1970s without making it back to the playoffs.

The first half of the 1980s were every bit as rough. Even when they made the playoffs in 1980, they lost in gut-wrenching fashion at home, to the Oakland Raiders, when league MVP Brian Sipe threw a fatal interception in the closing seconds that allowed Oakland to win the game. It was forever known as "Red Right

88", as that was the name of the play that Sipe falsely called in the huddle. Two years later, they returned to the playoffs but they lost to the Los Angeles Raiders, as they had moved out of Oakland by that point. The Cleveland Browns were tough and being led by the Defensive Rookie of the Year, Chip Banks.

Nevertheless, they failed to make it back to the playoffs the following two seasons, which led to the off-season of 1984 going into 1985, where the course of Cleveland Browns football would be forever changed. They had been slowly building a dynamic nucleus of young talent, and it would be up to newly appointed head coach Marty Schottenheimer to mold it all together. Schottenheimer had taken over for former head coach Sam Rutigliano midway through the 1984 season, and led the Browns to a 4–4 record in his time as coach.

Marty Schottenheimer was a former professional football player drafted in the seventh round of the 1965 American Football League by the Buffalo Bills. He was a linebacker for the Buffalo Bills during their 1965 AFL Championship season. He played well in Buffalo and was eventually selected to the AFL All-Star Team. Schottenheimer retired from football in 1971 and spent the next several years away from the game until deciding to return as a coach in 1974. He became the linebacker's coach for the Portland Storm of the World Foot-ball League. In 1975, he returned to the NFL as he was hired as a linebackers coach for the NFL's New York Giants, and in 1977 became defensive coordinator.

In 1980, he was hired as the defensive coordinator for the Cleveland Browns and took over for head coach Sam Rutigliano midway through their disappointing 1984 season. Schottenheimer was a hard nose coach, but one the players liked and respected. The team's owner, Art Modell, believed the move to Schottenheimer was exactly what the team needed to end their playoff drought.

The lineup boasted All-Pro tight end Ozzie Newsome who was in the midst of a Hall of Fame career. Nicknamed "The Wizard of Oz", Newsome had a stellar career at the University Alabama, starting in all four years that he attended school there. Newsome accumulated 102 receptions for 2,070 receiving yards and sixteen touchdowns. His 20.3 average yards per catch was a Southeastern Conference record for over twenty years. Newsome was named the

Alabama Player of the Decade for the 1970s as he was a two-time All-SEC player (in 1976 and 1977). He was drafted by the Cleveland Browns with the twenty-third overall pick in the 1978 NFL Draft. He had a great first season with the Brown and Orange and was voted the Cleveland Browns' Offensive Player of the Year, which was unheard of for a rookie at that time but Newsome fit the billing. In 1984, he set a record for most yards in a game (191), which was later broken by Josh Gordon. It was also good enough to earn him his second pro bowl selection.

Joining Newsome on the offense side of the ball was running back Kevin Mack. He was selected by the Cleveland Browns in the first round (eleventh overall) of the 1984 NFL Supplemental Draft of USFL and CFL Players. He was a bruising back out of Clemson University, and was the power back that Marty Schottenheimer was counting on to move the chains or plunge ahead for six points at the goal line.

Kevin Mack would join Earnest Byner in the backfield. Byner was drafted the prior season out of East Carolina University. He was a quick back and also an excellent pass catcher out of the backfield. Earnest Byner had a solid rookie season as he ran for 426 yards on only seventy-two carries. He was a backup to Mike Pruitt but the Cleveland Browns knew that Byner would step up his role big time in 1985 if given the opportunity. The two would soon prove to be a dangerous combo that many team defenses struggled to contain.

Also returning to the offensive scheme was second year wide receiver Brian Brennan. He was out of Boston College and had a strong rookie showing in 1984 despite poor quarterback play from Paul McDonald. Used mainly as a punt returner, Brennan made the most of his time lining up as receiver. Brennan was impressive as he caught thirty-five balls and racked up 455 yards. It was clear that Brennan would also be a major part of the offense moving forward.

Brian Brennan talks about his transition from playing with Doug Flutie at Boston College, to being drafted and playing pro-football in Cleveland:

> *"I had gone to Brother Rice High School in Detroit, which is a very prestigious high school known for its high football standards. It was a smooth transition to Boston College because I was used*

to being around high caliber athletes. However, when I went from Boston College to the Cleveland Browns, it was a significant change. The speed and size of the athlete itself was much more accomplished on the pro level. It was a big change to get used to, especially the quickness of the defensive backs I would have to face. All of them were so much quicker than I was used to facing against in college. The hitting was a large difference as well when you consider the force of the blow. I had played in the Big East and it was pretty good back then, but it was still a big step up in competition."

Brian Brennan goes on to talk about playing for Coach Schottenheimer:

"Marty is a bright person, so playing for a guy like that...you knew that our strategy would be very sound. He wasn't going to leave any stone unturned in preparation. He knew everything; he knew what every player's assignment was on offense and what every player's assignment was on defense. He even knew what every player's assignment was on special teams. He knew every assignment for every person on every play. Because of this, he always had us very well prepared for each game and each play. It works well when you have some skilled players with a coaching staff that they believe in because of how detailed their preparation was. It was a good formula and we felt that, with Marty at the helm, he would always put us in the proper situations. We knew where to be on every single play and weren't about to spin our wheels... this was made possible by the work we did in practice that week under the leadership under Marty. From a player's standpoint, everyone had faith in him and belief in his mottos of one play at a time. He would express that we just needed to beat the man in front of you. Those are things we lived by and when you do those things and believe in the coach...believe in the players around you...it leads to success on the field."

The defense also had several players returning to the lineup, including star defensive back Hanford Dixon. He was drafted by the Cleveland Browns out of the University of Southern Mississippi with the twenty-second pick in the first round of the 1981 NFL Draft. He looked increasingly better his first four years in the league. He finished the 1984 season with five interceptions and was becoming a player that opposing quarterbacks looked to avoid throwing too.

Dixon would be joined by Frank Minnifield in the backfield and they would quickly become a dynamic duo. Frank Minnifield was considered too small for college football at just five foot, nine inches and 140 pounds, but used heart and hustle to walk on the University of Louisville's football team, earning a scholarship spot for his final three years. He joined the USFL out of college as he went on to play for the Chicago Blitz and eventually the Arizona Wranglers. Minnifield left the USFL in 1984 and played his rookie season with the Cleveland Browns alongside Dixon. He would become known for his aggressive bump-and-run coverage and hard-hitting style. His career took off playing with Dixon and he was eventually voted to the NFL 1980s All-Decade Team as selected by voters of the Pro Football Hall of Fame. The Cleveland Browns' fans fed off the energy brought on by Dixon and Minnifield; thus, the "Dawg Pound" was created. It was the side of the stadium packed with fans near the goal line, known for their antics during the Cleveland Browns' home games at the old Cleveland Municipal Stadium inspired by Dixon's "barking" to teammates.

Clay Matthews was anchoring the defense; he was the hungry linebacker who was eating up quarterbacks with sacks every chance he got. He finished 1984 with twelve sacks and three forced fumbles. Matthews was a beast and wide receivers would fear going on a short slant route anywhere near where he was roaming. He was a first round pick of the Cleveland Browns back in 1978, and was having a stellar career. He was the perfect style of linebacker to wreak havoc in Marty Schottenheimer's defensive scheme.

Football was in the bloodline of Matthews. His father, Clay, played offensive tackle for the San Francisco 49ers for one season before having to leave the team and fight in the Korean War. As a paratrooper in the United States Army, he was part of the 82nd Airborne Division. He eventually returned home from the war and played three more seasons for the 49ers before retiring.

Matthews' brother, Bruce, would go on to play offensive guard and center for the Houston Oilers and Tennessee Titans for nineteen seasons, eventually earning NFL Hall of Fame honors. It was always a thrill for the Matthews boys for them to line up across from each other when the Houston Oilers played the Cleveland Browns. Their sons Clay the III, Bryce Matthews, and Jake Matthews all wound up playing in the NFL as well.

The table was set as the nucleus was slowly taking shape on both sides of the ball. Marty Schottenheimer seemed to have the pulse of the team in his hands and the Cleveland Browns were looking strong overall. However, they still had one glaring weakness, and that was Paul McDonald at quarterback. McDonald had started all sixteen games in the 1984 season and struggled doing so. He threw for 3,472 yards and fourteen touchdowns, but also threw a frightening twenty-three interceptions. The Cleveland Browns made a move in the off-season to replace McDonald with the veteran Gary Danielson, but also had a plan in place to secure a much bigger and younger name, to eventually become the face of the franchise. That young man's name was Bernie Kosar!

Chapter Two

Bernie Kosar

One of the most beloved Cleveland Browns of all time was quarterback Bernie Kosar. Number nineteen was a fan favorite during his entire career in Cleveland. He was drafted in the summer of 1985 and made an instant impact upon his arrival. He was behind center during three separate trips to the AFC Championship game. He never took the Cleveland Browns to the Super Bowl, but he did come closer three times than any other quarterback in team history. He possessed pin-point accuracy and an ability to read defenses like no quarterback before him ever did. He was a record setter for most passes in a row without an interception in team history, tossing 308 in a row during the 1990–1991 season.

Bernie Kosar was born in Youngstown, Ohio and grew up in Boardman, Ohio. Needless to say, he was a Cleveland Browns' fan. He was a standout quarterback at Boardman High School where he received All American Honors in his senior season there. He was also a star pitcher on their baseball team.

Kosar was highly touted out of high school and chose to play his college ball at the University of Miami. They ran a passing oriented style offense that was tailor-made for a man of Kosar's skills. Kosar was red-shirted in 1982, but then he started all twelve games as a freshman in 1983. He completed 61.5 percent of his passes for 2,328 yards and fifteen touchdowns, leading the Hurricanes to an 11–1 regular season, and a berth in the Orange Bowl against top-ranked Nebraska. It was an incredible season for a freshman to have, and it had the nation talking about Kosar and his chances of leading the Hurricanes to a possible upset over high-powered Nebraska.

Kosar led the Hurricanes to a 31–30 upset win over the Nebraska Cornhuskers. The Miami University Hurricanes were now National Champions thanks to Kosar's great play. His performance in the game was so good that it earned him MVP of the Orange

Bowl honors. It proved that despite his young age, Kosar was mentally and physically skilled years ahead of what his youth would indicate. He had the ability to lead, which was almost unheard of for a freshman quarterback in such a big moment.

The 1984 season proved to be another masterful one as he set Hurricane season records with 3,642 yards and twenty-five touchdowns. He was also a second-team All-American, and finished fourth in Heisman Trophy voting. Kosar's career completion percentage of 62.3 percent is still a Hurricanes' record. He played his final college game in the 1985 Fiesta Bowl against UCLA; Kosar completed thity-one of forty-four passes for 294 yards. He also had two touchdown passes and one interception in the 39–37 loss.

Kosar decided to leave college early and because of his superior intelligence he was able to finish his academic qualifications way ahead of pace. He graduated from college with a double major in Finance and Economics. He took eighteen credit hours during the spring of 1985, and an additional six credit hours during the summer in order to graduate early. He was so smart it just made his play on the field even better because coaches knew he could make adjustments to any strategy he saw within a second's notice.

Before Kosar could graduate college, however, there was a little drama regarding his eligibility to play in the National Football League. Under National Football League rules at the time, only seniors and graduates could be drafted. Kosar, who was scheduled to graduate over the summer from the University of Miami's Business School with a double major, had two years of college eligibility remaining and made it clear he would only enter the Draft if he could play for the Cleveland Browns. He even went as far as to say he would skip the normal NFL Draft if that's what it took.

On April 10, the National Football League's spokesman, Joe Browne, announced that if Kosar decided to play in the 1985 season, then the league would hold a Supplemental Draft for him and other eligible players. The Cleveland Browns and Kosar both eventually got their way, and Kosar was selected by the team in the supplemental draft.

Bernie Kosar arrived in Cleveland at a perfect time because the Browns were in desperate need of solid quarterback play coming off of a 5–11 season. Despite the fact that the plan was for Kosar to sit behind starting quarterback Gary Danielson to observe and learn for a season, fans knew that it was only a matter of time before Kosar would get his chance to shine.

Kosar was always in command of the huddle.
Photo courtesy of George Lilja

Joining Bernie Kosar on the Cleveland Browns's team would be fellow rookie, wide receiver Reggie Langhorne from Elizabeth City State University. He was a third round Draft pick and would be a nice compliment to Brian Brennan. Langhorne would become one of Kosar's favorite targets as the years went on. Langhorne discusses his decision to turn pro and what it was like to be drafted by the Cleveland Browns:

> *"When I came out of high school, my initial dream was to be in the military, however because of several scholarship offers I decided to go to college instead. It worked out well as I was eventually drafted into the NFL. I was lucky to have a hard enough work ethic and skills to turn football into a career. I didn't realize the rich history of football in Cleveland until I arrived and got to be a part of the organization. I grew up watching the Redskins and Raiders, so Cleveland was never a team on my radar."*

Also arriving in the beginning of the 1985 season was safety Felix Wright. He took the non-conventional way to the NFL, as he played several seasons in the Canadian Football League with the Hamilton Tiger Cats after playing his college ball at Drake University. He signed with the Cleveland Browns in the 1985 off-season, and was ready to come in and make an impact. He explains the circumstances that brought him to Cleveland:

> *"It was a no brainer for me at that start as I was just going to play for the highest bidder because that means they are the team that is the most interested in you. It was awesome because at the time I didn't even realize what kind of opportunity I had. I didn't know too much about Bernie Kosar until I arrived in Cleveland. When I arrived, I learned that he was locally brought up in Boardman, Ohio and was a superstar there. He had a great college career at Miami and made a point of wanting to come play for the Browns and he got his chance to play here through the supplemental draft which was awesome. I hold Marty Schottenheimer in high regard; he is my favorite coach of all time because he is the one who gave me the opportunity to play for the Browns. He believed in me from day one when I came and worked out for the Browns. He told me that if I kept doing what I was doing, I would be the man on defense and make some things happen. It took me a couple of years to crack into the starting lineup, but he gave me a chance and he was fair...as a ballplayer, that is all you ask for is a coach to be fair and give you equal opportunity, which is what he did for me which put me*

in a great position to go out and do what I did for six years with the Browns."

Blocking on the offense line that year was George Lilja, who had come to the Browns in 1984; his prior experience was with the Los Angeles Rams and New York Jets. He describes what it was like to play for Cleveland during this exciting time:

"I was able to come to a football rich town. It was quite the difference from when I played with the Rams. The Rams had made the playoffs while I was there and couldn't even sell out their home stadium. I cannot imagine the Cleveland fan base ever having that problem...they would normally sell out weeks in advance in Cleveland. I remember noticing right away in Cleveland how close the fans and players were. The fans would be waiting for us to get to our cars in the parking lot to cheer and get autographs. They were so passionate and involved with you, so we got to know them very well and quickly. We also stayed in town after the season was done so we got to know them as our neighbors. The athlete nowadays doesn't have that bond with the fans because they leave town once the season ends. I have such fond memories of being in Cleveland, and the winning...and the big wins and just going far into the playoffs. It was great because the fans became your friends throughout your playing days there."

Lilja also recalls playing for head coach Marty Schottenheimer very fondly:

"I remember him being a very smart football coach. As a defensive coordinator, he was a master of putting defenses together that allowed us to win. I will always be thankful to Marty because he gave me the first chance to start in the NFL in 1985, and he left me there the whole year. He really did give me my first chance to get a good taste of playing in the NFL full time. He did a masterful job of using his players in the right way with the proper talent being used to put us in the perfect position to win. He was just such a smart coach!"

Bernie Kosar would get his chance much sooner than anyone thought when starter Gary Danielson injured his shoulder in the fifth week of the season. The Cleveland Browns were 2–2 at that point and in need of a spark. Kosar was able to supply them with that spark as they won the first game he played in—a 21–7 road victory against the San Diego Chargers. It was the beginning of a three-game winning streak that also saw victories over the New England Patriots and division rival Houston Oilers. It was after the three-game winning streak that Bernie Kosar and the young Cleveland Browns hit their first serious road block and suffered through a brutal four-game losing streak. It began with a nail-biting 21–20 home loss to the Los Angeles Rams, followed by a 14–7 home loss to the Washington Redskins. From there, they were on the road and lost back-to-back divisional games. First, it was a 10–9 squeaker against the hated Pittsburgh Steelers and then a 27–10 drubbing from the Cincinnati Bengals.

Offensive lineman George Lilja gives his thoughts on why Bernie Kosar made such a good quarterback, despite his young age:

> *"Bernie had come in as a new player the year I was there, and started almost right away because of the injury to Danielson. He came in and was very mature and also very smart. He had a great vision and set of eyes to see the defense clearly. He had great leadership skills and didn't hesitate to talk with receivers, linemen, and running backs between plays. He could read defensive backs better than any quarterback I have ever played with. He would meet with Webster Slaughter, Brian Brennan, and Reggie Langhorne to discuss with them the defensive tactics they were up against during the game. He was always thinking three or four plays ahead. As far as leadership skills, he knew how to take command of that huddle better than anyone I have ever seen before or since. There was one time when a rookie wide receiver ran the wrong route and then shouted at Bernie after the play. Kosar kicked him out of the huddle and set him straight. The player never did that again! The rookie got the message and became a solid receiver in the league. Bernie would rather have ten guys on the offense and play with ten, if the eleventh guy wasn't willing to be a true team player. He was so mature that even as a rookie he was able to take respect and command of the huddle, his teammates and his opponents...he was that good, that early. It was a joy to play with him. Years later, he became great at commentating Cleveland Browns' pre-season games as well. It allowed his knowledge to come out with what he sees on the field. It is hard to get a quarterback that good who can see the game ahead of him...his vision down the field and command*

of the huddle. He is one of the smartest quarterbacks to have ever played."

Bernie Kosar and his young upstart team showed their reserve once again as they rebounded to journey on an impressive three-game winning streak to put themselves right back into playoff contention. They won a 17–7 battle at home against the Buffalo Bills followed by a 24–7 victory against the Cincinnati Bengals the following week at home. They finished their three-game tear with a 35–33 shootout win against the Giants in blistery New York. They were clinging to hope with a 7–6 record. It wasn't bad considering they were playing with a rookie quarterback, and being trained by a man coaching his first full season as a NFL head coach. They lost two road games against the Seattle Seahawks and the New York Jets; but mixed in between was a home win against the Houston Oilers to finish the season with a modest 8–8 record.

The AFC central teams were weak that year, and the mediocre record still allowed the Cleveland Browns to actually win their division and to sneak into the playoffs. Their first round opponents were the Miami Dolphins who were led by a couple of legends. Miami's head coach was one of the most successful men in the history of the league, Don Shula. He was a legend and the Miami Dolphins were coming off a Super Bowl run where they had met with defeat against the San Francisco 49ers and Joe Montana only a year before.

The lead quarterback for the Miami Dolphins was the highly-touted and much respected Dan Marino. He was widely regarded as one of the best in the league and before his career would end many years later, he held almost every single passing record. Marino was coming off of a season where he passed for an incredible 4,137 yards and thirty touchdowns. His main target was Mark Clayton with 996 yards and four touchdowns. Nat Moore caught seven touchdowns and piled up 701 yards. Mark Duper was a Miami fan favorite and he went for 650 yards with three touchdowns. Bruce Hardy added to the excitement with 409 yards and four touchdowns while running back Ron Davenport chipped in with eleven touchdowns of his own.

They scored touchdowns with seemingly ease, and their place kicker Fuad Reveiz converted fifty extra points along with twenty-two field goals. Their punter Reggie Roby only had to punt fifty-nine times. They were a scoring machine and picked by many to return to the Super Bowl. It was a highly anticipated showdown with the 1985 remarkable Chicago Bears' defense. The Miami Dolphins offense had recently handed the Chicago Bears their only loss of the season on televised *Monday Night Football*, and the nation wanted to see a rematch. Before any of that could happen, however, the Dolphins would have to get past a hungry young Cleveland Browns' team.

The game took place on January 4, 1986 in front of a packed house at Joe Robbie Stadium in Miami, Florida. The Cleveland Browns were not intimidated by the high-powered offensive attack of Dan Marino and the Miami Dolphins. They were a confident bunch that knew Coach Marty would have them well prepared for the challenge. The Dolphins struck first on a fifty-one yard Fuad Reveiz field goal to advance up 3–0. Bernie Kosar rallied the Cleveland Browns right back down the field and connected with tight end Ozzie Newsome on a sixteen yard scoring strike to put the Browns ahead 7–3. The Cleveland Browns remained hot, and in the second quarter had their rushing tandem on full steam as Earnest Byner stormed through for a twenty-one yard touchdown rush that put the underdog Browns ahead 14–3 heading into halftime.

As the second half of the game began, an upset looked even more possible as the Cleveland Browns remained red hot and Earnest Byner was continuing his amazing season. Byner ripped off a sixty-six yard touchdown rush that put the Cleveland Browns in front 21–3, and caused the Miami Dolphin fans a serious panic. They didn't remain panicked long, however, as Dan Marino proved to everyone once again why he was one of the greatest to ever lace up a pair of cleats.

Down 21–3, Marino began another epic comeback. He hit Nat Moore on a six yard touchdown pass midway through the third quarter and put the Dolphins back in the game, down 21–10. Marino remained hot and led another scoring drive capped off with a thirty-one yard Ron Davenport touchdown run to bring the score to 21–17. It was another Ron Davenport one yard touchdown run in the fourth quarter that completed the Marino comeback and gave the Dolphins the 24–21 lead. It was good enough for them to hold onto, and the Cleveland Browns were knocked out of the playoffs after coming so close to reaching the AFC Championship game.

The Miami Dolphins failed to reach the Super Bowl against the Chicago Bears as everyone had hoped to see; instead they were beaten badly at home the next week by the New England Patriots 31–14. Tony Eason managed to lead the Patriots to the Super Bowl instead where they were shut down by the Chicago Bears 46–10.

It was a great first season for the new offense led by Bernie Kosar as the threat of a passing quarterback allowed the running game to find holes against defensives concerned with stopping the passing attack. The Cleveland Browns used this ploy and focused the majority of their offense on running the ball. It was an incredible year as both Kevin Mack and Earnest Byner rushed for one thousand plus yards each. Running backs coach Steve Crosby had to have been pleased with the supreme effort by his dueling running backs. Earnest Byner rushed for 1,002 yards on 244 attempts and scored eight touchdowns. Kevin Mack was even more impressive with 1,104 yards on 222 attempts and scored seven touchdowns. It was the kind of season that most running back combinations would never be able to repeat.

The Cleveland Browns' defense had a few highlights as well. Chip Banks led the team with eleven sacks, and Reggie Camp was close behind with 8.5. Clay Matthews continued to shine and impress weekly as he once again led the team in tackles, this time with eighty-eight on the season. Strong Safety Al Gross capitalized on the tight coverage of both Frank Minnifield and Handford Dixon on the outside corners to force opposing quarterbacks to go over the middle, leading Gross to secure five interceptions—a team high in that category.

The offense scored a total of 287 points for a 17.9 per game average. It was only twenty-third of the twenty-eight teams in the National Football League. Their defense was the spotlight as it only allowed 294 points for an 18.4 point per game average, which was seventh in the entire NFL. While most of their offense did come on the ground, they also had a variety of success in the passing game. Ozzie Newsome led the team with sixty-two for 711 yards and scored five touchdowns. Brian Brennan caught thirty-two balls for 487 yards but failed to score a touchdown. Brian Brennan did have a touchdown with the special teams, however, when he returned a punt for one. No other wide receiver had more than ten receptions. It was clear that the running game would have to continue to carry the load until the passing game became fully in sync under a full season with Bernie Kosar at the helm.

George Lilja was on the offensive line and explains why they had so much success:

> *"With the talent we had on offense, it allowed us to have a great running attack. We had a great offensive line coach named Howard Mudd who meshed very well with the players who played for him. He was able to utilize our talents to bring out the best possible results. We worked really hard that whole season to perfect our running blocking schemes. We ran so many running plays, and made sure to be in the right place at the right time. We had an attitude that even though the other team knew we were going to run the ball, there was still nothing they could do about it. We just kept pounding away at defenses even when they knew we were going to run the ball. I think there was one game when we played Cincinnati that we only threw eight passes the whole game and still won the game. That shows you just how geared we were. We had some great players on the offensive line in Cody Risien, Dan Fike, Mike Baab and Paul Farren. We all really enjoyed playing with each other and I think that helped as well. We had a lot to be proud of with Earnest Byner and Kevin Mack both running for over one thousand yards."*

Despite the commitment to running the ball and his not starting until almost mid-way through the season, Bernie Kosar still put up respectable numbers. Kosar tossed eight touchdowns and threw for 1,578 on 124 completions in ten starts. He led the Cleveland Browns on two fourth quarter game-winning drives. The only downside was his lack of mobility as he was sacked nineteen times for a loss of 121 yards. Nevertheless, it was a promising sign for the new leader of the orange and brown. Little did anyone truly realize, but the best for Bernie and the boys was yet to come; the momentum was just getting started, and the next ten years would be one wild ride!

Chapter Three

A Mile High Challenge

Heading into the 1986 season, the Cleveland Browns had found their franchise quarterback. It was time to put the final touches on the team, and make a serious run at the championship. Marty Schottenheimer was returning as head coach alongside Lindy Infante to run the offense. Dave Adolph was to handle the defense, and a young fiery coach named Bill Cowher was to coach the special teams.

When training camp began at Lakeland Community College in Kirtland, Ohio, the Cleveland Browns were fresh off of drafting a talented young receiver named Webster Slaughter out of San Diego State University who would help them for many years to come. Slaughter would line up alongside Brian Brennan and Reggie Langhorne to make up one of the deadliest receiving corps in the NFL. Cleveland Browns' General Manager Ernie Accorsi drafted Slaughter in the second round based on the strong recommendation of the Browns' Hall of Fame Receiver Paul Warfield, who was an unofficial scout for the team in 1986.

Because of the supplemental draft picking of Bernie Kosar the year before, along with various other trades, the Cleveland Browns were without a first round pick, third round pick, and sixth round pick. This made every selection in the NFL Draft even more important. With that being said, Slaughter ended up being the only one from their draft class that would make any kind of impact on the team, and the only draft pick to play for more than one season. Fifth round pick Nick Miller, and both seventh round picks Jim Meyer and Mike Norseth only played one NFL season. Other draft picks in later rounds such as Danny Taylor, Willie Smith, Randy Dausin, and King Simmons also never advanced out of their first NFL season.

Gary Danielson was still hurt when the 1986 pre-season began, and Bernie Kosar was once again ready to seize the opportunity. He took the starting position from Danielson and never looked back. Kosar excelled in the high-flying offensive scheme put in place by offensive coordinator Lindy Infante. He also had a solid relationship with head coach Marty Schottenheimer, which would lead to bigger and better things as time went on. Of course, there would be clashes at times as Kosar's "let it fly style" would not always mesh with the sometimes conservative approach of Coach Marty.

The season began in Chicago, Illinois as the Cleveland Browns lost a wild shootout—41–31 to the Chicago Bears at Soldier Field. Bernie Kosar threw for 289 yards and connected on a touchdown pass to Brian Brennan. The Cleveland Browns' defense struggled and could not contain the defending Super Bowl Champion's attack as they scored all game long. Walter Payton carved up the Browns' defense for 113 yards and a touchdown. Payton also caught numerous balls and scored a touchdown through the air as well. Quarterback Jim McMahon threw for 135 yards and a touchdown. It was the Bears' special teams and defense that did the real damage with a ninety-one yard Dennis Gentry kickoff return for a touchdown, followed by a Wilber Marshall fifty-eight yard interception return for a touchdown. The Browns saw just how far they had to go to become a better team after the first week's shellacking at the hands of the defending Super Bowl Champs.

The Cleveland Browns bounced back the following week with a close 23–20 win against the Houston Oilers in the Astrodome. The Browns rode a fourteen point fourth quarter, complete with a fifty-five yard touchdown pass from Kosar to Langhorne. The defense held when it needed to, and the Cleveland Browns departed Houston, Texas with a 1–1 record. Kosar was held in check, only connecting on eleven passes, but he made the most of them with 180 yards and the key late touchdown.

The Browns returned to Cleveland the following week to take on their state rivals to the south, the Cincinnati Bengals, in their home opener. It was a disappointing effort as the Cleveland Browns were crushed in front of their own home fan-base. It was actually tied 13–13 late in the third quarter when the Bengals decided to go on a run. Two touchdown runs from Larry Kinnebrew from four and two yards out, combined with a twenty-five yard Jim Breech field goal, led to the 30–13 blowout loss to the Cincinnati Bengals. The Browns' offense failed to score a touchdown, as their only trip for six came on a Frank Minnifield fumble return.

The Cleveland Browns responded from the disappointing start to the season by ripping off an impressive three-game winning streak. They beat the visiting Detroit Lions 24–21, highlighted by an eighty-four yard punt return for a touchdown by Gerald McNeil. They stayed hot the following week with a 27–24 win in Pittsburgh. Kosar threw for 186 yards and a touchdown in the win. They capped off the three game tear with a 20–7 home victory over the Kansas City Chiefs. Kosar stole the show with 287 passing yards and two touchdowns to bring the Cleveland Browns record to 4–2. The kid from Boardman, Ohio was becoming a man in front of everyone's eyes. On a week by week basis, he just kept getting better.

The Cleveland Browns lost a heart-breaker in week seven at home against the visiting Green Bay Packers. It was a fourteen point second half rally by the Packers that secured them the 17–14 win. Bernie Kosar had 222 yards with two touchdowns but that simply wasn't enough.

They responded to the Green Bay loss with another three-game winning streak. This time, they beat the Vikings in Minnesota by a score of 23–20. They also took down the Colts in Indianapolis with 24–9 before returning home to beat the Miami Dolphins 26–16. It was a great run that saw all sides of their game click on all levels. The winning streak came to a halt, however, as they lost in Los Angeles to the Raiders 27–14.

A major turning point in the season came in week twelve as they held a 7–4 record; they proceeded to win their final five games including thrilling overtime wins at home against the Houston Oilers and Pittsburgh Steelers. The overtime wins against their divisional rivals further showed their dominance at home games, and the rising prominence that the Cleveland Browns had in the division. They mixed in road wins at Buffalo and Cincinnati with another home win against the San Diego Chargers. The Cleveland Browns were now 6–2 at home and 6–2 on the road. They finished 12–4 overall, which was the best record in the AFC at that time. The four game win improvement was much more than anyone could have hoped for. The mix of young talent with excellent veteran leadership was creating a great team for the Cleveland Browns!

Bernie Kosar played great all season as the permanent leader of the team. Kosar started all sixteen games, completing 310 passes for 3,854 yards and seventeen touchdowns. He only threw ten interceptions but was sacked thirty-nine times for a loss of 274 yards. The amount of times he hit the dirt was the only concern, as they needed to keep the young superstar upright. As good as he was, he couldn't read defenses or throw touchdown passes while laying on his back.

The running attack cooled off as Kevin Mack was held to 665 yards with six fumbles in only twelve games as he missed four due to injury. Earnest Byner was also held out of nine games due to an injury and only ran for 277 yards. To supplement the loss of Byner's injury was a scrappy running back named Curtis Dickey who stepped into the role and helped the Browns when they needed it the most. Dickey ran for 523 yards and scored six touchdowns off the bench for Cleveland. He was drafted a few years prior with the Baltimore Colts in 1980. He was a rookie sensation for Baltimore as he rushed for eleven touchdowns in his rookie year. A few years later during the 1983 season for the Colts, he rushed for 1,122 yards and four touchdowns. Unfortunately, injuries kept him from reaching his full potential, and the 1986 season with Cleveland would be his last.

Without the two-headed rushing monster in the backfield, the Cleveland Browns relied heavily on the wide receiving crew who rose to the occasion. The rookie Webster Slaughter caught forty passes for 577 yards and four touchdowns. Reggie Langhorne continued to improve with thirty-nine catches for 678 yards and scored one touchdown. Brian Brennan joined in the fun with fifty-five catches for 838 yards and six touchdowns. Tight end Ozzie Newsome continued to be a valued veteran presence as he mentored the young receiving crew as well as contributed with 417 yards on thirty-nine catches and three touchdowns.

The special teams led by Coach Bill Cowher also had something to boast about that season as their tiny kick returner Gerald "Ice cube" McNeil returned kicks for 997 yards and one touchdown. He stood at five foot, seven inches and weighed in at 145 pounds, but he was a beast when it came to kick and punt returning. Place kickers Matt Bahr and Mark Mosely also teamed up to kick twenty-six field goals and gain forty-four extra points.

Leading the defense with five interceptions was the top dog Hanford Dixon. The shutdown corner of Frank Minnifield had three interceptions of his own, and the tandem continued to shut down passing attacks each week. Clay Matthews continued to impress as he led the team with eighty-nine tackles. Carl "Big Daddy" Hairston led the team in sacks with nine. They were a fierce and well-rounded attack team!

Wide receiver Reggie Langhorne explains why the offense clicked so well that season and beyond:

> *"Bernie and the offense really started to come into effect that second year together. It didn't hurt to have great running backs such as Kevin Mack and Earnest Byner along with Hall of Fame tight end Ozzie Newsome along with the combination of Brian Brennan and Webster Slaughter. The offensive line did a great job protecting Bernie and giving us the opportunity to be successful. We had two one thousand yard running backs in the backfield as well. We all worked together to master the Lindy Infante offense and get to the pinnacle of the game. We pushed the envelope as far as we could with the offensive talent that we had."*

Brian Brennan also gives his insight as to why that season went so well:

> *"It seemed like every year I played for the Cleveland Browns things seemed to go pretty well. That year, in particular, we had a lot of good players. We had a pretty solid offensive line and a great running game with Kevin Mack and Earnest Byner. We had some strong receivers and also a good third down back with Herman Fontenot. We were able to execute and it helped that Bernie Kosar made very few mistakes. I honestly think we were just better than the other teams from a personnel standpoint."*

The Cleveland Browns' fever was at an all time high as the fans were falling in love with their young quarterback. A group of fans went as far as to come up with a popular song in tribute to Kosar.

"Bernie Bernie, Oh yeah, how you can throw!
Yeah, yeah, yeah, yeah, yeah
Bernie Bernie, oh baby, Super Bowl!
He came from Miami and was oh so young,
Rifles to the Wizard, my, what a gun!
Takes the snap, drops back and looks down the field,
Brennan breaks open and the victory is sealed.
Bernie Bernie, oh yeah, how you can throw!
Yeah, yeah, yeah, yeah, yeah
Bernie Bernie, oh baby, Super Bowl!
The dogs are barking and all having fun,
Bernie will lead us to that place in the sun.
He has style and class at age twenty-three,
The MVP of the AFC!
Bernie Bernie, oh yeah, how you can throw!
Yeah, yeah, yeah, yeah, yeah.
Bernie Bernie, oh baby, Super Bowl!
Cody and Baab keep blitzes at bay,
Give Bernie some time to make the big play.
Bernie Bernie, oh yeah, how you can throw!
Yeah, yeah, yeah, yeah, yeah
Bernie Bernie, oh baby, Super Bowl!
We gotta go, Super Bowl, We gotta go!
Go Browns!

While the fans were writing songs about them, the players were working on media ventures of a different kind, including cinema fame. In the middle of the 1986 season with the hype growing, some of the Cleveland Browns' players got together to create a seventeen minute short film that would forever live in the sports lore of Cleveland fans for many years to come. It was called "Masters of the Gridiron", and starred such players as Mike Baab, Hanford Dixon, Clay Matthews, Dan Fike, Bob Golic, and many more.

The previous season the Chicago Bears had filmed a rap video entitled, "The Super Bowl Shuffle", and it was completed with a big Super Bowl win later that year. The Cleveland Browns couldn't sing, and chose to go a different route. It was a film with their players dressed as He-Man type characters and featured them fighting against ninjas, bears, and an evil lord in hopes of capturing an elusive ring. The film itself was produced by Lolis Garcia-Baab, the wife of Cleveland Browns' offensive lineman Mike Baab.

It was around the same time that the United Way was starting to get involved with the National Football League, and the film was to raise money for the charity. Baab, who was in his fifth season with the Browns in 1986, had already become a fan favorite in Cleveland. Even prior to the video, a small subsection of fans in the old Cleveland Municipal Stadium had started calling themselves "Baab's Barbarians", and would dress in medieval costumes and bring fake swords into the facility. Oftentimes, Baab would emerge from the huddle and make a gesture towards the group where he'd raise a fake sword. It was another clear example of the passionate connection the Cleveland Browns' players had shared with their fans. It was silly, but their fans got behind it passionately. In addition to the Browns' players, additional cast members included a trained bear and Tiny Tim, a colorful ukulele player. Tim would later have that same ukelele smashed over his head by Jerry the King Lawler on an episode of World Wrestling Federation's *Monday Night Raw* in 1993. He wasn't known for his athletic prowess, which brought even more quirkiness to the film. The video was a massive local success upon its release and quickly sold out of the approximately 40,000 copies that were initially produced.

The great season earned them a first round bye and home field advantage throughout the playoffs. They would take on the New York Jets in the first round on January 3, 1987, in one of the most memorable playoff games in NFL history. Kosar would throw for 489 yards in a double overtime thriller that fans still talk about nearly thirty years later.

The New York Jets boasted a strong line-up that was bound to give the Cleveland Browns fits all day on both sides of the ball. Coached by Joe Walton, the 1986 Jets had gone 10–6 and finished second in the AFC East Division. Their offense was coached by Rich Kotitie, while the mastermind behind the defense was Cleveland Browns' future head coach Bud Carson. The Jets were coming off a strange season that saw them go on a nine game winning streak at one point to run their record to 10–1, before enduring a five game losing streak to back their way into the playoffs. The New

York Jets crushed the Kansas City Chiefs in the wild card round by a score of 35–15 to earn the right to play the Cleveland Browns.

Quarterback Ken O'Brien was coming off one of his best seasons as a pro. He threw for 3,690 yards while connecting on twenty-five touchdown passes. His problem was his inability to scramble and get out of the pocket before getting sacked. He was sacked an incredible forty times for a loss of 353 yards. He also panicked quickly because of all of the sacks and was pressured into throwing twenty interceptions. The vaunted Cleveland Browns' defense would need to keep the pressure on O'Brien early and often.

The New York Jets had some big play threats to go with O'Brien's strong arm. Wide receiver Al Toon had a great season himself. He caught eight touchdown passes and also went for 1,176 yards. Toon wasn't the only Jets receiving threat that season, however, as Wesley Walker also caught for 1,016 yards and scored twelve touchdowns. The feature back was Freeman McNeil who had an above-average season as he rushed for 856 yards and five touchdowns. He would have had more but their main scoring back was Johnny Hector who was used at the goal line, as he scored eight touchdowns on only 164 rushing yards.

The New York Jets' defense was built around one man with a high profile reputation. Mark Gastineau was one of the elite pass rushers in the NFL that season, and numerous seasons beforehand. He was a five-time pro bowler with over one hundred sacks in his first one hundred games. He was quick and fierce, and those traits struck fear in opposing offensive lines. In 1984, he set an NFL record with twenty-two sacks, which led the NFL for the second year in a row along with sixty-nine tackles and one fumble recovery for a touchdown in 1984. He was voted the UPI AFC Defensive Player of the Year. Gastineau was nationally famous for doing his signature "Sack Dance" after sacking an opposing quarterback. Prior to the 1986 season, he was featured on the cover of *Sports Illustrated* alongside New York Giants star linebacker Lawrence Taylor. The SI Jinx hit Gastineau as his 1986 season was hampered by injuries and cut into his sack and tackle totals. He was hampered by groin and abdominal muscle ailments and then by a damaged left knee that required arthroscopic surgery. He returned for the playoffs and the Jets would need a big game out of him to stop the high-flying passing attack of the Cleveland Browns' offense.

The Jets jumped out to a 7-0 lead when quarterback Pat Ryan hit Wesley Walker with a forty-two yard pass for a touchdown. The Browns rallied back later in the first quarter to tie the game with a Kosar to Herman Fontenot thirty-seven yard pass for a tying touchdown. The teams would also trade field goals before the half was over, and went into the locker room for halftime tied at ten apiece.

The New York Jets added another field goal in the third quarter to take a 13-10 lead. They scored again in the fourth quarter on a Freeman McNeil twenty-five yard rush to expand the Jets lead to 20-10. The Cleveland Browns had lost six straight playoff games dating back to 1970 and this one looked bleak as well. The Browns had been struggling to move the ball; they hadn't scored since the second quarter. Their running game was struggling—only twenty-one yards on fifteen carries.

The Cleveland Browns were in deep trouble and running out of time. It was then that Bernie Kosar realized that he needed to carry the weight and lead a desperation comeback before they were sent home sulking for the winter. A crucial mistake committed by All Pro Jets defensive star Mark Gastineau gave the Browns new hope. With the Cleveland Browns facing a second down and twenty-four from their own eighteen yard line, Gastineau was called for a roughing—the passer penalty that gave the Cleveland Browns one last opportunity. If he hadn't committed that bad penalty, the Jets would have more than likely gotten the ball back and ran out the clock. The play had originally resulted in an incomplete, so instead of having a 3rd-and-24 situation, the fifteen yard penalty on Gastineau gave the Browns a first down at their own thirty-three. From there, Kosar drove the Cleveland Browns the remaining sixty-seven yards to a touchdown, which cut the Jets' lead to 20-17 on a Kevin Mack one yard rumble past the goal line.

The Cleveland Browns' defense managed to hold the New York Jets one more time, giving the ball back to Kosar on their own thirty-three with only fifty-one seconds left to play. Kosar led them on another incredible drive, which allowed placekicker Mark Mosely to tie the game with seven seconds to go on a twenty-two yard field goal. Ozzie Newsome made the comment about Kosar's ability to lead them back after the game:

> *"He was not going to be denied. He was going to find a way to win that football game."*

It was only minutes prior that the game looked like defeat; now two incredible drives led by Kosar put the game into overtime. Neither team could break through and score in the first overtime, which sent the game into double overtime. The Cleveland Browns did have a chance to win it early in the first overtime but placekicker Mark Mosely had shanked an easy twenty-seven yarder wide right.

Bernie Kosar was not going down without a fight and stepped up once again to lead the Cleveland Browns on a game winning drive in double overtime, capped off by the winning twenty-seven yard field goal to send the Browns' fans into frenzy, and the team into the AFC Championship game. The game winning drive witnessed Kevin Mack take over. He had a run for four yards, a pass reception for six, and then three straight runs later in the drive for fifteen, four, and seven yards to set up the chip shot field goal. Marty Schottenheimer was quoted as saying:

> *"I have never experienced or seen a comeback like that. After it was all over and just before we said our prayer in the locker room, I told the players to listen...you could still hear the people cheering for us. This is a victory...a game...a moment all of us will remember for the rest of our lives."*

Wide receiver Brian Brennan reflects back on the emotions of that wild game:

> *"The Jets were a very good team loaded with talent but I believe we were a better overall cohesive team. We had great resolve back then and Bernie Kosar instilled a lot of confidence in us, so we knew we could come back any time and get a score at any time. We had Webster Slaughter who was a big play guy, and also Reggie Langhorne who was a very physical and strong receiver. Herman Fontenot was also a big play guy who could make things happen. Earnest Byner and I were more of possession ball carrying and receiving guys. We had a lot of options and ways to execute plays to result in points when the chips were down such as they were in that game. Despite the lead the Jets had on us,*

Bernie instilled great confidence in us and we were able to stick to the task...not feel sorry for ourselves, and not feel defeated. It was the same thing with the defense with our big linebackers like Clay Matthews and Eddie Johnson. Guys like Chip Banks, Frank Minnifield, Hanford Dixon and several others...we were loaded on defense. We stuck in the game and never gave up...the emotion went from rejection to elation."

Mark Gastineau never truly recovered from his momentous mistake late in the fourth quarter that kept the Cleveland Browns' flickering hopes alive. Following the game, Gastineau said that he hadn't been guilty of roughing and that he was *"just following through."* Joe Walton, the New York Jets' head coach would only say:

"It was a very key play, Mark was just trying to do the best he could do."

Gastineau would continue to do strange things that kept fans questioning his morals and overall character. In 1987, he was the only NFL player to cross the picket line in that year's players' strike, citing his need to pay alimony. After leading the league in sacks eight weeks into the 1988 season, he suddenly decided to retire from the game. At the time of his retirement, Gastineau was the NFL's all-time leader in sacks. After his career ended, he would spend time in prison due to several disputes with the law, including domestic violence and drug possession in 1993. In 2000, Gastineau spent eleven months in Rikers Island for parole violations. Did his life spin out of control because of the controversial roughing penalty against Cleveland?...one may never know!

The following week on Sunday, January 11, 1987, the Cleveland Browns welcomed the Denver Broncos into Cleveland Municipal Stadium. It was only twenty-one degrees with the wind chill, and for the second straight week, the freezing cold fans of Cleveland, Ohio were about to witness a classic.

The 1986 Denver Broncos were led by head coach Dan Reeves who was in his sixth season. He was a former player and performed in two Super Bowls during his professional playing days with the Dallas Cowboys. He also went to three Super Bowls as an assistant coach with the Dallas Cowboys once his playing career was done. He was from the Tom Landry coaching tree and became the youngest head coach in the NFL in 1981 when he took over in

Denver. He had brought the Denver Broncos to the playoffs twice before, losing to the Seattle Seahawks in the 1983 Wild Card game, and the Pittsburgh Steelers in the 1984 Divisional round playoff game. Dan Reeves was determined that this year would be different!

The Denver Broncos had a strong start in the season, winning their first six games. They finished with a 11–5 record and were the AFC Western Division Champions. They were led by a man who would eventually go down as one of the greatest quarterbacks in the history of the NFL. John Elway was coming off of a season where he only threw for nineteen touchdowns and 3,485 yards. But what the stats didn't show was his exceptional killer instinct and ability to put a team on his shoulders and lead a game winning comeback against any opponent at any time.

John Elway had been drafted number one overall by the Baltimore Colts in the 1983 NFL Draft. It was a draft that also saw future Hall of Famers Jim Kelly and Dan Marino selected in the first round. Elway had said for weeks prior to the draft that he would not play for Baltimore if they selected him, and demanded a trade the second that they did. He even threatened to quit football and play baseball for the New York Yankees instead. He was coming off a great career at Stanford University and carried a lot of stroke coming into the league. His power play with the Baltimore Colts eventually worked, and he was traded to the Denver Broncos. Elway was the proto-typical perfect quarterback, a laser arm with great vision downfield; he also had great mobility and could scramble away from the very best defensive linemen in the league. John Elway was only at the beginning of a great career with Denver, and beating the Cleveland Browns was his first major mission to accomplish. For years to come, John Elway remained one of the most hated men in Cleveland because of his incredible games against the hometown Browns.

The Denver Broncos were coming off of a 22–17 win against the defending AFC champion New England Patriots. John Elway was ready to lead his three top receivers Mark Jackson, Vance Johnson, and Steve Watson into battle against the stingy Cleveland Browns' secondary. The Duke and his Three Amigos would have their hands full. They would also rely on their top running back

Sammy Winder, who was coming off a season that saw him rush for 789 yards and nine touchdowns.

The Cleveland Browns got off to a hot start as Bernie Kosar again hooked up with Herman Fontenot on a first quarter touchdown pass to put the Browns ahead. The Broncos would respond with ten straight points of their own before Cleveland could answer with a field goal to close out the first half 10–10. They appeared to be following the same script from the prior week.

By the late fourth quarter, the Cleveland Browns and Denver Broncos had exchanged field goals and the game remained tied, 13–13. With a little over five minutes remaining in the game, Kosar hit Brian Brennan on a beautiful forty-eight yard touchdown pass to put the Browns ahead 20–13. Brian Brennan talks about the incredible emotion of that game and play:

> *"When I caught the pass from Bernie with a little over five minutes to go in the game, I really thought that would seal our victory. The defense had been playing so well...only giving up one touchdown at that point. I really felt that we were going to continue on to the Super Bowl in Pasadena that year. I was on the sidelines after that catch...almost shaking with excitement. I was excited that it was a play that I was involved with in front of our own Cleveland Browns' fans that looked as though it was going to propel us to a Super Bowl. It is hard to describe the feelings you have, but they were chalked full of excitement and brimming with joy."*

It looked like it was over when on the following kickoff, a Denver Broncos' miscue put them on their own two yard line with their backs against the ravenous dog pound. With 5:32 left in the game, it would take a near miracle for the Bronco's to come back. The 79,915 fans in attendance in Cleveland were screaming and cheering as they were certain they were on the doorstep of a championship. What happened instead was a legendary ninety-eight yard drive led by John Elway that tied the game and sent it into overtime.

The drive was a thing of beauty, directed by a quarterback who simply refused to lose. John Elway started the drive with a short pass to Sammy Winder. A few plays later, Elway scrambled out of the pocket and ran for eleven yards and a first down. He then connected on a twenty-two yarder to Steve Sewell and backed that up with a twelve yard connection to Watson. All of a sudden, the Broncos had the ball on Cleveland's forty yard line with still two minutes to work. After an incompletion pass on first down, the Cleveland Browns' defense managed to sack Elway for an eight yard loss, which set up a very long third and eighteen. Elway refused to panic, and even after a bad snap, managed to recover and throw a twenty yard rocket down the field to an open Mark Jackson to keep the drive alive at the Cleveland Browns' twenty-eight yard line.

The hostile crowd was no match for Elway, as he continued to lead the drive. He connected on a fourteen yard pass to Sewell that put them on the Browns' fourteen yard line. Two plays later, it was John Elway on a bad ankle, scrambling for a nine yard run to move the ball down to the Browns five yard line. With thirty-nine seconds to go, he found Jackson in the middle of the end zone and sent the Cleveland Browns' fans into quiet mode. John Elway threw the ball so hard that Jackson was quoted later as saying:

> *"I felt like a baseball catcher and that was his fast ball, outside and low. Elway had unlimited potential and promise for years... on that drive, he finally reached it!"*

The scoring drive came out of nowhere as on the two previous fourth-quarter drives, Elway only led them to nine and six yards on each. Before the drive, they still only had 216 total yards all day. Their only touchdown had come off a short thirty-seven yard field following a costly Cleveland Browns' fumble. One of Karlis's two previous field goals was also the result of a short field that had followed an interception. It was later revealed that Elway actually had a bad left ankle, which made it even more impressive.

Elway had been confident all week going into the game. He was asked mid-week about the tough Cleveland defense and his bad ankle. He shrugged off the concerns and said:

> *"The ankle is fine, I could play now if I had to. There are no dominating teams in the NFL. What about the Giants, anybody can beat them. The weather is all in your mind!"*

The Denver Broncos' defense had also been stifling all day for the second year phenomena Bernie Kosar to have to deal with. Broncos' assistant coach Joe Collier had prepared a special defensive strategy to stop Kosar and the Cleveland Browns' high-profile attack. They decided they weren't going to blitz, instead they would drop seven or even eight defenders into pass coverage and had its stunting lineman force the pressure on Kosar, who was not known for his mobility. The pressure worked as Kosar had one of his worst games of the year with two interceptions and several dropped interceptions. The tactic helped rattle Kosar because everyone was covered downfield.

The Broncos wasted no time in overtime moving the ball down the field. John Elway connected with tight end Orson Mobley for twenty-two yards. A couple of plays later, he connected with Watson for twenty-eight more yards. They then had three straight runs by Sammy Winder to keep the ball moving. From there, it was their place kicker Rich Karlis booting a thirty-three yard field goal just barely between the goal posts to win the game. Many who witnessed the kick will swear that it was no good. The Cleveland Browns had lost in the cruelest of ways. Bernie Kosar finished with two touchdown passes and 259 yards, but it wasn't enough to stop destiny.

It was two magical drives by John Elway that let the league know he had officially arrived. It was two scoring drives, one of ninety-eight yards and one of sixty yards. He ran for twenty yards and threw for 128 yards combined on both drives. He was quoted as saying:

> *"You know how you'll think, the night before, about how you'd like to do great things in the game, well this is the kind of game you dream about."*

Brian Brennan had to watch the drive from the sidelines after making what he and Cleveland thought was the game-winning catch just minutes before. Brennan goes on to recall the agony of the moment:

> *"It was painful to watch the Broncos march down the field…it was an 'oh no' feeling! I had feelings of worrisome and nausea to be honest with you. All of sudden, as we were watching it develop from the sidelines, it became clear that these guys were going to score. We were in just disbelief that they were going down the field like that."*

Felix Wright discusses why there was such a defensive breakdown on that final drive by Denver in regulation:

> *"It's tough to look back at it...it seems like everywhere the media always talks about that game. It will come playoff season and especially if Denver is in the playoffs, they will bring up the history and they played so well. So, we have to listen to it everywhere. John Elway, you have to take your hat off to him as he is an awesome quarterback. He was able to get the job done every time he needed to get it done. It was just one of those deals where he had a good drive at the end of the game. It was really the only good one he had all game as we had pretty much shut him down until that point. I think we got too conservative on defense. Pretty much the whole game we had handled their offense well until that point. We got too conservative and went into the prevent mode. I think when you do that you open up opportunities and you get less aggressive. We had the bend not break mentality and he was able to take full advantage of it for that particular series. Back in that day, that's what you do when you were up. It was common for teams to go into their prevent defense, all teams did it, it just backfired on us. I think we learned our lesson from it when we got back in the opportunity again the following year in games...we changed it up and didn't go into the prevent anymore. It is what it is, and I give a lot of credit to John Elway and the Broncos as they both played very well and they did what they needed to do."*

Offensive lineman George Lilja also reflects back to the big game and the near miss at going to the Super Bowl:

> *"It was one of my biggest highlights of playing in the NFL, and also one of my biggest lowlights. We did play a very good team in Denver, and it was so close. I remember that drive vividly because it was finally hitting me that we had a chance to go to the biggest event in football and all of sports for that matter. I remember looking up into the stands and seeing my wife to give her the thumbs up. They had ninety-eight yards to go in such a short amount of time. It was such a slow death, and you can't take anything away from John Elway as he was great enough to put that drive together. I remember it being third and very long after a sack...and Elway coming back to connect on a long pass to keep*

> *the drive alive. Everything went right for them...even after the snap hit a running back moving in motion...Elway still recovered to make a beautiful play. It was one of the hardest games for me to get over. It took me a good three months to emotionally recover from that game. We are trained as professional athletes to move on from a loss but it is not easy when it is the last game of the year and you have all offseason to think about it. I will always be proud of how far we got and how excited the city was for what we did that year even though we lost that game. The fans even cheered as we ran off the field as their way of saying 'thank you for the great season' despite the loss. It remains one of my great memories but also one of my darkest memories to overcome."*

George Liljas goes on to talk about the slumped and depressed atmosphere in the locker room after that brutal loss:

> *"To play at that level, you have to be ready to handle anything perfectly and emotionally correct. But to lose a game so close like that...it really does bring tears to your eyes. You have to be able to wrestle with the emotions of the game, and that locker room was awfully quiet. Coach Marty told us that we were going to dedicate ourselves to bringing us back to this exact same spot and winning it next time! Ironically, they returned the next year and got so close again. People try and make you feel better but there is really nothing else you can do. It's something you always think about and know in your gut that we had it! What can you really say, it was quiet and I heard some sobbing...I just never wanted to have to feel that again. We had to take something like that, a negative, and use it as a positive motivator to come back and work even harder the next time because we never wanted to have that horrible feeling again!"*

Despite the heartbreaking loss to Denver, the Cleveland Browns had a lot to be proud of. They came within minutes of winning the AFC Championship Game, and had a young quarterback in only his second season. They were one of the most impressive teams in the entire league, and lost not only to a future Hall of Famer in Elway, but a team that caught the right breaks at the right time. Several times on the drive, the Browns had the Broncos in a third and long situation, but simply could not put them away. Fans have spoken for years about the greatness of Elway and the drive, but no one can take away from the supreme effort that the Cleveland Browns' players, coaches, and fans gave on that epic Sunday. One thing was for sure, the Cleveland Browns were determined to return to the Super Bowl the following season at all costs.

The upcoming NFL Draft would be crucial for the Cleveland Browns once again. This time around, they had a full complement of picks, and had to ensure to make each one count after the horrible draft the previous season. Things started off ominous when they selected Mike Junkin with their first pick in the draft out of Duke University. He was supposed to be the final piece on the defense as he was a linebacker tasked with covering the whole field on every play. It was a hefty price to pay for the Browns as they traded Chip Banks along with their first and second-round picks to the San Diego Chargers for their first and second-round picks. Banks had been one of the best players on the Cleveland Browns' defense for several years, and this was a risky move. The pick of Junkin was the fifth overall selection in the Draft, making it even more important that he live up to the potential and not be a bust.

This pick would be scrutinized for years to come, however, as Mike Junkin went down as one of the biggest first round busts in NFL Draft history. The reason for his failure on the Cleveland Browns' team was a-plenty. Perhaps the biggest reason was the unrealistic expectations bestowed upon him by Marty Schottenheimer who insisted that scout Dom Anile had watched him play, and compared his playing style to "a mad dog in a meat market." Despite the high praise from Dom Anile, he still made a point of stating that Junkin wasn't worth more than a middle round pick, not the fifth overall selection. Coach Marty was not willing to trust his scouts, and instead overruled his scouting staff and insisted that they take Junkin.

The original plan that the Cleveland Browns had for Junkin was for him to be the starting outside linebacker opposite Clay Matthews. This was a risk in itself because Junkin had played inside linebacker in college. They were already switching his role, and messing with his confidence. Even with the high praise from Marty, the transition proved to be a difficult one for him to make. Mike Junkin didn't make things any easier for himself or the Cleveland Browns by engaging in a sixteen day holdout. For a rookie switching positions from his normal college position to miss that much time in the beginning of camp is always a huge mistake, and this was no different. He eventually came to terms on a deal with the Cleveland Browns for four-years worth just under two million dollars.

Offensive lineman George Lilja was in charge of blocking for Kosar. Photo courtesy of George Lilja

The holdout caused him to miss the first pre-season game against the St. Louis Cardinals. He eventually got to play in the second pre-season game against the New York Giants, but didn't see any action until the second half, and then failed to record a single tackle. It became even clearer that the Browns may have made a terrible choice with Junkin. By the end of training camp, he had already lost his chance at the starting job to play alongside Clay Matthews; instead, the Browns opted to start Anthony Griggs over Junkin.

Things never really improved for Junkin as he ended up missing most of the season due to an injury and landed on the injured reserve list. He would play one more season for the Cleveland Browns following that, before getting traded to Kansas City. Junkin's horrid two-year stint in Cleveland would earn him the eighth biggest Draft bust of all time honors by *ESPN Magazine* in a 2009 article. Many fans and media members would also agree that he is one of the top five worst Cleveland Browns' first round draft picks of all time as well. By the time his short NFL career was done after only three seasons—one with the Chiefs after two with the Browns—he had only played in twenty games while only starting in seven of them. Things never quite did work out for the "Mad Dog in a Meat Market."

The Cleveland Browns used their second round pick on a center out of Miami, Florida named Gregg Rakoczy. He was a decent pick who would end up only playing three seasons with the Browns; while not a lot, it was still more than their other recent draft picks. In the third round, they took a bruising fullback Tim Manoa from Penn State. He brought a physical style to the backfield but also a winning history as he was a member of the 1986 national championship team.

The only other selection of note was on placekicker Jeff Jaeger. The Browns had Matt Bahr as their reliable starting kicker which made the pick a strange one. However, due to a number of circumstances with Bahr, Jaeger ended up playing in ten games and broke all of the Cleveland Browns' rookie scoring records with seventy-five points. It was the only season for him. The next season, he left for the Raiders.

With the expectations high, they began their new season on a rocky note. They had split their first two games of the season with a 28–21 loss in New Orleans against the Saints before beating the Pittsburgh Steelers 34–10 in the second week at home. The third week, a highly anticipated rematch against the Denver Broncos was canceled because of the sudden players' strike. This was a giant letdown for the fans who had been hoping for some early season revenge against John Elway and the Denver Broncos.

The following week with replacement players in front of an upset and small crowd in New England that only saw 14,830 fans show up, the Cleveland Browns won 20–10. Still using replacement players, the Browns lost the following week at home against the Houston Oilers 15–10. Gary Danielson took over at quarterback the following week and the Browns routed the Bengals in Cincinnati 34–0.

Bernie Kosar and the normal starters returned to the team the following week and the Cleveland Browns beat the Los Angeles Rams 30–17 at home in front of 76,933 loyal fans. They would suffer their third loss of the season the following week in San Diego, 27–24 in heartbreaking fashion. They rebounded from the loss with three straight wins against the Atlanta Falcons, Buffalo Bills, and Houston Oilers. The momentum and excitement of their winning streak came to an end as they dropped two straight games to the San Francisco 49ers and Indianapolis Colts. The Browns once again rebounded and closed out the year with a three-game winning streak—wins over the Cincinnati Bengals, Los Angeles Raiders, and Pittsburgh Steelers finished off the wild 10–5 regular season.

Bernie Kosar threw for 3,000 yards for the third straight season as the Cleveland Browns went 10–5 and captured the AFC Central Division Championship once again. As usual, the running game remained strong as Kevin Mack returned to full-time duty and went for 735 yards on five touchdowns. Earnest Byner went for only 432 yards but scored eight touchdowns. The receiving corps continued to do their job as well. Webster Slaughter caught seven touchdowns and piled up 806 yards. Brian Brennan remained consistent and caught forty-three passes for 607 yards and six touchdowns.

Their first round playoff matchup was against the Indianapolis Colts at home in Cleveland. The Colts had an up-and-down season that never saw them win or lose more than two games in a row. They finished with a 9-7 record and won the AFC Eastern Division. Head coach Ron Meyer had the Colts ready to go. They were led by quarterback Jack Trudeau who split time in the starting role with Gary Hogeboom throughout the season. They relied heavily on their running game as they had Future Hall of Famer running back Eric Dickerson carrying the ball the majority of the time. He had rushed for 1,011 yards and scored five touchdowns. Joining Dickerson in the backfield was Albert Bentley who rushed for 631 yards and scored a team high with seven touchdowns.

The first round playoff game took place on Saturday, January 9, 1988 in Cleveland, Ohio in front of a packed house of loud and passionate fans. It was cold that day—sixteen degrees with eight miles an hour winds, and a five wind chill factor. The Browns had to focus on the task at hand and not look ahead to the possible rematch with Denver. Needless to say, Coach Marty would have the boys well prepared and focused on the game!

From the very beginning, the playoff game had all the makings of a shootout. Earnest Byner kicked off the scoring with a ten yard pass and catch from Bernie Kosar for seven quick points. The Colts would battle right back and tie the game with a two yard touchdown pass from Jack Trudeau to Pat Beach. As they entered the second quarter, the scoring continued when Bernie Kosar connected on a thirty-nine yard scoring strike with Reggie Langhorne to put the Cleveland Browns ahead. The Indianapolis Colts continued to show their strength, and battled back once again with a Jack Trudeau nineteen yard touchdown pass to Erick Dickerson to tie the game at fourteen apiece heading into halftime.

Offensive coordinator Lindy Infante kept the offense on high alert as they came out of the locker room running and gunning for more points. Earnest Byner rumbled in the end zone from two yards out and the Browns reclaimed the lead by a score of 21-14; they held it the rest of the third quarter. The now healthy and returning Matt Bahr kicked a twenty-two yard field goal to start the fourth quarter and put the Browns ahead by ten.

The Cleveland Browns kept the pressure on when later in the quarter it was Brian Brennan catching a two yard touchdown pass from Bernie Kosar to give them a hefty 31-14 lead. The Colts answered with a one yard touchdown run from Albert Bentley. It was at that point that the Cleveland Browns' defense stepped up to the challenge, and on the Colts next possession, Frank Minnifield picked off a Jack Trudeau pass and returned it for a forty-eight yard interception touchdown return. *Whew*! This put the Cleveland Browns ahead where they stayed and hung onto win the game 38–21, earning a rematch with John Elway and the Denver Broncos. This time, however, they would have to travel to the hostile environment of Mile High Stadium in Denver, Colorado.

On Sunday, January 17, 1988 the Cleveland Browns arrived in Denver looking to extract revenge from their prior season's championship game loss. The atmosphere was intense in Colorado with the hostile fans and the brutal altitude issues causing numerous Browns' players to have to resort to chewing wads of Big Red bubble gum just to keep moisture in their mouth. Safety Felix Wright describes the game and the conditions:

> *"the atmosphere was awesome, everyone made such a big deal about the altitude and how our lips would be dry and affect our breathing...and it did! I know a couple of times before we went, we practiced in Florida and also Mexico to prepare for it. I don't think you can prepare for over a week's time...I think it's just something you have to live with to feel comfortable with. I don't think it had anything to do with the outcome of the game. It was just one of those deals when you get out there between the lines, you have to play football and make things happen. In that particular game, they played well right off the bat and we didn't play up to our standards that we usually did in the first half. That happens in football...sometimes you will have halves where you don't play well and other halves where you play really well. We played well in the second half to get back in the game...I believe I had an interception early on and we scored...and just started coming right back at them."*

The Denver Broncos were also a team on a mission, having lost the prior year's Super Bowl to the New York Giants 39–20. John Elway played well, throwing for 304 yards, but it wasn't nearly enough to get past the accurate Phil Simms and the New York Giants. Elway and the Broncos knew that the only thing that stood between them and a return trip to the Super Bowl was a highly motivated Cleveland Browns team desperate to erase the bitter memories of the prior season's heartbreak ending.

The Denver Broncos were coming off of a great 10–4–1 season—a record good enough for first place in the AFC Western Division. They were a nasty team full of confidence and swagger; they didn't fear the Cleveland Browns, and were planning on strategically outplaying them two years in a row.

John Elway was coming off of another strong season under offensive coordinator Mike Shanahan's scheme. Elway threw for 3,198 yards and nineteen touchdowns. His numbers would have been even higher had he not missed out on four games because of the players' strike. He also had four game-winning drives. The game was never over if #7 had the ball in his hands, no matter the size of the deficit. His main target was once again Vance Johnson, who accumulated 684 yards on forty-two catches with seven touch downs. Ricky Nattiel was another big play threat with Elway as he went for 630 yards on thirty-one catches, scoring twice. Mark Jackson also remained a key part of the passing attack with 436 yards and two touchdowns. As usual, the running game played second fiddle to Elway and his rocket arm, but feature tailback Sammy Winder ran for 741 yards and scored six touchdowns.

Mile High Stadium was packed with loud and ravenous fans who would not allow the cool temperatures to rob them of their excitement. It was only twenty-nine degrees, with a crisp wind chill that made it feel much colder all afternoon. John Elway was once again about to show everyone why he was the future of Pro Football not only in Denver, but within the entire league.

Elway came out on fire and wasted no time leading the Denver Broncos straight down the field on an impressive scoring drive. Elway capped off the drive with a beautiful eight yard touchdown passing strike to Ricky Nattiel. The Duke and his Three Amigos were merely getting started. A little bit later in the first quarter, it was Steve Sewell scoring from one yard out to put the Broncos firmly ahead 14–0 after the first quarter was completed. The Cleveland Browns got on the scoreboard in the second quarter with a twenty-four yard Matt Bahr field goal. Denver had a 'right back at you' answer with a one yard Gene Lang scoring run, which gave the Broncos a commanding 21–3 lead heading into halftime.

Bernie Kosar and the Browns refused to go down without a fight. Kosar wasted no time connecting on an eighteen yard touchdown strike to Reggie Langhorne to pull within eleven at 21-10. John Elway was not impressed, or even concerned as he promptly answered the Kosar scoring strike with one of his own. Elway connected with Mark Jackson on a brilliant eighty yard touchdown pass to put the Broncos ahead 28-10. Denver's Mile High Stadium was full of momentum with roaring fans.

The latest John Elway touchdown pass put the Cleveland Browns in a serious hole. With their backs against the wall, it was time for Bernie Kosar to lead an epic comeback. It began with a thirty-two yard pass for a touchdown to Earnest Byner to pull them within eleven again at 28-17. The rally was far from over as on the next drive, they scored again on an Earnest Byner four yard touchdown rumble to pull them within four at 28-24. The Broncos answered with a thirty-eight yard Rich Karlis field goal to advance 31-24 heading into the fourth quarter. The game was shaping up to be a thriller as the Browns battled back to tie the game 31-31 on a beautiful four yard touchdown pass from Bernie Kosar to Webster Slaughter. The Cleveland Browns had scored twenty-eight second-half points, and clearly had stolen the Denver Broncos' momentum.

Elway once again would answer with a drive of his own capped off by a twenty yard touchdown pass to Sammy Winder. The Broncos led 38-31 with only a few minutes remaining. Kosar would have to repeat what Elway did the prior season if the Cleveland Browns were going to be able to push the game into overtime. Bernie Kosar remained hot and led the Browns right back down the field into scoring position with only a few minutes remaining in regulation.

As the Browns had the ball inside of the eight yard line, it seemed like it would only be a matter of moments until they scored to tie the game. Seconds later, Kosar handed off to Earnest Byner who was stripped from behind by Jeremiah Castille before he could score. The ball bounced into the hands of the Denver Broncos... and just like that...the Cleveland Browns had come up short again in the championship game.

The play would live on in infamy and forever be known simply as "The Fumble." When Marty Schottenheimer was asked about it later, he said that the blame was not entirely on Byner because Webster Slaughter was supposed to take ten steps then block Castille to the outside. Instead, it was Slaughter getting caught up watching the play, and missed his assignment to block Castille. Schottenheimer was positive that Byner never saw Castille coming in on the play.

Years later in an ESPN Classic Films documentary, Castille was asked about the play and had this to say:

> *"I was thinking...I got burned the last time I tried to bump-and-run [Slaughter]...so instead I stepped back six-to-eight yards before the snap, so I could better see the play unfold. I saw it was a draw play and that Byner had the ball. I remember thinking that Byner ran all over us that entire second half, so there was no way I was going to tackle him. Instead, I went for the ball the whole time."*

It was a bitter pill to swallow after the tremendous comeback effort from Kosar, who finished the game with 356 yards and three touchdowns. Fans and media tend to harp on Byner for the costly fumble, but if it wasn't for him they would have never even gotten that far. Byner, to his credit, finished with sixty-seven rushing yards on fifteen attempts with one touchdown. He also caught seven balls for 120 yards and a touchdown. He piled up 187 total yards and scored twice. He had an amazing game, but sadly, no one chooses to remember that. Too often, Earnest Byner takes the blame for that loss and he shouldn't. Coach Shottenheimer was quoted as saying in the documentary years later entitled, *The Fumble* as saying:

> *"Earnest was the reason we were still in the game at that point. He had several heroic runs and catches over the course of the second half that allowed us to have a chance to tie the game at thirty-eight. All of these heroics, unfortunately, were overshadowed by a single draw play from the eight- yard line."*

Kevin Mack helped provide the one-two punch with a twelve carry sixty-one yard rushing effort of his own. Webster Slaughter led the Browns' receivers with four catches, fifty-three yards and a touchdown. They played well enough to win in the second half... they just came up a little bit short.

John Elway was far too much to stop as he threw for 281 yards and three huge touchdowns. Elway was on fire from the very beginning and it was no surprise that the Denver Broncos piled up thirty-eight points, despite facing one of the best defenses in the league. Elway's main target was Mark Jackson, who racked up 134 yards and four catches with one touchdown. Ricky Nattiel stepped up and pulled down five catches for ninety-five yards and a touchdown. It was just too much for the Cleveland Browns to hold off, and the 38–33 loss was just another brutal way to end the season. The Denver Broncos would go on to get blown out in the Super Bowl 42–10 at the hands of the Washington Redskins a few short weeks later.

Felix Wright goes on to recap another heartbreaking loss:

"Football is a game of momentum, you get it going and it's hard for the other team to stop. We made it close and made things happen, then... unfortunately, we had an accident down there by the goal line late in the game. We were going to go in and score...and we had a few missed assignments that kind of caused that fumble. That's what happens in football. It was a tough loss no doubt, although the fumble would have just tied the game, it didn't guarantee us a win. We still don't know if we would have won it if we did tie it up...you just never know."

Wide receiver Brian Brennan gives his thoughts on the atmosphere and brutal loss to Denver once again, that year on the road:

> *"Once again, I felt as though we had the better team. It's not as easy to win as many games as we did again, and make it to the AFC Championship Game. It was hard because we felt we were the better team and we didn't play particularly well in the first half...digging ourselves a large hole. It's hard to play there and it's a loud atmosphere. We felt we were prepared and excited to play them again. The way we lost with the fumble was devastating, not just for Earnest Byner, but for all of us. It wasn't his fault because one play doesn't make a game. We should have never been in that situation to begin with. It was just so devastating... simply brutal!"*

Heading into the 1988 NFL Draft, the Cleveland Browns were desperate to make the right choice with their number one pick after swinging and missing the prior season with Mike Junkin. This time, the Browns selected Clifford Charlton, another linebacker, out of

Florida University. Charlton had some prestige coming out of college being a two-time All SEC player in 1986 and 1987, as well as a First Team All American in 1987. Sadly for the Cleveland Browns, though, Charlton never reached his potential in the pros. After only thirty-one games in which he started just one, he suffered a severe knee injury that tore the MCL and ACL ligaments of his knee and prematurely ended his professional career.

The defense would have the help of a new and talented draft pick joining the team with their second round selection of Michael Dean Perry. He was the younger brother of Chicago Bears All Pro defensive tackle William 'the Refrigerator' Perry who had been dominating the league since his arrival with the Bears in 1985. In fact, because of the death of his father, Michael Dean Perry was taught how to play football by his older brothers. They taught him well because Michael Dean went on to play his college ball at Clemson University and set the school record of twenty-eight sacks. The Cleveland Browns wasted no time choosing him in the second round of the 1988 NFL Draft.

The Cleveland Browns' defense also benefited from the addition of rookie safety Thane Gash out of East Tennessee University. Gash was a speedy outside linebacker during his college-playing days at Florida, where he earned All American honors. He was also a first-team All-SEC selection in 1986 and 1987, and a first-team All-American and team captain in 1987. His fifteen forced fumbles, forty-nine career tackles for a loss, and twenty-five quarterback sacks still rank first, fifth and fourth, respectively, on the Florida Gators' all-time career records lists. The Cleveland Browns were stocking up on talent for another run at the AFC Championship Game.

Few people could have ever predicted just how crazy the season would become nor as quickly, as things started to change. Marty Schottenheimer along with quarterbacks coach Marc Trestman were about to have their hands full with all kinds of injuries and issues. Bernie Kosar was hurt in the very first game of the season on the road in Kansas City. Kosar only had a chance to attempt eight passes before getting knocked out of the game from a crushing blow.

Former starter and now backup, Gary Danielson, came back into the game but was unable to get the Browns' offense moving. After three quarters of play, the Browns only had three points on the board. Lucky for them, the defense was lights out, and up for the task as they completely shut down the Kansas City Chiefs' attack led by Bill Kenney. He was held to zero touchdown passes and two interceptions. The Cleveland Browns' ravenous defense kept the Chiefs guessing all day. The Browns' defense also held the Chiefs' top rusher, Paul Palmer, to only twenty-eight yards on the ground.

Despite their great defense, the Cleveland Browns' offense continued to play poorly. Gary Danielson threw for 170 yards, but had zero touchdowns and one interception. The Browns never gave up and kept their heads in the game despite missing their leader. It wasn't pretty, but Matt Bahr was able to convert on the go ahead field goal late in the fourth quarter to give the Browns the 6–3 win. The Browns' defense could take full credit for the win as they held the Kansas City Chiefs' offense to only 149 total yards, zero touchdowns and two turnovers. The Cleveland Browns fled from Kansas City with a lucky and generous 1–0 record.

However, the Cleveland Browns weren't so lucky the following week when the New York Jets came to town to open up play at Municipal Stadium. The Browns' offense was in a slump all day, only earning twelve first downs, once again not scoring a touchdown, and only getting one field goal. They got crushed by the New York Jets 23–3 in front of a packed house of fans. The offense only mustered up 222 total yards. Quarterback Gary Danielson converted thirteen of twenty-three passes for 154 yards before getting knocked out of the game with injury. The Browns had to turn to third string backup quarterback Mike Pagel who went seven for fourteen, achieving seventy-three yards with no touchdowns and one interception. The Browns knew they were headed for a long grueling season if they couldn't get the quarterback situation under control. The offensive line's inability to stop incoming pass rushers and keep their quarterback vertical was starting to become a major problem.

The following week, the Cleveland Browns turned things around at home on *Monday Night Football* against the Indianapolis

Colts. They stuck with third string quarterback Mike Pagel because of the injuries to the two players in front of him, and Pagel led them to a 23–17 win. Mike Pagel went twenty-three of thirty-eight for 255 yards and completed touchdown passes of fourteen yards to tight end Ozzie Newsome and seventeen yards to speedy wide receiver Webster Slaughter. The Colts made it close late in the fourth quarter with a Clarence Verdin seventy-three yard punt return, but the Cleveland Browns hung on to win.

Mike Pagel and the Cleveland Browns' team were unable to work their magic the following week as they traveled to Cincinnati, Ohio. The Bengals were great that season; they ended up going 12–4 and making it all the way to the Super Bowl. On that particular Sunday against the Browns, they erupted for seventeen points in the second quarter and the Browns couldn't quite make a comeback. They pulled to within seven in the fourth quarter on a Kevin Mack three yard rush, but it was too little too late and they fell to 2–2 with a 24–17 loss. Pagel completed twenty-four of forty-eight passes for 254 yards and one touchdown. The running attack was non-existent that day, and it really hurt the Browns. To compound matters, the Browns could not stop the three-headed rushing monster of the Cincinnati Bengals—James Brooks, Icky Woods, and Stanley Wilson—who combined for 213 rushing yards and two touchdowns. It allowed for quarterback Boomer Esiason to only have to complete eight passes in the win.

A quarter of the way into the season, the Cleveland Browns had already used three starting quarterbacks, and were desperate for answers to get the train back on the tracks. They traveled to Pittsburgh the following week with Mike Pagel remaining at the helm. However, quarterback play would have little to do with the Browns 23–9 victory that Sunday. Matt Bahr kicked three field goals combined with a seventy-five yard interception for a touchdown by Brian Washington that was more than enough for the win. They coupled their solid defense with a strong running game as Earnest Byner hadseventy-eight yards on twenty carries. Tim Manoa was also a bright spot chipping in with eighty-two yards on eighteen carries including a touchdown.

The Browns failed to keep the momentum of the win as they were beaten the following week at home against the lowly Seattle

Seahawks. They only scored one touchdown in a 16–10 loss. After the latest injury to a quarterback, this time it was Mike Pagel going down, and they literally had to call retired veteran quarterback Don Strock off the golf course to start.

Don Strock came into replace the injured Pagel who had gone two for eight with only twenty-three yards and an interception. Strock did his best to compete, but the rustiness of his game was apparent as he threw twenty passes, connecting on twelve for 151 yards and one interception. It was a rough loss that brought the team back to .500.

With a full week of practice and geared up, Don Strock came back strong the following week and threw two touchdown passes in the 19–3 victory at home against the Philadelphia Eagles. Strock connected on a fifteen yard touchdown strike to Webster Slaughter in the third quarter, then capped it off with an eighteen touchdown pass in the fourth quarter to Reggie Langhorne. It was part of a 189 yard passing day that put the Cleveland Browns back over .500 at 4–3.

After splitting the first two games against the Seahawks and Eagles, they flew to Phoenix to take on the Cardinals. It was the eighth game of the season and Bernie Kosar had finally returned to start under center. Eight games in, they had already gone through four quarterbacks before being able to get their starter back. Kosar didn't waste any time getting back into the fold as he tossed a three yard touchdown pass to Ricky Bolden to start the first quarter and give the Browns a 7–0 lead. Kosar remained hot as he launched a twenty-nine yard touchdown pass to Reggie Langhorne in the second quarter to extend the lead to 14–0. The Cardinals came roaring back with two touchdowns of their own to tie the game before Matt Bahr hit a forty-six yard field goal to close out the first half and send the Browns into the locker room up 17–14.

Bahr would tack on another field goal to start the second half and put the Browns ahead 20–14. The Cardinals would not go away, however, and came back to actually take the lead when quarterback Cliff Stout hit Robert Awalt for a twenty-one yard touchdown pass to give the Cardinals a 21–20 lead. Bernie Kosar and the Cleveland Browns were not to be denied. They made Kosar's first game back a memorable one as he connected with

Reggie Langhorne on a twenty-five scoring strike that would put the Browns ahead for good as they tacked on safety points and won 29-21. They were halfway through the season, had started four quarterbacks, but the record was on the plus side at 5-3 with reason to be optimistic.

The Cleveland Browns looked to remain hot as they returned home the following week to take on the Cincinnati Bengals at Cleveland Municipal Stadium. Bernie Kosar struggled all game, completing only eighteen passes and was picked off twice. Fortunately for the Browns, other members of the team stepped up their game and helped them pull off the 23-16 win, their third straight! The Cleveland Browns' defense played hungry all day, holding Boomer Esiason to zero touchdown passes and 173 yards. They also shut down Icky Woods and James Brooks for a combined ninety-five yards rushing.

At 6-3, the Cleveland Browns were looking like a serious contender once again to win the division if they could keep up their strategic winning ways. The Houston Oilers had different plans, however, as they punished the Browns all day inside of the Astrodome. The Oilers combined rushing touchdowns from Alonzo Highsmith and Mike Rozier along with a passing touchdown from Warren Moon to Ernest Givins for the 24-17 win. Reggie Langhorne had a rare twenty yard rushing touchdown, but it was not enough to win the game.

Things would not improve for the Cleveland Browns. The following week, as they traveled to Denver, they were once again blown out in embarrassing fashion by a score of 30-7. John Elway had no problems displaying showmanship in excellent quarterbacking as he torched the Browns' vaunted defense for 207 yards, two touchdowns and zero interceptions. The Browns lost to Denver again, and it was becoming more apparent that Elway had pretty good insight into their game. The brutal loss dropped the Browns' record to 6-4. At times, it seemed like Elway could beat the Browns in his sleep. They would have to overcome him if they ever wanted to reach the next level.

The Cleveland Browns were determined to turn things around once again after two straight brutal conference losses. Their arch rival, the Pittsburgh Steelers were coming to town and the Browns were eager to release their frustration against their hated rivals. The Cleveland Browns built a big lead early in the game, and were unstoppable. Bernie Kosar threw touchdown passes to Reggie Langhorne and Derek Tennell. Frank Minnifield chipped in with an excellent special teams effort play as he returned a blocked punt for a touchdown. On this day, the Steelers were no match for the inspired Browns' attack. Cleveland won 27-7, improving their record to 7-5 three quarters of the way into the season.

The Cleveland Browns traveled to Washington, D.C. the following week and knocked off the Redskins 17-13. Kosar was held without a touchdown; nevertheless, Kevin Mack rushed for 122 yards and a touchdown in the win. The Browns remained hot and won their third straight game the following week with a nail-biting 24-21 win at home against the Dallas Cowboys. Dallas was terrible that season with a 3-13 record, but they gave the Browns all they could handle that day. Herschel Walker ran the ball 24 times for an impressive 134 yards and a touchdown. Kosar was up for the challenge as he responded with 308 yards with three touchdown passes to Reggie Langhorne, Herman Fontenot, and Clarence Weathers. It was the capper on another three-game winning streak that saw the Cleveland Browns improve to 9-5.

With the playoffs within their grasp, the Cleveland Browns traveled to sunny Miami, Florida the following week for what turned into an epic shootout against Dan Marino and the Miami Dolphins. It was a wild affair that saw yet another injury to Bernie Kosar.

Dan Marino began the scoring in the second quarter as he passed to Mark Clayton for an eleven yard touchdown pass. Bernie Kosar responded with a thirty-nine yard scoring strike to Earnest Byner. After a thirty-three yard Matt Bahr field goal, the Dolphins struck again on a Dan Marino to Jim Jensen touchdown pass, also in the second quarter. Fuad Reveiz capped off the scoring with a thirty-five yard field goal to give the Dolphins a 17-10 halftime lead.

The second half started off the same way the first half ended, with another scoring drive from the Miami Dolphins. This time, it was a Dan Marino touchdown pass to Lorenzo Hampton to extend the Dolphins' lead to 24-10. The Browns continued to show their resilience with a rare Bernie Kosar touchdown scramble to pull within 24–17. Sadly for Cleveland Browns' fans, that was the last they would see Kosar play in the 1988 season. He was hurt soon after, and this time, he was done for good.

The fourth quarter began with Dan Marino throwing yet another touchdown pass, this time connecting with Mark Clayton on a nine yard scoring strike. The score was 31–17 and things were looking bleak for Cleveland with Kosar out of the game. Don Strock was called upon to step up once again. He did not disappoint as he led another furious rally. Strock connected with Reggie Langhorne on two separate fourth quarter touchdown passes to tie the game. It was an unbelievable comeback and happened with just a little too much time on the clock. Dan Marino, who was known for his numerous fourth-quarter game-winning drives, had yet another one. It was Lorenzo Hampton rumbling in for a one yard rush in the closing seconds to secure the win for Miami, 38–31.

Heading into the final week of the season, the Cleveland Browns were 9–6 and needed a win at home against the Houston Oilers to sneak into the playoffs. It would be up to aging veteran backup Don Strock to get them there. Strock played his college ball at Virginia Tech in 1973, his senior season, and had led the nation in total passing and total offense. The strong season allowed him to finish in the top ten for the Heisman vote. His career at Virginia Tech was so impressive that in 1985 he was voted into their Hall of Fame.

Strock was drafted by the Miami Dolphins in the 1973 Draft and spent fourteen seasons there, most of them, as a backup to the great Bob Griese and later on an even better Dan Marino. Strock just had that luck of always being behind a legend. He had a vast amount of post-season experience as he was on the Dolphins's team when they won the Super Bowl in 1973 as an unbeaten team. He was also a part of both teams that lost in the Super Bowl, once in 1983 to the Washington Redskins and then again in 1985 against the San Francisco 49ers. Now, for the first time in years, Strock would play in a pressure-packed game that would ultimately decide if the Cleveland Browns would reach the playoffs, or for the first time in four years, be forced to go home early.

It was roughly twenty blistery degrees on Sunday, December 18, 1988 when the Houston Oilers visited Cleveland. Houston was also hungry for the win because they knew if they won, it would knock the Browns out of contention; also, if they lost, they would have to return the following week right back to Cleveland and face the Browns in the first round.

The Houston Oilers got off to a good start with Tony Zendejas hitting a thirty-nine yard field goal followed by a thirty-six yard interception touchdown return by Domingo Bryant to put the Oilers ahead 10–0. The Cleveland Browns' defense put up points of their own when Michael Dean Perry scored on a ten yard fumble return for a touchdown. The Oilers advanced with two more Tony Zendejas field goals from forty-two and thirty-five yards to close out the half and give the Oilers the midway lead of 16–7.

The Oilers wasted no time in expounding upon that lead early in the third quarter when Warren Moon connected with Haywood Jeffires on a seven yard scoring strike to put Houston ahead 23–7. The Browns were finally on high alert, and got themselves back into the game with a two yard touchdown pass from Strock to Byner followed by a two yard touchdown rush by Byner to start the fourth quarter. The Browns were still down two by a score of 23–21 but suddenly were showing signs of life.

Despite all the odds being against them, and having a fourth string aging by the second quarterback, the Cleveland Browns showed the heart of a lion and the fight of a champion by completing the comeback with a twenty-two yard touchdown pass from Don Strock to Webster Slaughter to win the game 28–23. The win secured home field advantage the following week in the divisional round against those same Houston Oilers.

Don Strock overcame three interceptions to pass for 326 yards, toss two touchdowns, and just competed all game long to keep the Browns in it. Earnest Byner continued to do his best to make up for the fumble in the prior season's championship game by scoring touchdowns via the air and ground game that day. The Browns were down but not out. They had reached the playoffs for the fourth straight season when everyone else might have folded.

For the season, the Cleveland Browns scored 304 points which was a nineteen point per game average, good enough for twentieth of twenty-eight in the NFL. Their defense remained the focal piece of the team and only allowed 288 points, which averages out to eighteen points per game, finishing a stout sixth overall in the NFL. Their great defense and even-keeled offense led to an overall differential of sixteen points, which was exactly one point per game better than their opponent.

Bernie Kosar led the team in touchdown passes with ten, and only had three interceptions with 1,890 yards passing. Despite only playing in nine games, Kosar was sacked twenty-five times for a loss of 172 yards. It was a growing problem that could not be ignored. Earnest Byner played in all sixteen games, avoiding the injury bug, but was held to only 576 yards along with five more fumbles. Kevin Mack, who only played in eleven games, chipped in with 485 yards on the ground along with three touchdowns, the same amount while playing in five less games than Byner. Felix Wright led the team with five interceptions. The Cleveland Browns' defense would need to be on top of their best game to try and stop the Houston Oilers' high-powered offense for the second straight week.

The coach of the Houston Oilers was Jerry Glanville, and he was out for blood after the Browns took home field advantage away from them the prior week. Glanville was a colorful character who loved to yell at the referees. He was quite comical at times, and the NFL video team often caught some of his barbs on camera. Glanville had the help of star quarterback Warren Moon to run his high tempo run and shoot offense. Moon excelled in the offense and threw for 2,327 yards with seventeen touchdowns that season. His numbers would have been even better but he missed six games that season due to an injury.

The main target of Warren Moon was Drew Hill, who caught seventy-two balls for 1,141 yards and ten touchdowns that season. Along with Hill was Earnest Givins who was also coming off of a great season that saw him catch sixty balls for 976 yards and scored five touchdowns. Also helping out with 302 yards and a touchdown was Curtis Duncan. They were a formidable receiving crew with Haywood Jeffires also coming into his own. The Oilers looked like a dominant offense for many years to come.

December 24, 1988 was not the normal Christmas Eve of parents wrapping last second gifts as the children wondered what Santa Claus would be bringing them the next morning. This one for both Cleveland and Houston fans was about earning a trip to face Buffalo in the divisional round the following weekend. Tension and drama were both at an all-time high as the two AFC Central Divisional rivals were about to square off for a third time.

The Cleveland Browns jumped out to an early 3–0 lead on a thirty-three yard Matt Bahr field goal. They were given good field position following a Felix Wright interception return. The lead and Don Strock both quickly left the game for the Browns as Houston knocked the aging quarterback out for good. He had been playing with a rubber band on his throwing hand, but it wasn't enough to keep him in the action as the Browns were forced to go back to Mike Pagel after Strock severely hurt his wrist. Meanwhile, as the Browns' quarterback cavalcade continued, the Oilers scored ten straight points, highlighted by a fourteen yard touchdown pass from Warren Moon to Allen Pinkett to give them the 10–3 lead.

The Browns battled back with two more Matt Bahr field goals of twenty-six and twenty-eight yards to slice into the Houston Oilers' lead. At halftime, the Browns trailed 14–9 in what was looking to be another game set to go down to the wire. Making the most of his opportunity, Mike Pagel connected on a fourteen yard touchdown pass to Webster Slaughter to give the Browns a 16–14 lead.

The Oilers refused to stay down for long though as they battled back to start the fourth quarter with a one yard Lorenzo White touchdown rumble. A little bit later on, the Oilers tacked on a forty-nine yard Tony Zendejas field goal to give them the 24–16 lead. Down eight points with time running out, the Browns went on a desperation drive led by Pagel, resulting in a two yard Webster Slaughter touchdown pass to bring the Browns within one point at 24–23. It would prove to be too late. The Cleveland Browns' season ended with the Houston Oilers win, 24–23.

It was an up and down game for both teams. Moon threw three interceptions but rebounded to toss a touchdown pass and 213 yards. Mike Pagel did his best off the bench coming into a critical game. Pagel threw for 179 yards and two touchdowns, but it simply wasn't sufficient to keep the Browns alive in the playoffs. Notably, the two teams combined for twenty-two penalties.

The Houston Oilers went on to face the Buffalo Bills the following week, losing to them by a score of 17–10. The Bills would be knocked off in the AFC Championship game by another AFC

Central team, the Cincinnati Bengals 21–10. The Cincinnati Bengals, despite being a heavy underdog, was narrowly defeated in a classic Super Bowl that season against the Joe Montana-led San Francisco 49ers.

Wide receiver Brian Brennan talks about the craziness of that season, and the challenges and advantages of working with several quarterbacks:

> *"It wasn't too bad because they were all seasoned quarterbacks. I mean Don Strock was very seasoned and so was Mike Pagel and Gary Danielson. We had the consistency of offensive coordinator Lindy Infante. We also had the consistency of having the same receiving core of Reggie Langhorne, Webster Slaughter and myself. Our running game was also very strong. With the good offensive line and threat of running and passing the ball well, it helped. It was the same exact offense and players, so we just plugged in a new quarterback and off we went."*

Wide receiver Reggie Langhorne had his best season as a Cleveland Brown player that year, despite the various quarterbacks. He discusses why he was able to improve his game, and the craziness of having to work with so many starting quarterbacks in one season:

> *"For me, it wasn't a problem; we had Kosar, Pagel and Danielson all get hurt which led to pulling Don Strock off the golf course in Florida. I really enjoyed catching the ball from Strock because he had a soft touch and early delivery. He had the great experience of someone who had played in the league for so long. The reason why my numbers improved so much was because of injuries to other players on offense such as Earnest Byner and Webster Slaughter. Those injuries made me the number one guy instead of the number two or three guy on the offensive game plan, and I was able to have some success. I became the guy to go to on third down and the guy to make the big play. As I said, the offensive line and the four quarterbacks all had to work together to make things work out. Marty Schottenheimer instilled in us how to act as a group on the field and we fed off of each other as players. We won for several years and that had a lot to do with it...our attitude of next man up. That attitude enabled us to continue winning despite all the big injuries we suffered that season.*

In what was viewed as a shock to many, that game would be the last for Marty Schottenheimer as the head coach of the Cleveland Browns. He could not agree on a contract extension amongst other personal issues with owner Art Modell, and the two agreed to part ways. Schottenheimer left behind quite a legacy. While in Cleveland, he held a 44–27 (.620) regular-season record and a 2–4 (.333) mark in the playoffs, including four playoff appearances, and three AFC Central Division titles.

Schottenheimer would be leaving behind some very big shoes to fill. The pertinent question was, who would fill them? Would they turn to someone already on the staff, or look outside the franchise for someone with prior head coaching experience? Marty had been the full-time head coach for four seasons, leading them to the playoffs each season. It was a perplexing move for Modell to make, but it was even odder when he looked to someone who made his name while working for the enemy to become the new head coach.

Chapter Four

A Change of the Guard

Without Marty Schottenheimer at the helm as head coach, the Cleveland Browns would need to succeed him with someone who could handle the talent on the team but also the ego of the team's owner. The fact that the team had been to the playoffs four years in a row and had one of the league's best offensive attacks would help make it a lucrative employment opportunity for any established coach looking to get back into the league, or any top-notch assistant looking to make a name for himself.

The solution for head coach came from the most unexpected place. It was a man who made his name being one of the most important assistant coaches of the Browns' hated divisional rivals—the Pittsburgh Steelers. The new head coach of the Cleveland Browns would now be Leon Carson, or as everyone knew him, "Bud."

Leon "Bud" Carson played his college football at the University of North Carolina as a Tar Heels' defensive back, but left after two years to enter the United States Marine Corps. Carson was tough, and his stint in the Marines helped to strengthen and make him tougher. However, military life wasn't for him long term, as his heart was with football. In 1967, he took a job on the coaching staff of Bobby Dodd at Georgia Institute of Technology (Georgia Tech). It didn't take Carson long to go from assistant to becoming the man in charge. Carson took over as head coach in 1967. It took Carson a little time to get caught up on recruiting and fix the mess left behind by Dodd as the Georgia Tech Yellow Jackets endured three straight losing 4–6 seasons before turning things around and going 9-3. He led the Yellow Jackets to a big win in the 1970 Sun Bowl 17-9 over Texas Tech.

The following season, the Georgia Tech Yellow Jackets took a step back under Carson and finished the season 6–6 complete with a disappointing 41–18 loss in the Peach Bowl against Ole Miss. He was let go by the University shortly thereafter. Most men would see this as a lethal blow to their NFL coaching dreams. Little did anyone realize at the time but it was the greatest thing that could have ever happened to Carson, as his life and career in coaching were about to go through the biggest resurgence possible.

Pittsburgh Steelers head coach Chuck Noll hired Carson as defensive backs coach to start the 1972 season. After only one season, Noll was so impressed with Carson that he promoted him to the defensive coordinator. Carson was influential in developing the famed "Steel Curtain" defense. It is widely regarded as one of the greatest defensive units and eras in the history of the National Football League. The defense boasts some of the all-time greats to play the game including Jack Lambert, Mel Blount, Jack Ham, and Mean Joe Greene. They gave up fewer points than any other AFC conference team in Pittsburgh's Super Bowl seasons of 1974 and 1975. In 1976, they set a record that may never be broken when they gave up fewer than ten points a game.

Carson was known as one of the top defensive minds in the game. He knew that his goal of becoming an NFL head coach would not happen while in Pittsburgh because Knoll was racking up Super Bowl championships, so he left Pittsburgh for the Los Angeles Rams; however, still not a head coach, he was asked to be the defensive coordinator there as well. With Carson handling the defense, the usually awful Rams turned things around that season and made it to the Super Bowl, losing to the Carson's former team the Pittsburgh Steelers as his "Steel Curtain" defense captured their fourth Super Bowl championship.

Carson's NFL coaching odyssey continued as he remained the defensive coordinator in Los Angeles for three more years before taking coordinator jobs in Baltimore, Kansas City, and then the New York Jets. While with the Jets, he helped turn their defense around and once again reminded the NFL that he had a brilliant tactical mind. It was only a matter of time before an NFL owner was willing to take a chance on Carson as a head coach. Art Modell was that owner. He took a chance, and hired Carson to be the eighth head coach in Cleveland Browns' history.

One of the biggest switches was going from the 3-4 defensive scheme of Marty Schottenheimer to the 4-3 aggressive attack that

Carson wanted to run. Carson had defensive coordinator Dan Radakovich in place to make sure things were ran his way, and heavy pressure was to be put on the opposing quarterback each week.

Reggie Langhorne describes the adjustment from Schottenheimer's strategy to Carson's defense strategy:

> *"Bud was more involved in the defense so I didn't get to spend a lot of time with Bud. For me, it was more of the same coming from a small school...my attitude was so what, it's still football and we have to play the game hard. No matter who you're playing for, the fact remains, the field is the same length and you need to do your job as the next man does his. If the scheme made sense, I knew we could get the job done. It didn't hurt that we picked up Eric Metcalf that year, who really lit it up for us that year as a rookie. Metcalf proved to be a great asset to the offense. So even with missing a few players on offense, he did a great job filling in and also on punt returns and kick returns. He also did an amazing job catching balls out of the backfield."*

Felix Wright gives his thoughts on the coaching change heading into the 1989 season:

> *"It worked out real well. I remember when Bud first came in... both him and Marty were defensive-minded head coaches. Bud had a different philosophy then Marty did; however, I think Bud was a little more aggressive when it came to attacking people on defense. I remember when Bud first came in, he wanted to switch my position.*
>
> *I didn't really like that because I liked the position I was already playing. I was a bit of a rebuttal because I really didn't want to switch positions, and didn't understand what he was trying to tell me at the time. He sat me down and explained to me that he wanted to move me from free safety to strong safety because the strong safety is the main cog in his defense and the position that needs to be able to call the plays...get the defense set and into position. Once he explained it to me and we got out and started practicing and putting it together, he did put me in good positions and make things happen...and I bought into the system like everyone else did. It worked out well for me as I ended up leading the league in interceptions. It was awesome, and I thank him for*

that. He was a great guy who knew so much football because he had been in it for so many years.

Bud Carson probably forgot more football than I would ever even know. He didn't know much about offense so Bernie and his crew with offensive coordinator Marc Trestman kind of handled that end of things. I remember the first game we played, we opened up in Pittsburgh and won 51–0, and I was thinking...wow this is pretty cool! Between the two coaches, I think both of them were good coaches, him and Marty. I think both of them ended up getting raw deals. Marty and management had a disagreement on offensive coordinators because they wanted to switch, and Marty didn't want to switch coordinators. Marty was a 'don't fix it if it is not broke' kind of guy. I believe in that philosophy as well. However, ownership always wins those deals and so Marty chose to leave and go to Kansas City, which was bad for the team's moral.

Brian Brennan weighs in with his thoughts on the coaching switch:

"We had the same group of talented players for the most part that we had in the prior seasons, although we may have a little older but still very talented. Bud knew that, and he wasn't going to come in and change a lot of things with a winning formula... why would he? We were all mature adults at that point. We knew how to win, and what was expected to win...and again, I think that speaks to the talent level we had as a team. Bud treated us as mature adults and delegated more of the responsibilities to the position coaches and even the players more so than Marty did, and it made for a solid team."

With the new head coach in place, General Manager Ernie Accorsi and Director of Pro Personnel Michael Lombardi had their work cut out for them to add talent to a roster that was starting to age. Carson made the decision to keep Marc Trestman on as his offensive coordinator, and now it was time to add another piece for Trestman to play with. They hit the Draft boards hard in search of youth and speed at key offensive positions.

Their first draft pick was the speedy Eric Metcalf, a small but fiercely quick running back and kick returner out of Texas

University. Metcalf is the son of former St. Louis Cardinal great Terry Metcalf. Not only did Eric have football in his blood, but he had lightning in his feet. He was the 1988 U.S. Track and Field Champion in the long jump, and a two-time NCAA Champion in the event while at Texas. It was a talent that he developed while in high school where he set records including the seventh longest distance ever posted indoors by a USA high-schooler with a jump of 7.75 meters.

Eric Metcalf continued to excel at track in college where he held the University of Texas long jump record at 8.44 meters. He went on to win the NCAA National Long Jump Championship in 1986 and 1988, and the SWC Long Jump titles in 1986 and 1987. He added on to those accomplishments by also becoming the United States Jr. National Long Jump Champion in 1986 and 1987. His hard work earned him the distinction of being a five-time All-American.

There was no professional track and field; however, there was professional football, and that is where Eric Metcalf looked to earn a living for himself and also follow in the footsteps of his father. Eric Metcalf excelled in his time at Texas as he was an All-Southwest Conference selection three times. He also was the 1987 Southwest Conference Player of the Year and a second team All-American. To this day, Eric Metcalf holds the distinction of being the only player in Texas history to lead the team in all-purpose yards all four years, and holds every school-receiving record for a running back.

Bernie Kosar coveted pass-catching running backs that could run wild in his pass happy offense, and the Cleveland Browns were fully aware of that when they drafted Eric Metcalf with their first round pick, and thirteenth overall pick. Earnest Byner was traded to the Washington Redskins before the start of the 1989 season for running back Mike Oliphant. Metcalf would be counted on to fill that void left behind by Byner.

The selection of Eric Metcalf became even more crucial when their other starting running back Kevin Mack got served with a six-month jail prison sentence just weeks before the season began. Mack had fallen into the wrong crowd of people and made a horrendous mistake. Mack, who was only twenty-six years old at the time, was arrested while sitting in his vehicle as the police searched his car and found eleven bags of cocaine, each worth approximately fifty dollars each at the time. Judge Richard McMonagle of Cuyahoga County Common Pleas Court sentenced Mack to the Mansfield Reformatory, but allowed Mack to apply for probation after serving at least thirty days.

The incident took place near East Tech High School, located in a neighborhood that had a reputation for drug trafficking. Not only did the arrest come as a shock to the Cleveland Browns' fans and Mack's teammates and coaches, but it also hit the owner pretty hard. Art Modell was truly shocked upon hearing the news. He was quoted as saying, *"I know Kevin Mack,"* Modell said. *"He's a very, very fine person and what this is all about is a shock to all of us."* With hindsight being 20/20, the Cleveland Browns would have never traded away Byner had they known the arrest of Mack was forthcoming. Mack would only end up serving one month of his six-month sentence.

With their second pick in the Draft, and the 31st overall pick, they chose wide receiver Lawyer Tillman out of Auburn. He was a big and lanky receiver that would give Bernie Kosar another viable target in the passing attack. Tillman had made a famous play in college, playing for Auburn against their arch rival Alabama in the 1986 Iron Bowl. It was his scoring on a late fourth-quarter play, and end around that led to Auburn upsetting Alabama for the win, and Tillman jumping up Draft boards.

The Cleveland Browns followed the two offensive picks with back-to-back draft picks to help things on the other side of the ball. They didn't have a third-round pick, but they selected defensive end Andrew Stewart with their fourth round pick. They followed that up by taking cornerback Kyle Kramer to further help a strong secondary. In the fifth round, they drafted another receiver, Vernon Jones from Maryland. The receiving additions of Vernon Jones and Lawyer Tillman would go along nicely with an already very deep-receiving core threat. The Browns' starting receivers were Webster Slaughter, Brian Brennan, Reggie Langhorne, and Gerald "Ice Cube" McNeil.

Quarterback Bernie Kosar was protected by his veteran line of offensive lineman consisting of Paul Farren, Ted Banker, Gregg Rakoczy, Cody Risien, and Dan Fike. Mike Baab had left the team in the offseason. Joining the rookie Eric Metcalf in the backfield was fullback Tim Manoa who would be counted on to pick up blitz assignments and help guide the rookie. Ozzie Newsome would continue to be the anchor of the offense and line up to catch balls at tight end.

The Browns' defense was stacked again with cornerbacks Frank Minnifield and Hanford Dixon to go along with safeties Felix Wright and Thane Gash. The linebackers were as fierce as ever as Clay Matthews, David Grayson, and Mike Johnson looked to make anyone coming across the middle against them pay for it with a thunderous hit. Second year sensation Michael Dean Perry would join forces with Al "Bubba" Baker, Carl "Big Daddy" Hairston, and Robert Banks on the defensive line to keep pressure on the opposing quarterbacks.

The Browns also possessed one of the quickest return teams in the NFL with rookie Eric Metcalf set to return kicks, and Gerald McNeil handling the punt-returning duties. The place kicking would be handled by the popular and reliable Matt Bahr. He was in his tenth NFL season, and viewed as one of the best kickers in the league. The punting job was won by Bryan Wagner.

Along with several new additions to the coaching staff and team roster, the Cleveland Browns would have to adapt to several new rule changes the NFL was laying out that season. Some of the more noticeable ones were after a penalty that occurs inside the last two minutes of the first half and inside the last five minutes of the second half, the game clock will start at the snap, instead of when the ball is spotted and the Referee signals it is ready to be played. If a receiver and a defender eventually establish joint control of a pass, the ball will be awarded to whoever was the first player to establish control of the ball.

With a rule that made zero sense and took away from the spirit of the game, the NFL stated that there would be a loss of timeouts or five yard penalties, to handle the problem of crowd noise when it became too loud for the offensive team to hear its signals. This was almost directly placed against the rabid fans of the Cleveland Browns, as their antics and crowd enthusiasm had caused multiple offenses to commit false start penalties and delay of games.

With more and more teams starting to run it and incorporate it into their offense, the "hurry up offense" was recognized as fully legal, and penalties for delay of game would be called against teams whose defenders faked injuries in order to slow down the tempo, unless those teams called for timeouts.

The Leon "Bud" Carson-led era of the Cleveland Browns would begin on September 10, 1989 from the steel city of Pittsburgh, Pennsylvania. Carson was in the same city where he had seen his best success in the NFL as the defensive coordinator of the vaunted steel curtain. The game was at Three Rivers Stadium in front of a packed house of Pittsburgh Steelers' enthusiastic fans.

The Steelers were led that year by quarterback Bubby Brister, who the games television announcer Joe Namath was quoted on the broadcast as saying, *"Brister all set to make things happen today."* Brister's main receiving threats were rookie receiver Derek Hill and Louis Lipps. In the backfield with Brister was rookie running back Tim Worley and veteran fullback and resident loud mouth Meril Hoge. However, despite the boast by Namath in the booth, the only thing that Brister was able to *"make happen"* was turnovers and bad plays as the Cleveland Browns crushed the Steelers from the opening snap!

The Cleveland Browns came out like a team on fire to impress their new head coach and help him take home a victory against his ex-team, and their hated rivals. The defensive scheme of "Bud" Carson paid immediate dividends when linebacker Clay Matthews took a fumble in for a touchdown and gave the Browns an early 7-0 lead. After a Matt Bahr field goal advanced them 10-0, the defense scored again with linebacker David Grayson taking another fumble in for a touchdown. At the end of the first quarter, it was Cleveland Browns seventeen, Pittsburgh Steelers zero, with both touchdowns being scored by the Browns' strategic defense. Despite the pre-boasting of Namath of the unproven Brister, it was the Cleveland Browns' defense that was truly making things happen that day.

The scoring spree for the Browns continued in the second quarter when Matt Bahr booted another field goal from twenty yards and put the Browns up 20-0. They captured their first offensive score when Tim Manoa rumbled in the end zone from three yards out later in the quarter. Matt Bahr capped off the first-half scoring with a successful thirty yard field goal to gleefully send the Browns into the locker room at halftime up 30–0.

The Cleveland Browns continued to press forward on the scoring in the second half as they opened up the third quarter with another Tim Manoa touchdown rumble. This one from two yards out, which put the Browns even further ahead by a score of 37–0. And, the defense wasn't done scoring yet either. Moments later, it was David Grayson scoring his second touchdown of the game, with a fourteen yard interception return. At the end of three quarters, it was the Cleveland Browns dominating the Pittsburgh Steelers 44–0. For the fun of it, the Browns would tack on one more touchdown with a Mike Oliphant twenty-one yard touchdown rushing strike.

When the blood bath was done, it was the Cleveland Browns fifty-one and the Pittsburgh Steelers zero. It was one of the biggest opening day blowouts in NFL history. Kosar didn't have to do too much as he had short fields to work on all day because of the incredible defensive play. He threw for 207 yards, including a fifty-one yard strike to Webster Slaughter to set up one of the touchdowns.

The newly minted three-headed rushing attack was not overly impressive, but they did get the job done when needed. Rookie Eric Metcalf had a modest twenty-eight yards on ten carries. Mike Oliphant, who was only seeing increased playing time because of Kevin Mack's imprisonment, ran for forty-eight yards on six carries, including the twenty-one yard touchdown strike. Tim Manoa rushed the ball nine times for only twenty yards, but did score twice from within the five yard line. Matt Bahr would have to ice down his foot on the plane ride home after kicking six extra points and three field goals for a total of thirteen points.

As for Bubby Brister, the man who Joe Namath claimed would *"really make things happen,"* went a meager ten for twenty-two passing with only eighty-four yards. Brister compounded those weak numbers with three interceptions and six sacks. The Browns' defense had dominated in the opening week, and put the rest of the AFC on notice! It was also the worst home game loss of legendary Pittsburgh head coach Chuck Noll's long coaching career.

The Cleveland Browns had their home opener a week later against their former playoff rival, the New York Jets. The Browns once again put up points with ease, but it was the Jets who actually scored first in this affair when running back Roger Vick scored a rushing touchdown from thirty-nine yards out to give the Jets an early 7–0 lead.

It wouldn't take the Browns long, however, to respond to the Jets' touchdown strike with one of their own when Bernie Kosar hit Webster Slaughter on a beautiful thirty-five yard pass for a touchdown, tying the game at seven points apiece. The defense once again rose up and took scoring matters into their own hands when Thane Gash intercepted a Ken O'Brien pass and took it back thirty-seven yards for the touchdown. The Browns held onto their lead, proudly exiting the field at halftime up 14–7.

The Jets came out motivated in the second half tying the game on a Ken O'Brien to Jo-Jo Townsell forty-nine yard touchdown pass. Not to be outdone, Kosar answered the O'Brien strike with one of his own, and connected with Tim Manoa on a six yard touchdown pass. After a Jets field goal, the Browns scored yet again with a Keith Jones nine yard touchdown rush. At the end of three quarters, the Browns led 28–17.

The Jets started the fourth quarter quickly with a Freeman McNeil one yard touchdown rush. Once again, the Browns would respond in kind as Bernie Kosar hit tight end Ozzie Newsome with a four yard touchdown pass. Matt Bahr followed up the Newsome touchdown with a twenty-one yard field goal to put the Browns up to stay at 38–24. Two games into the "Bud" Carson era, and the Browns were 2–0.

The Cleveland Browns' defense proceeded to dominate as they picked off Ken O'Brien four times. They had interceptions by Thane Gash, Mike Johnson, and two by Felix Wright. They also achieved three sacks by Al Baker, Michael Dean Perry, and Andrew Stewart. Although Bernie Kosar was held to 196 yards, he did manage to get in three touchdown passes at critical moments in the game. As a team, the Browns only rushed for eighty-five yards on twenty-three attempts. Needless to say, those numbers would have to improve or the Browns would soon be in trouble. The Browns had scored eighty-nine points in two games, but their running game had little to do with it.

The following week, the Browns traveled to Cincinnati where they suffered their first loss of the season against the Bengals 21–14. They looked good in the first half as Bernie Kosar threw touchdown passes to Eric Metcalf and Tim Manoa, but the Bengals pressed forward with scores of their own each time. The Browns were shut out in the second half, and fell to 2–1 in the process.

Bernie Kosar looked sharp as he threw for 203 yards and two touchdowns, but also tossed an interception along the way. Their running game continued to be a problem as they once again struggled to get anything going. Their running game was held to ninety-twoyards on twenty-one carries. Perhaps the biggest concern of those numbers was that thirty-two of the ninety-one yards came on end-a-rounds with their receiver Gerald McNeil and not yardage from their actual running backs.

The Browns managed to bounce back from their first loss of the season by doing something they had not done since 1974—they beat the Denver Broncos the following week in Cleveland. This was a statement win and game for "Bud" Carson as one of the biggest reasons his predecessor Marty Schottenheimer was let go was his inability to beat Denver.

The game itself was a surprising defense showcase by both professional teams. It came down to field goals as Cleveland place kicker Matt Bahr made three of five, from thirty-six and forty-eight yards again to win it as time expired. The final score was 16–13. Denver quarterback John Elway was held in check with only six completions, which was a career game low. The Browns defense had carried them to this win, and improved their record to a stout 3–1 under their new head coach, Leon "Bud" Carson.

Nevertheless, the Cleveland Browns didn't have much time to bask in the glow of their Denver win, as the very next week saw a heartbreaking loss to the Miami Dolphins in a game once again dominated by defense. The Browns lost to the Dolphins by a score of 13–10. The ending came in overtime on a thirty-five yard Pete Stoyanovich field goal. Kosar threw for 234 yards but had zero touchdowns and two interceptions.

They couldn't bounce back, and lost the following week's game at home against Pittsburgh 17–7 in another lackluster effort. Their offense was suddenly cold, and would need to get things together quickly for the rookie head coach. It was a puzzling loss, due to the fact that they had destroyed the Steelers on the road 51–0 just six weeks earlier.

The Cleveland Browns were determined to get back on the winning end of things the next week when the Chicago Bears came to town. It was *Monday Night Football*, and the Browns were eager to showcase their skills on primetime television. The eyes of the football nation would be on them, and they didn't want to disappoint.

The Cleveland Browns got things started right when rookie Eric Metcalf scored on a three yard dump off pass from Kosar to give the home team an early 7–0 lead. It was the only score of the first half as the Browns were once again entrenched in a stiff defensive battle. The Browns' defense under Carson's strategic leadership continued to be their strength all season long, and this night would be no exception.

Matt Bahr put the Browns back on the scoreboard early in the third quarter when he converted a successful thirty-one yard field goal. Eric Metcalf would be the next player to join in the scoring as he hit the hole hard and scored on a seven yard rush to put the Browns ahead 17–0 to close out the third quarter. The Browns would end all doubt early in the fourth quarter as Bernie Kosar broke a Cleveland Browns' record by connecting with Webster Slaughter on an absolutely incredible ninety-seven yard touchdown pass. It was a record that stood for fifteen years.

The Bears finally got on the scoreboard a short time later with a Jim Harbaugh touchdown pass to Wendell Davis. It was too little too late, and after a thirty-five yard Matt Bahr field goal, the Cleveland Browns took the victory by an impressive final score of 24–7 in front of a joyous hometown crowd. This home-winning game was highly relevant for the team because they had the opportunity to showcase their strategic and dominant skills in front of a national television audience. This big win would go a long way in helping restore their confidence after the previous rough two game patches.

Bernie Kosar had another strong performance as he completed twenty-two of twenty-nine passes for 281 yards and two touchdowns with zero interceptions. The rushing game continued to struggle, however, as Eric Metcalf was held to only sixteen yards on twelve carries. The defense once again dominated, holding Bears' quarterbacks Jim Harbaugh and Mike Tomczak to only thirteen completions and 169 passing yards, most of which came in mop-up prevent defense time.

Following their big Monday night win, it appeared as if the short week of practice took its toll on the Browns's team. The following Sunday as the Houston Oilers invaded Cleveland Municipal Stadium, the Browns were shut out in the first half against their heated divisional rival and trailed 10–0 after a beautiful Warren Moon to Haywood Jeffires thirteen yard touchdown pass. They also scored on a twenty-three yard Tony Zendejas field goal.

Down 10–0 against the Oilers, head coach "Bud" Carson would have to light a fire underneath his team before they left the locker room for the second half. The Browns were 4–3 at this point, and still unsure in many ways if Carson was the man for the job. This would be his chance to show that he could make vital half-time adjustments, and help pick his team up off the canvas.

Whatever adjustments were made and whatever words of encouragement were said during halftime clearly worked as the Cleveland Browns emerged out of the locker room as a team on a mission. Bernie Kosar led a drive down the field in which he capped off with a rare five yard touchdown scramble. The Browns scored again the next time they touched the ball as Kosar led another scoring drive when he connected with Webster Slaughter on a dazzling eighty yard touchdown strike to give the Browns a 14–10 lead.

Warren Moon and the Houston Oilers answered the back-to-back touchdown drives out of Cleveland with one of their own, capped off by a Mike Rozier one yard touchdown rush. This score would put the Oilers ahead 17–14. The Browns refused to stay down long, and progressed to score on another long touchdown pass from Kosar to Slaughter—this one was seventy-seven yards and gave the Browns a 21–17 lead heading into the fourth quarter. Notably, that was three extremely long touchdown passes to Slaughter in two weeks. Slaughter would end up finishing the game with four catches for 182 yards—this made for an incredible and unheard of forty-six yards per catch average. It was the biggest and best stretch of Webster Slaughter's career.

Up 21-17, in the fourth quarter, the Cleveland Browns were out for blood and wanted to take the lead for good with another big time strike. And, they did exactly that as they ran a trick play to catch the Oilers offguard and it worked. They were beginning to think that there was nothing the flashy rookie Eric Metcalf couldn't do—return kicks, catch touchdown passes, run for touchdowns, and now throw touchdown passes as he took the ball and completed a halfback pass to Reggie Langhorne for a touchdown. This trick play sent the Cleveland Browns' crowd into a frenzy and gave the Browns a 28-17 win.

It was a big win for the Cleveland Browns and improved their record to 5-3 at the midway point of the season. Bernie Kosar threw for 262 yards and bounced from two interceptions to toss two touchdown passes and run for one. Despite the red hot passing attack, the running game still could not get out of the blocks. Eric Metcalf had a healthy seventeen attempts, but only rushed for forty-eight yards. The bulk of his offense continued to come on kick returns and pass catches out of the backfield.

The Cleveland Browns' defense held their own against the excellent run and shoot passing attack of the Houston Oilers. Warren Moon completed fifteen of twenty-five pass attempts for 241 yards and a touchdown. Despite his solid numbers, when the Browns' defense needed the stops in the second half, they always got them and held the Oilers to a meager seven second half points. The Browns kept the pressure on Moon and finished with three sacks, two more for Thane Gash, and one by Andrew Stewart.

The Cleveland Browns would look to extend their two-game winning streak as they traveled to Tampa Bay, Florida the following week to take on the lowly Buccaneers. It would-n't take long for an all and all shootout to soon develop as both offenses had something to prove.

The battle would be between Bernie Kosar and the man who replaced him as quarterback for the Miami University Hurricanes in college when Kosar left for the Cleveland Browns. Vinny Testaverde had a stellar college career in replacement of Kosar, even winning the Heisman Trophy in 1986. Testaverde was so impressive that he later became the number one overall draft pick in 1987 by the Tampa Bay Buccaneers. No one could have foresaw on this particular day in 1989 just how crucial Vinny Testaverde would become in the eventual downfall and departure of Kosar from Cleveland, but more on that later!

Vinny Testaverde was off to a rough start as the leader of the Tampa Bay Buccaneers and with the Cleveland Browns' excellent defense coming to town, it didn't look like this game was going to change his luck anytime soon. However, much like sports often teaches us, that is why the games are played on the field and not on paper. Testaverde was up for the challenge, and the Buccaneers entered the field trying to score right away. They drove right down the field on the Browns' defense to start the game, and capped off the impressive drive with a one yard touchdown rush from Lars Tate.

Bernie Kosar and the high voltage Browns' offense were still on a high, riding the cusp of a two game winning streak. Their confidence was building once again, and they looked to take the attack right at the Buccaneers' defense. The Browns were unfazed by the early deficit and took the ball right down the field to score. The rookie running back Eric Metcalf continued to prove that he could do more catching passes out of the backfield than taking handoffs, as he caught a screen from Kosar and took it twenty-four yards for a thrilling touchdown to tie the game at seven points apiece.

Two quick touchdowns were on the board, but the scoring explosion for both teams was just getting started. It was a great day for rookies on the Cleveland Browns' team as Lawyer Tillman was the next one to cash in on the weak Tampa Bay defense. Kosar dropped back to pass, and connected with Tillman on a nice seven yard touchdown strike in the back end zone to put the Browns on top 14-7.

The Browns' defense had been known for scoring touchdowns on interceptions and fumbles all season long, and this contest would be no different as they added to that lore when safety Felix Wright picked off a Testaverde pass and returned it twenty-seven yards for a Cleveland Browns' touchdown! The defense was not done showing off yet, and on the very next drive, it was linebacker

Thane Gash picking off Testaverde and returning it fifteen yards for yet another defensive touchdown to put the Browns ahead 28-7 midway through the second quarter. It was a combined thirty-five points in a little over twenty minutes of game play, but the scoring wasn't even close to being done yet as twenty-one more combined points would occur before halftime. What a thrilling game this was turning out to be.

Vinny Testaverde answered on the next drive with a sharply thrown nine yard touchdown pass to James Wilder. Bernie Kosar fired right back, connecting with seldom used Derek Tennell on a nicely placed four yard touchdown pass. Testaverde responded yet again, and capped off the first half scoring with a nice two minute drive good enough to place Tampa Bay in field goal position to try one before the end of the half. Buccaneers place kicker Donald Igwebuike wasn't exactly headed for Canton and the Hall of Fame, but he was good enough on this attempt from fifty-three yards to keep the Buccaneers in striking distance headed into the locker room at half time. It was the Browns leading the Buccaneers 35-17 after a wild and action-packed first half. It was November 5th, and seventy-one degrees in Tampa that day, and both teams were sizzling like the hot weather!

The Tampa Bay offense picked up where they left off to start the second half, and completed another scoring drive with a nine yard touchdown pass from Testaverde to James Wilder to pull the Buccaneers to within eleven points at 35-24. The score remained the same as both offenses cooled off for the rest of the third quarter.

The Browns' offense came alive, and got back into scoring mode when Eric Metcalf broke off a forty-two yard touchdown run to put the Browns ahead 42-24 in the fourth quarter. The rookie Metcalf was putting together an impressive first season; despite his low overall rushing stats, he was still proving that he could score in a variety of ways. The Buccaneers would soon answer with a one yard touchdown run by Lars Tate, but it was simply too late. They won 42-31, which improved their record to 6-3 and placed them in the thick of the AFC playoff chase.

Bernie Kosar finished the game with only 164 passing yards, but was very effective as he completed nineteen of twenty-two pass attempts with three of them for touchdowns. Testaverde showed the best and worst of his game as he threw for a superior 370 yards on twenty-seven completions. Testaverde threw three touchdowns but his Achilles heel of interceptions crept up once again by tossing four picks. The Browns secondary feasted on the fact that Testaverde attempted fifty passes, with two sacks and the interceptions by Felix Wright, Thane Gash, Robert Lyons, and Frank Minnifield.

At 6–3 and winners of three straight, the "Bud" Carson-led Cleveland Browns then traveled to Seattle to take on the Seahawks in the hopes of remaining hot and securing another road victory. The Seattle Kingdome was rocking—it was considered one of the loudest places to play because of the high volume of noise the crowd was able to produce in the dome. The Browns were up for the challenge and their defense was looking to shut down future Hall of Fame Seattle Seahawks receiver Steve Largent.

As the Cleveland Browns focused on stopping Steve Largent, the Seahawks quarterback Dave Kreig was able to find a wide open Brian Blades to open the scoring in the first quarter with an eight yard touchdown pass to put the Seahawks ahead. The Browns were unable to score, and the first quarter ended with the Seahawks up 7–0.

Despite their early lead, the Browns stuck to their game plan and shutout the Seahawks' offense the rest of the game. The Seahawks did not score a single point after the first-quarter touchdown. The Browns secondary held Largent in check as well, only allowing him to catch four balls for a minuscule thirty-three yards.

As the Browns' defense was holding serve, the offense snapped things back into high gear and started throwing and running the ball all over the dome. A Tim Manoa touchdown run tied the game heading into halftime. Then, a Kosar third-quarter touchdown pass to Lawyer Tillman combined with a Matt Bahr fourth-quarter field goal sealed the game for Cleveland as they walked away with a victorious 17–7 win.

Bernie Kosar passed for 173 yards and a touchdown with zero interceptions. Rookie running back Eric Metcalf helped out with seventy-five yards on nineteen carries while Tim Manoa chipped in with sixty-fove yards on fourten attempts. Despite the early touchdown toss by Dave Krieg, the Browns' defense shut him down the rest of the game, and he was held to a meager 141 yards with three interceptions to Handford Dixon, Felix Wright, and Clay Matthews.

On November 19, 1989, with a 7-3 record, the Cleveland Browns were set to play at home—the biggest game of their season—the one game they circled on the calendar when the schedule first came out. It was their former coach Marty Schottenheimer and the Kansas City Chiefs coming to town. Schottenheimer had less than a stellar exit out of town, so he was looking for revenge and made sure his team was fully prepared. For the Cleveland Browns, this game was the beginning of a four-game slide that nearly ruined their season.

For all the hype of Schottenheimer returning to the sidelines in Cleveland, the game itself provided very little action as it was a defensive battle all the way. In fact, there was only one offensive touchdown the entire game. It came on a third-quarter touchdown run by Eric Metcalf to put the Browns ahead 10-7. The Chiefs' lone touchdown came earlier in the same quarter as their defense converted a fumble into a three yard return by Neil Smith.

The game was pushed into overtime on a Nick Lowery field goal that made it 10-10. It was an awful game for Lowery, as that conversion was the only one he made all day, missing two others including one in overtime. The Browns could not move ahead, and the game ended in a very anti-climactic 10-10 tie. They didn't beat their old coach, but they didn't lose to him either.

It was clear that the lack of a running game had once again hurt the Browns in the 10-10 tie against Kansas City, as they ran the ball thirty-seven times, but only for seventy-eight yards for an embarrassing 2.1 yard average. Sadly for the Browns, their offense would remain in a scoring coma. They lost the following Thursday, on Thanksgiving Day to the Detroit Lions 13-10. Their defense continued to play great, but it simply wasn't enough to carry the anemic offense. Things got even worse the following week with a 21-0 shutout loss at home against their interstate rivals, the Cincinnati Bengals. The embarrassing shutout loss dropped their record to 7-5, and placed their playoff hopes in serious jeopardy.

Things went from bad to worse the following week when they traveled to Indianapolis to take on the Colts. The Browns led

17–7 late in the third quarter but could not hold the lead, and the Colts eventually forced overtime 17–17. Just when it seemed like the Browns would have a chance to turn things around in overtime, bad luck struck once again as Bernie Kosar was picked off by Mike Prior and he returned the interception fifty-eight yards for a touchdown and a Colts win. The once promising Browns' season now looked nearly doomed as their record dropped to 7–6–1 and their playoff hopes were now on life support.

With every game now becoming a 'must win' for the Brown and Orange, the real drama and wild antics began to truly unfold when the Minnesota Vikings invaded a blistery Cleveland Municipal Stadium on Sunday, December 17th. It was a wild affair that kept every fan and every media member guessing just what would happen next. And, the weather didn't help the situation. It was a freezing two degrees outside with a twelve miles per hour wind that made it feel like minus fifteen degrees with the wind chill. Nevertheless, Cleveland fans showed why they are the best in the sports nation when they packed Cleveland Municipal Stadium despite the team's four-game winless streak and the freezing conditions. Their Browns' team had faced challenges all season long and bounced back; they were determined that this would be the start of their final playoff surge.

The Cleveland Browns' fans had good reason to have such strong faith in their team. This was a franchise that had made the playoffs four straight seasons, and had one of the league's best quarterbacks. If it wasn't for a play or two over the last couple of seasons, they quite possibily could have had one or even two Super Bowl rings. This particular game on this extremely cold day in many ways symbolized one last hope for the team and city that perhaps the good times were not over just yet. With the weather condition being a huge factor, and the Browns running game struggling all season, the challenge would be even greater as throwing the ball would not be the number one option.

The Minnesota Vikings had a strong offense that season with the recently traded for running back Herschel Walker in the backfield leading the way. Walker was one of the best in the game and the Vikings recently traded away countless draft picks to Dallas for the services of Walker. It was a trade that Dallas would later use to build their dynasty of the 1990s. They had duel-receiving threats with the dangerous Anthony Carter and tight end Steve Jordan. The issue they faced was not having a true number one quarterback as Wade Wilson and Tommy Kramer juggled time behind center.

Due to the blistery weather, both offenses struggled to move the ball in the first quarter. It was an old nemesis from a very bad memory that scored the first points of the game when barefooted placekicker Rich Karlis put one through the uprights from 44 yards out to put the Vikings ahead 3–0. Karlis was the same kicker that hit the game winner in Cleveland against the Browns for the Denver Broncos three years earlier in the AFC Championship game to win it in overtime. The Browns' offense remained ice cold and scoreless as the Vikings led 3–0 heading into halftime.

"Bud" Carson was a master at making halftime adjustments, and did so once again as the Browns were able to come out and score to begin the third quarter. A Bernie Kosar five yard touchdown pass to Ron Middleton put the Browns on the board and in the lead 7–3. The lead wouldn't last long, however, as Minnesota's Herschel Walker blitzed in the end zone from twenty-six yards out to regain the lead 10–7. Bernie Kosar and the Browns' offense were determined not to go away quietly and answered again, this time with a sixty-two yard bomb touchdown pass to Reggie Langhorne to give the Browns a 14–10 lead heading into the fourth quarter.

The drama would intensify as Minnesota quarterback Wade Wilson departed the game with a twisted knee, and was replaced by backup Tommy Kramer. The move paid off right away. Tommy Kramer connected with Steve Jordan for a two yard touchdown pass. Minnesota re-claimed the lead 17–14. Tommy Kramer had completed passes of twenty and twenty-four yards to Steve Jordan to highlight an eight-play, fifty-seven yard drive.

As time ran down in the fourth quarter, and the Browns were staring their fourth straight loss in the face, Bernie Kosar and the offense had one last drive in them to avoid defeat. With the winds whipping, the sky darkening, and the cold weather cooling off any playoff chance the Browns had, Kosar and the crew drove down the field one last time to get Matt Bahr in a last ditch field goal position. Bahr rewarded his team's faith in him and made the crucial thirty-two yard field goal to send the game into overtime for the second straight week, and fourth time that season for Cleveland. Clearly, the Browns were motivated to win, regardless of the weather.

The Cleveland Browns' previous three overtime games had not gone so well—one tie and two losses. At this point, they could not afford even a tie or a loss. It was win, or the season would be over. Nearly ten minutes had elapsed in overtime play, and no team had yet to score. With time winding down, and the anxious crowd looking on, Kosar hit Reggie Langhorne for a thirty-nine yard strike that placed the Browns in field goal range.

With just over five minutes left in overtime, the Cleveland Browns' strategic decision was to send Matt Bahr in the game to attempt a thirty-two yarder to win the game. He had a kick of the same distance late in the fourth quarter to send the game into overtime. The thought was that the Browns were trying the kick on third down in case of a bad snap or a botched hold, that way they could just land on the ball and try it again on fourth down. However, the real reason they were trying the kick on third down and not fourth quarter became crystal clear as Pagel, the backup quarterback who holds on field goals, took the snap and rolled right, hitting Waiters at the ten who then turned up field wide open for the easy game-winning touchdown. The trick play came at the perfect time and was handled beautifully. The reason they tried it on third down was because if it failed, they could still kick on fourth down. Needless to say, Minnesota was caught completely off guard.

The Cleveland Browns were now 8-6-1 and amazingly right back in the mix for the AFC Central Division Championship. Their upcoming opponents were the 9-6 Houston Oilers and they would have to travel to Houston, Texas to play them in the Astrodome. It was a heated rivalry, and the year before had become even nastier when Houston eliminated Cleveland from the playoffs.

The game was on the eve of December 23rd. It promised to be a thrilling Christmas Eve for the Cleveland Browns and Houston Oilers' football fans. It was the Saturday night showcase, and both teams knew the extreme importance of the game. It was a hostile crowd in Houston as the dome was packed and very loud; however, the Browns were not intimated and sought to demolish Houston with reckless abandon.

Matt Bahr got the scoring going early with a thirty-two yard field goal. Bernie Kosar would then assist on the next drive with a sixty-eight yard touchdown pass to the speedy Eric Metcalf. It was another fantastic play from Metcalf as he continued to prove that his speed kills. Bernie Kosar remained hot and connected on a long pass to Webster Slaughter later in the second quarter for a forty yard touchdown pass to put the Browns ahead 17–0. It was a commanding lead, and settled the outrageously loud Houston crowd.

Warren Moon finally got the high-octane Houston Oiler Run and Shoot offense in gear and led the Oilers on a twenty point run. During this stretch, he connected on two touchdown passes to Drew Hill, which were wrapped around a pair of Tony Zendejas field goals. This momentous explosion combined with the Oilers' defense shutting down the Browns' offense, gave the Oilers a 20–17 lead with just a few minutes to play in the game.

The Cleveland Browns' playoff hopes appeared bleak until Bernie Kosar led the Browns back down the field. He silenced the dome by carving up the Oilers' secondary and putting his team into scoring position. It was the returning Kevin Mack who made a heroic return by rumbling into the end zone from four yards out in the closing moments to give Cleveland the division clinching win!

Bernie Kosar looked sharp all night long as he passed for 228 yards and a pair of touchdowns. Webster Slaughter had three big catches for sixty-six yards. Eric Metcalf was limited to a pass catching back and only took four handoffs. The bulk of the carries went to the returning Kevin Mack who was given twelve carries for sixty-two yards. Warren Moon played one of his best games of the season with an incredible 414 passing yards and two touchdowns. It was an epic effort out of Moon, but not enough when it mattered the most.

The AFC Central proved to be one of the best divisions in football as it ended up sending three teams to the playoffs. The Cleveland Browns won the division, and the Houston Oilers and Pittsburgh Steelers both went to the playoffs as wild cards despite all three teams winning nine games. What helped the Cleveland Browns is that they only had six losses; because of the tie to Kansas City, their winning percentage was slightly higher than both the Oilers and Steelers.

This was the last season in which the NFL used a ten-team playoff format. The league would expand the playoffs to twelve teams next season. Joining the Cleveland Browns in the playoffs were the Buffalo Bills who finished at 9-7, and their old playoff rivals, the Denver Broncos who took the number one overall seed in the AFC with an 11-5 record. It was such a tight race to get into the playoffs that the Colts, Dolphins, Bengals, Chiefs and Raiders all finished with eight wins and only one game out.

The NFC was clearly the dominant conference that season as all six of their playoff teams won double-digit games including the San Francisco 49ers with fourteen wins, the New York Giants with twelve wins, the Philadelphia Eagles and the Los Angeles Rams with eleven wins, and the Minnesota Vikings with ten wins. So dominant was the NFC that season that they had two ten-win teams not even making the playoffs in the Green Bay Packers and Washington Redskins.

To the Cleveland Browns, however, none of that meant anything, they were just happy to win the division and return to the post-season. They wanted to win and get a chance at revenge against the Denver Broncos. They scored 334 points, which is an average of 20.9 per game, it was fourteenth of twenty-eight teams in the NFL. Their defense allowed 254 points for only 15.9 points a game—it was stellar fourth in the entire NFL. Even more impressive was their differential of eighty points, an average of 5.0 per game.

It was a bumpy road along the way but an overall solid regular season with Bernie Kosar tossing eighteen touchdowns and throwing for 3,533 yards. Kosar's mobility continued to suffer by the week as he was sacked thirty-four more times for a loss of 192 yards. It was an average of two sacks every single game.

Kosar's two most dependable targets that season were Reggie Langhorne and Webster Slaughter. Langhorne had sixty catches for 749 yards and two touchdowns. Slaughter caught sixty-five balls for 1,236 yards and six touchdowns. Lawyer Tillman turned out to be a giant bust, and showed no signs of cracking the top four receivers as he only caught six balls for seventy yards in fourteen games. Out of the six balls he caught, two of them were for touchdowns, however.

The sensational rookie Eric Metcalf showcased his skills in several different ways. He caught fifty-four passes for 397 yards and four touchdowns—very impressive for a rookie tailback. He also rushed for 633 yards and scored six rushing touchdowns. He scored ten touchdowns overall, and combined for over a thousand yards. On top of running and catching the ball, Metcalf also stood out on the return team as he returned thirty-one kickoffs for 718 yards and a 23.2 yard average.

By the time Mack returned from prison, he only played in four games and rushed for 130 yards. Tim Manoa filled in nicely with 289 yards and three touchdowns. Several players found the end zone from the back field as Keith Jones, Barry Redden, and Mike Oliphant all had one-rushing touchdown as well.

Placekicker Matt Bahr looked great at times and shaky at others as he converted sixteen of twenty-four field goal attempts. He only made one over fifty yards, and that had the Browns' coaching staff mildly concerned heading into the post-season. The punting game of Bryan Wagner also looked weary at times as his overall average was just less than forty yards a punt.

As 77,706 fans packed a frigid Cleveland Municipal Stadium on January 6, 1990 to watch their hometown Cleveland Browns play the Buffalo Bills who won the AFC East with a 9-6 regular season record, they all had one thought on their minds—beat the Bills and earn a rematch with the Denver Broncos the following week. The task would not be easy, however, as the Buffalo Bills were a team on the rise and deserved their playoff seed.

The Buffalo Bills reminded fans and media members around the NFL of a young talented Cleveland Browns' team. The Buffalo Bills had a high-scoring offense and a hard-hitting defense. It was a similar formula that Cleveland had built a few years earlier. The Bills were led by quarterback Jim Kelly who was coming into his own in the NFL. He threw for 3,130 yards and twenty-five touchdowns during the 1989 season—it was a season in which he missed three games due to injury. He ran Marv Levy's no huddle fast-paced offense to perfection.

As many people may now know, and a lot of others don't, Jim Kelly was actually drafted by the Buffalo Bills in 1983 after a strong college career at the University of Miami, but chose not to go to

Buffalo, instead opting to play in the newly formed USFL instead. Kelly put up impressive numbers during his career at Miami. He had 406 completions on 646 attempts for 5,233 yards and thirty-two touchdowns. Jim Kelly would eventually be inducted into the University of Miami's Hall of Fame in 1992.

Kelly was part of the vaunted 1983 draft class from which other legends Dan Marino and John Elway were also selected. Kelly did not want to play in cold weather and told Buffalo he would not play for them. It was almost the fashionable thing to do as the number one pick John Elway refused to play for the Baltimore Colts, and threatened to leave and play baseball full time for the New York Yankees.

Kelly made the most of his time in the upstart USFL while suiting up with the Houston Gamblers, who played in the climate-controlled Houston Astrodome. It was during this time that he became familiar with the run and shoot style of offense ran by Coach Mouse Davis. In his two seasons at Houston, Kelly threw for 9,842 yards and eighty-three touchdowns, completing sixty-three percent with an average of 8.53 yards per attempt with forty-five interceptions.

His incredible play was good enough to earn him the USFL MVP in 1984. He set a league record that year with 5,219 yards passing and forty-four touchdown passes. Kelly's USFL records eclipsed those of fellow league quarterbacks Doug Williams and Steve Young, both of whom would advance to solid NFL careers themselves after departing the USFL.

So in the demand was Kelly that when the Houston Gamblers folded, Kelly went to the New Jersey Generals and was positioned to be their starting quarterback. The hype for Kelly was at an all-time high when he appeared on the cover of *Sports Illustrated* while holding a General's helmet, but the league folded before he could ever take a single snap with the Generals.

The Buffalo Bills' front office was intelligent when it came to legal matters such as contracts and rights, and made sure to retain Jim Kelly's full NFL rights during his time with the USFL. Kelly decided to join the Bills in 1986 after the USFL folded. The Bills were happy to have him aboard finally to help rebuild what would quickly become one of the NFL's best young teams.

Head coach Marv Levy was a proprietor of the no huddle offense, and in Buffalo they called it the "K-Gun Offense." It was a fast-paced offense that denied opposing defenses the opportunity to make timely substitutions. The offensive scheme required multiple formation calls in a huddle, so that after each play was completed, the Bills would forgo a following huddle; instead they chose to line up for the next play where Kelly would read the defense and audible the play. This led to mismatches and defensive communication breakdowns. The success of this style was one of the biggest reasons that the Bills were considered one of the NFL's most successful and dangerous offenses. The Browns' defense would have their work cut out of them trying to stop their high-octane attack.

One of the primary reasons that Jim Kelly and the Buffalo Bills were so good at running the K-Gun was that they had multiple players with excellent talent on the offensive side of the ball. Kelly's primary 'go-to' wide receiver was physical wide out Andre Reed. In the 1985 NFL Draft, Reed was drafted by the Buffalo Bills in the fourth round with the 86th overall selection. It would turn out to be one of the biggest steals in NFL Draft History as Reed ranks near the top in nearly all NFL career statistical receiving categories. He went over one thousand yards four times in a sixteen year career, is tenth in NFL history in total career receptions with 951. In 1989, he caught eighty-eight balls for 1,312 yards and nine touchdowns. It was clear that this future Hall of Famer, combined with the strong and accurate arm of Jim Kelly, was set to give the Cleveland Browns' secondary fits all day.

Don Beebe lined up on the other side of the line as the duel-receiving threat for Jim Kelly to go to when Andre Reed drew the double coverage. Don Beebe was not the typical looking receiver as he stood at only five foot, eleven inches and weighed 185 pounds. He played with the heart and emotion of someone twice his size, and it led to an impressive NFL career. He came from little known Chardon State College, and emerged as a rookie in 1989 to become a vital part of the Bills' passing attack.

The passing attack wouldn't be the only thing the Cleveland Browns' defense would have to worry about as the Bills also possessed a stout running game led by Thurman Thomas who was also coming off of a fantastic season. In sixteen games during the 1989 season, Thomas had gotten 298 carries which he turned into 1,244 yards and six touchdowns. He was an excellent pass catcher out of the backfield and caught an incredible sixty passes for 669 yards and six more touchdowns. They were MVP type numbers for the second year back out of Oklahoma State.

As good as the Buffalo Bills offense was, their defense was every bit as stout as it prominently featured all-pros at almost every position. The defensive line play was led by future Hall of Famer Bruce Smith who had recently signed a massive monetary free agent deal just prior to the regular season. They also boasted a highly talented line backing core of Carlton Bailey, All Pro Cornelius Bennett, Shane Conlan, and another All Pro in Darryl Talley. The leaders of their shutdown defensive secondary were cornerback Nate Odomes, and free safety Mark Kelso. Both teams were loaded with talented and skilled players, and this one was set to be an instant classic.

Despite the cold temperature of twenty-eight degrees with a seven mile per hour wind chill that made it feel more like twenty-one degrees, neither team's offense let it affect them and thus a shootout would occur. The field was very icy because of the weather, and it would come into play right away when Matt Bahr lost his footing and slipped during a forty-two yard field goal attempt during the game's first drive and could not get the kick off, costing the Browns a chance at three quick points.

The Bills jumped on the chance to work with a good field position. On their second play from scrimmage, Kelly threw a short pass to Andre Reed when Felix Wright slipped while going into coverage, leaving Reed wide open and he ended up taking the ball seventy-two yards to the end zone to start the scoring and put the Bills ahead 7–0.

The Browns were able to bounce back from the early deficit and scored on a Matt Bahr forty-five yard field goal as well as a fifty-two yard touchdown pass from Bernie Kosar to Webster Slaughter to give the Browns their first lead of the game at 10–7. The lead would not last long, however, as Jim Kelly hit James Lofton on a beautiful thirty-three yard touchdown pass to allow Buffalo to reclaim the lead. The Browns refused to stay down and drove back down the field, capped off by a Bernie Kosar to Ron Middleton three yard touchdown pass to give the Browns a 17–14 lead heading into halftime.

The Buffalo Bills would get the ball first coming out of the locker room to start the second half; however, the Browns' defense was ready to shine on the big stage on the opening drive. It was Browns' defensive back Mark Harper who intercepted a pass from Kelly on the Cleveland forty-six. Kosar then connected with his favorite wide receiver Webster Slaughter for another touchdown pass, this one forty-four yards, to increase their lead to 24–14.

Buffalo would not be intimidated. Kelly responded with a six yard touchdown pass to running back Thurman Thomas making the score 24–21. Thurman Thomas was putting together the game of his life, and actually tied an NFL playoff record with thirteen receptions for 150 yards before the afternoon was over.

With the Buffalo Bills pulling within three points and keeping everyone on the edge of their chilled seats midway through the third quarter, it became rookie running back Eric Metcalf's time to shine with the world watching. Metcalf returned the ensuing kickoff ninety yards for a touchdown to give his team a 31–21 lead. The fans were up out of their seats cheering. It was another good play in a rookie season for Metcalf. Shortly after the big touchdown return, the third quarter ended, and the tension began to thicken in the frigid air.

Down ten points heading into the fourth quarter, the Buffalo Bills knew they had to do something quickly. And, they did. They drove the length of the field and had place kicker Scott Norwood attempt and make a thirty yard field goal. Shortly after, Matt Bahr made one for the Browns, and it was 34–24 midway through the fourth quarter.

Jim Kelly and the Buffalo Bills refused to stay down. Kelly soon drove Buffalo seventy-seven yards to score on a three yard touchdown pass to Thomas. Moments later, Scott Norwood slipped on an icy patch on the field while attempting the extra point, causing him to miss it and keep the score at 34–30. This was a crucial miss because it kept the lead at four for Cleveland and not three, meaning that if Buffalo had gotten the ball back, they would have to score a touchdown to win it, rather than a field goal to tie it.

With seconds left on the clock, and the Buffalo Bills in position to try and win the game on offense, the Browns' defense was on high alert and ready to step up one more vital time. Kelly took the snap at the Browns eleven yard line and dropped back to pass, and found a wide open fullback Ronnie Harmon in the end zone. Call it luck, fate, or just destiny, but Harmon dropped the ball. The Browns would not allow another chance as linebacker Clay Matthews picked off Jim Kelly on the very next play to seal the victory for the Cleveland Browns, and book a return trip to the AFC Championship game to face the Denver Broncos once again.

The Cleveland Browns won with a total team effort as every phase of their team stepped up. Their secondary held Don Beebe to only one catch for seventeen yards and dropped Beebe on his head the one time he did catch the ball. They needed to hold Beebe in check because as mentioned prior, Thurman Thomas got loose for thirteen catches and 150 yards. His other running mate, Andre Reed, caught six balls for 115 yards. The problem for Buffalo was that the passing game was all they had because the Browns' stout defensive line held the Bills' running game in check all day. The Browns only allowed Thurman Thomas to rush for twenty-seven yards on ten carries. Lifelong Browns' fan Bob Lamb from North Olmsted, was at the game and had these comments:

> *"It was so cold that my friend and I kept warm by holding a hot dog warmer in our hands for heat. But the cold was worth it... it was the most exciting sporting event I have ever been too. The emotion of the crowd was one of the loudest I have ever heard. The game was thrilling and when Clay Matthews intercepted that final pass to seal the victory, I was just so happy we won! I couldn't believe it, and I truly thought that was a sign we would go all the way!"*

Bernie Kosar continued to improve upon his storied post-season presence with another excellent showing—he threw for 251 yards on twenty completions and had three touchdowns. He only missed nine passes all day and did not have any interceptions. Not only was Kosar able to throw for a nice amount of yards but he also did a fabulous job of spreading the ball around and getting everyone involved in the offensive game plan. Webster Slaughter caught three passes for 114 yards and two touchdowns. Reggie Langhorne caught six balls for forty-eight yards, and tight end Ozzie Newsome contributed with four catches for twenty-five yards.

The Cleveland Browns were headed to the AFC Championship game for the third time in four seasons, and for the third time, it was the John Elway-led Denver Broncos standing directly in their path to the Super Bowl championship. The Broncos possessed the best record in the AFC that season as they had won eleven regular season games and held the overall number one seed in the playoffs for the AFC. The Broncos were fresh off a one-point nail-biting win the prior week against the Pittsburgh Steelers 24–23, and ready for another epic battle against the Browns. The Broncos were aware that, despite their two earlier wins in the prior playoff games against Cleveland, they could not take anything for granted with all of the talent that the Cleveland Browns possessed.

The nucleus of the Denver Broncos' coaching staff and ownership team had remained in place over the years as well with Dan Reeves still calling the shots from the sidelines as head coach. The defense was run by Wade Phillips, son of legendary Houston Oilers' coach Bum Phillips. Chan Gailey was in charge of the offense, but more often than not his main job was to stay out of the way and let John Elway run the show. The team was owned by one of the most respectable men in sports, the revered Pat Bowden. General Manager John Beake knew not to change much with the roster prior to the season, but he was smart enough to draft rookie sensation Steve Atwater, a safety out of Arkansas.

The addition of Atwater was key as he was part of a ball hungry secondary that combined for fourteen interceptions. They were led by Tyrone Braxton, who led the team with six interceptions in which he returned for 103 yards and a touchdown, while also recovering two fumbles. Every bit as good as their secondary was their line backing core and defensive line. Bleake signed veteran defensive end Ron Holmes, who recorded nine sacks. Holmes, along with veteran linebackers and fan favorites, Karl Mecklenburg who had 7.5 sacks and four fumble recoveries along with Simon Fletcher who had twelve sacks, gave the Denver Broncos' one of the quickest defensive lines in the AFC.

Their offense had an excellent rookie edition of its own as Bleake added running back Bobby Humphrey. It was an excellent move as he rushed for 1,151 yards, caught twenty-two passes for 156 yards, and scored eight touchdowns. The young running back was able to give the Broncos a powerful running attack that they lacked but sorely needed in their previous seasons.

For the first time in recent memory, some in the national media and local Denver fan base did have some minor concern about John Elway as he had played inconsistently during the regular season. Shockingly, though, he threw just as many interceptions as touchdowns (18) and put up a meager 73.7 passer rating. He couldn't blame his struggles on his receiving core because they continued to play up to snuff. His favorite target, Vance Johnson, put up the best numbers of his career with seventy-six catches for 1,095 yards and seven touchdowns. It was a large drop off to get to the second leading pass catcher which was Mark Jackson with only twenty-eight for 446 yards. The mission for any defense was basic—shut down Elway throwing to Vance Johnson—and their chances at success would greatly increase.

Unlike in prior years, this Denver Broncos' team showed signs of vulnerability as their regular season had been filled with ups and downs. They began the season 6–1, with their only loss being against Cleveland, but then went just 5–4 the rest of the way, including a 2-game losing streak, and losing three of their last four regular season games. They had the talent, but at times it seemed that they lacked focus. They would need to be in top form as the Cleveland Browns were out for revenge and a championship win.

It was January 14, 1990—this author's eighth birthday—and 76,005 people packed Mile High Stadium in Denver, Colorado. As television announcers Dick Enberg and former San Francisco Super Bowl winning coach Bill Walsh prepared to call the action for NBC's televised game, both the fans and players alike were in high expectation of another classic game that would be gripping down to the closing moments. How could anyone expect anything less after the dramatic ending to their regular season game, as well as their past two AFC championship games?

The one skill that made up for Bernie Kosar not having even decent mobility was his ability to not make mistakes; he would rather take a sack than throw an interception. That's why it was so shocking when he threw an interception to Denver's safety Dennis

Smith late in the first quarter. The Broncos made the Browns pay for the early turnover just five plays later when place kicker David Treadwell converted a twenty-nine yard field goal to allow Denver to draw first blood.

The mistakes for Cleveland continued to occur the next time the Broncos would touch the ball. It was defensive back Frank Minnifield who stumbled while trying to bump receiver Michael Young at the line of scrimmage, enabling Young to race past him and catch a pass from Elway for a seventy yard touchdown reception. This was a very costly mistake for Cleveland as it put the Broncos ahead 10–0, a lead they would hold through the rest of the first half.

As the Cleveland Browns entered the locker room for halftime, they had to take solace in the fact that despite how bad they were playing, they were still only down by ten points. Coach "Bud" Carson had been a master of making halftime adjustments all season and this would be no exception as the Browns came out and started the second half with all guns firing. Bernie Kosar led them on a seventy-nine yard, eight-play drive that was capped off with a twenty-seven yard touchdown pass to Brian Brennan. The catch by Brennan was made while falling down and juggling the ball; he made the catch, quickly scrambled up, and ran it in for the score. That play stands as one of the greatest catches in NFL history and made it a three-point game.

The Broncos, however, had no intentions of allowing Cleveland back in the game. John Elway led the Broncos' offense on a touchdown drive, highlighted by several long passing plays. It was capped off with a five yard touchdown toss to tight end Orson Mobley. Cleveland had knocked starting running back Bobby Humphrey from the game, but his backup Sammy Winder had no issues picking up where he left off and ran for twenty-two important yards on that drive.

The mistakes for Cleveland just kept coming—down 17–7 and desperate to get their defense off the field so their offense could have a shot of coming back, they made another a critical error. It was a severe lack of judgment when Cleveland's defensive back Kyle Kramer was called for fifteen yard spearing penalty on Elway's twenty-five yard run, setting up Winder's seven yard touchdown run that gave the Broncos a whopping 24-7 lead with 4:19 left in the third quarter.

Bernie Kosar always took time out for the fans.
Photo courtesy of Anna DeLuca

This was a critical time for the Cleveland Browns' team. Their mistakes created a huge hole for the shaky Browns' team and they desperately needed something good to happen to get them back in the game. Bernie Kosar was not going down without a fight, though, and remembered the epic comeback in Denver just two seasons prior. Kosar shook off the bad start and began demolishing the Broncos' secondary. Kosar, once again, showed that he excelled at moving the ball around to get it down the field as he completed passes to Reggie Langhorne, Lawyer Tillman, and Webster Slaughter for gains of twenty-seven, fifteen, and sixteen yards. Kosar then connected with Brian Brennan on a ten yard touchdown completion that breathed life into the faltering Browns' team. The team's effort had their passionate fans praying for one more chance at the Super Bowl.

Down 24–14 in the closing moments of the third quarter, the Cleveland Browns received their first big break of the afternoon when defensive end Al Baker forced Broncos' running back Melvin Bratton to fumble the ball. An alert defensive back Felix Wright recovered the ball and returned it twenty-seven yards to the Denver one yard line. This heads-up play helped set up Tim Manoa's two yard touchdown run. They closed the gap to 24–21 as the third quarter desperation expired.

Sadly for the Cleveland Browns' entire organization and devoted fans, the fourth quarter meant that it was John Elway's time to take over once again, and the three points were the closest Cleveland would come. The Broncos began their fourth quarter tear as Elway completed his first two passes to Vance Johnson for forty-three yards. With the Browns' defense on the decline, Elway went for broke and hooked up with Winder for a thirty-nine yard touchdown completion to put the Broncos ahead 31–21.

The Cleveland Browns had no answer for the Elway touchdown pass. Then, the Broncos kicked two field goals on their next two drives to secure the game. The final score was Denver Broncos thirty-seven and Cleveland Browns twenty-one. It was a bitter end to a thrilling season for Cleveland.

Bernie Kosar didn't have one of his better games as he was picked off three times. He did throw for 210 yards and two touchdowns, but it simply wasn't sufficient enough to stop fate. Brian Brennan played a good game including the amazing catch; he finished with fifty-eight yards on five catches and scored two touchdowns. Down big early and often, they never really had a chance to get the run game started and Metcalf only had three carries for four yards. Kevin Mack was not much better as he ran the ball six times for thirty-six yards. The Denver Bronco's luck would finally run out the next week when they got embarrassed in the Super Bowl, getting blowed out by the San Francisco 49ers by a score of 55–10.

Brian Brennan shares why he thinks the Browns couldn't get past Denver once again:

> *"There wasn't a mental block on our part...I sure don't remember there being one. Sometimes the ball just bounces the wrong way. The first loss, we probably should have not gone into the prevent defense. The second loss, we started slowly then had to have a furious rally to get back in the game. It ended with a very ill times fumble. The third loss, they were just a better team than us, but with the first two games we felt that we were the better team...when I look back on it now almost thirty years later."*

Reggie Langhorne has his feelings on why, despite all their success, the Browns couldn't seem to get past Denver:

> *"It wasn't just one thing. We got behind in the fumble game and had to really press the envelope to get back in the game. Maybe that's something that we needed to do from the start of that game until waiting until we got that far down. Playing against one of the greatest quarterbacks like John Elway didn't help matters, but then our defense stepped it up and allowed us to get back into the game. We then had the fumble and...it is what it is... things happen in games. The Drive year was just one of those things, we had them third and eighteen, and John Elway throws a completion, and we end up losing. Those were two key plays in two great seasons that ended up keeping us from the Super Bowl. We won a lot of games during that stretch and have a lot to be thankful for to even be there, but I can honestly say John Elway beat us in those games. He was the better quarterback for his team. We couldn't do enough to stop it. The one thing it does for us as players who lived through it is it makes us even closer. The players on those teams still have a bond from what we went through. Even now in our fifties, we still have respect for one another.*

With three runs to the AFC Championship game in five years and their quarterback still in his prime, it seemed like only a matter of time before the Cleveland Browns would finally break through and win a Super Bowl championship. They still had a better roster than most teams in the AFC as well as the veteran leadership to get them there. Their coach seemed like a good fit for the job, and the fans were passionate. What could possibly go wrong?

Chapter Five

Rebuilding with Bill

Headed into the 1990 season, the Cleveland Browns felt that they were still a relatively complete team that could stand toe-to-toe with any other team in the league. They did have a few areas that they wanted to strengthen with running backs nearing the top of the list. The lack of a consistent running game had hurt them several times the prior season, and with Eric Metcalf being more effective of a pass catching back they looked to select more of a between the tackles bruiser style running back in the draft.

The pass happy attack of offensive coordinator Marc Trestman was no more as he left to become the quarterback coach in Minnesota. It seemed like an odd move for him to leave a coordinator position to take a position coaching job. Perhaps, Trestman saw the writing on the wall for what the Browns and their fans were about to endure in the 1990 regular season.

The new offensive coordinator was Jim Shofner, who ended up playing a much larger role before the season was over. Shofner knew a thing or two about running the ball from his days playing running back in college at Texas Christian University. He excelled at TCU and led the Southwestern Conference in rushing in 1957 with 682 yards. He also scored six touchdowns that season.

Shofner was selected by the Cleveland Browns in the 1958 Draft but saw little playing time as he was behind Jim Brown on the depth chart. After realizing that he couldn't outplay Jim Brown, he allowed the Cleveland Browns to move him to cornerback starting in 1959 where he would excel. Remarkably, during his six-year stretch with the Browns, they failed to make the championship game. It was towards the tail end of the Paul Brown era, and the Cleveland Browns couldn't seem to break through for one more coveted championship opportunity.

Jim Shofner decided to call it quits after only a six-year career with the Cleveland Browns following the 1963 season. As fate would have it, the Cleveland Browns would win the NFL championship the following season in 1964—the last major championship any Cleveland team has won since. Shofner would not remain on the sidelines long, though, as he eventually would return to professional football as the defensive backs coach of the San Francisco 49ers in 1967. Shofner would remain in San Francisco through the 1973 season, also serving as quarterbacks coach and wide receiver coach. His time in San Francisco was a success. While there, he helped 49ers quarterback John Brodie win the Most Valuable Player award with an incredible year in 1970.

Shofner left San Francisco to return to TCU in the winter of 1973 to become their new head coach. Things went horrible for Shofner as the team endured a twenty game losing streak, and Shofner won just twice in three seasons before resigning in 1977 with a 2-31 record. After failing as the head coach of his alma-matter, he returned to the NFL, again with the San Francisco 49ers. He was the quarterbacks coach once again but would only stick around for one season; he returned to Cleveland following the 1977 season.

Shofner's mission was to get a once-promising coaching career back on the right track with Cleveland as his previous two stops did not go well. The return to Cleveland ended up being the best thing to happen to Shofner as things went extremely well there. He was the quarterbacks coach and had the prestigious task of molding a young gun slinger named Brian Sipe. Shofner proved to be just the man for the job as in 1980 he helped Sipe throw for more than four thousand yards and win the NFL Most Valuable Player award.

The Houston Oilers witnessed his success first-hand in their two battles against the Cleveland Browns that season, and offered Shofner the job as their offensive coordinator in the winter of 1981. He accepted the job, but only spent two seasons there as things once again did not go well. His coaching odyssey next led him to Dallas, Texas where he would become the quarterback coach of the Cowboys. He seemed to perform better when he was just a quarterback coach, and not responsible for the heavy duties that come with a coordinator position.

Shofner's time with Dallas ended poorly following the 1985 season, and the Cowboys had seen enough. Despite how poorly things went in Dallas, he still managed to land yet another offensive coordinator position for the St. Louis Cardinals who would eventually move to Phoenix during his time there. His time with the Cardinals never led to much success, however, and he left them following the 1989 season to once again return to the Cleveland Browns. This time as the offensive coordinator, it was his third different team to have that role with. He had a lot of success there as the quarterback coaches in years past and hoped to reclaim some of that magic once again.

Dan Radakovich had left Cleveland and it was now Jim Vechiarella in charge of the defense. He had broken into the NFL in 1983 as the linebackers and special teams coach for the Kansas City Chiefs. He spent three years in Kansas City before leaving for the Jets to spend three more years in the same role. This was his first chance to be a coordinator and he wasn't about to pass it up.

The Cleveland Browns were heading into the season with two new coordinators and some aging veterans on both sides of the ball. It was crucial that they drafted correctly and for their specific need. As mentioned, the running game struggled and with the need for a power back becoming clear, they focused all their efforts on making sure their first selection would make an immediate impact out of the backfield. They already had Eric Metcalf, but they still needed a back to bust open holes instead of run to the outside.

They would also need to be smart with their picks, and make sure each one hit because they were without a first round pick. They had traded it away previously to the Green Bay Packers, so they would have to wait until the 45th overall pick in the second round to start drafting.

The wait would seem like an eternity as they saw several running backs get scooped off the board early. Blair Thomas went number two overall to the New York Jets. Emmitt Smith went seventeenth to the Dallas Cowboys and would go on to become the NFL's all-time leading rusher. Darrell Thomas went nineteenth to the Green Bay Packers, Steve Broussard twentieth to the Atlanta Falcons, Rodney Hampton twenty-fourth to the New York Giants, and Dexter Carter twenty-fifth to the San Francisco 49ers. It was a total of six running backs off the board in the first round alone. The run on running backs would continue in the second round with

Reggie Cobb going to the Tampa Bay Buccaneers, and Anthony Thompson going to the Phoenix Cardinals. A few picks later, it was Anthony Johnson being selected by the Indianapolis Colts followed by Harold Green being selected by the Cincinnati Bengals. Then, it was the Buffalo Bills turn to pick. Despite already having Thurman Thomas, they decided to join the running back party and drafted Carwell Gardner. By the time the Browns got around to picking at forty-five, there were already eleven running backs off the board. The Cleveland Browns could not afford to choose unwisely on their pick.

The Browns selected Leroy Hoard with the 45th overall pick in the 1990 NFL Draft, a bruising running back out of Michigan. He had a superior college career, winning the 1989 Rose Bowl MVP honor. Hoard explains how he first decided to even play football as a child:

> *"I enjoyed playing football and being around the sport as all my friends played it as well. I didn't play competitive football until my junior year of high school. I just wanted to be around my friends as they all played and we ran track together as well... since we were kids, we just wanted to do everything together. The reason I didn't get to play my freshman and sophomore years was because I transferred schools and moved out the district, so I had to sit out.*
>
> *I was ready to play by year three. I didn't look at it as a future profession...I was just having fun with it until I got to college. It was one of those things where I said, hey, you know what; let's get a free education out of this. So from that standpoint, I went about it that way. I was glad I gave it a try. It finally sunk in that I made it when I got drafted. Until that point, I may have never taken it as serious as some other guys did. I didn't treat it as a life or death situation. I made sure that I had fun and made sure that throughout my whole career, I still enjoyed doing it. I think I had more success because I only had fun doing it."*

Leroy Hoard took a certain sense of pride with him into the NFL as the Cleveland Browns were known for always having great running backs. He goes on to explain how he felt:

> *"I was very fortunate that in every step of my football career, the coaches that I played for and my father required me to play football the way I played. So when I left high school, I was blessed to have Bo Schembechler as my coach. We all know how Big Ten football is. When I left Michigan and went to Cleveland, I was in my element as the style of football required there was something I was very used to already playing in the Midwest. It was a style of football I knew I could play well to be successful in that division. It was also a style of football I knew fans wanted to watch. The Cleveland fans didn't want to see flashy, they wanted to see effort and hard work. The fans there want to see you give your full effort no matter what the results on the football field turned out to be. That was how I had played my whole life so I kind of fit right in. The fans really liked me because I was just being me, which allowed me to fit in."*

The Cleveland Browns looked for Leroy Hoard to compliment Eric Metcalf in the backfield. It was a lightning and thunder combination with Metcalf's speed combined with Hoard's power. Both men would be counted on heavily to perform well in their roles so the other one could come in at any time and force the defense to adjust on the fly.

After the first pick went towards offense, the Cleveland Browns used their next four picks to address defense. They selected defensive end Anthony Pleasant out of Tennessee State with their third round pick. Pleasant worked out well for the Browns and played five strong seasons for them.

With their secondary now lacking a defensive back as Hanford Dixon retired in the offseason, they needed to fill that hole and selected Harlon Barnett out of Michigan State with their fourth round pick. Later in the sixth round, they chose another defensive back, Randy Hilliard from Northwestern State University. They hoped one of these two men could fill the spot left behind by Dixon. Sandwiched between the two defensive backs was fifth round selection Rob Burnett, a defensive end out of Syracuse. The Browns hoped that these additions would help solidify what was already a strong defense.

The Cleveland Browns' upper brass, coaching staff, players and passionate fans began the 1990 season full of hope. Why wouldn't they? They had been to the playoffs five straight seasons; the core of their offensive was back. They had two young running backs and one of the smartest quarterbacks in the league. If they could just stay healthy and find a way to get back into the playoffs, this could very well be the year they finally got past the Denver Broncos and reach championship kingdom.

The season started well enough, at home against their division rival Pittsburgh Steelers. The Cleveland Browns won the game but there were many concerning issues that jumped out. Despite the defense looking stellar once again, the offense failed to score a single touchdown. The lone touchdown for Cleveland was from their defense when Anthony Blaylock returned a fumble 30 yards for a touchdown. They tacked on two field goals by new kicker Jerry Kauric for the 13–3 win. It was nice for the Browns to get a win in their opener game against their hated rivals but the warning signs of a disappointing season were apparent everywhere they looked.

The Cleveland Browns only achieved eleven first downs and a meager 158 yards. The long-awaited return to a dominant running game never got off the ground as Leroy Hoard didn't even play, and Eric Metcalf only had eight carries for six yards. Also concerning was that Metcalf had zero catches. The passing game wasn't much better as Kosar stumbled in the opener and only tossed thirteen completions for 120 yards. The weather was a perfect sixty-eight degrees with a nice eight miles per hour wind blowing through, good playing conditions that lousy offense could not be blamed for.

The Browns had a bad feeling in the pit of their stomachs as they entered week two of the season. Despite their opening week victory, the signs of regression indicated that they needed a strong effort to get things kick-started and rebound from the slow start. They believed that a trip to play the New York Jets would be good antidote for them. It wasn't. They were out beat 24–21.

Once again, the offense had its struggles and the Cleveland Browns trailed 24–7 near the end of three quarters. Their lone touchdown at that point was a ninety-eight yard kickoff return for a touchdown by Eric Metcalf to start the game. They managed to get their first offensive touchdown late in the third quarter with a Bernie Kosar to Reggie Langhorne four yard touchdown pass. They tacked on a fourth-quarter touchdown run by the rookie Leroy Hoard, but it was too little too late as they lost 24–21.

Bernie Kosar threw for 233 yards on twenty-one pass completions from forty-one attempts with one touchdown and no interceptions. Eric Metcalf had nine catches for fifty-four yards while Webster Slaughter caught four balls for sixty-three yards. Reggie Langhorne contributed with five catches for sixty-nine yards and a touchdown. The running game continued to be stuck in the mud as Hoard rushed for twenty-nine yards on six carries and Eric Metcalf had nine yards on six carries. For Metcalf, that was now a total of fourteen carries for fifteen yards in two games.

Things began slide as they returned home the following week and were beaten by the visiting San Diego Chargers 24–14. Yet again, their defense did the early scoring with a Mike Johnson sixty-four yard interception touchdown return in the first quarter. Leroy Hoard also had a one yard scamper for a touchdown but it simply wasn't enough. Bernie Kosar looked good for his part as he threw 232 yards with no interceptions but the rest of the offense would sputter.

Their running game only put up forty-four total yards as the dynamic duo of Hoard and Metcalf continued to be a total disaster. Leroy Hoard had fourteen carries but only converted them into thirty-four yards. Eric Metcalf continued to struggle as he had five carries for a minuscule ten yards. The defense didn't do much better, allowing little known San Diego quarterback Billy Joe Tolliver to put up twenty-four points against them.

Any signs of the season turning around at 1–2 were forgotten the following week when the Browns visited their old coach Marty Schottenheimer in Kansas City to take on the Chiefs. Kansas City is one of the toughest locations in sports for a visiting team to have to play, and this day would be no different for the orange and brown. Schottenheimer realized that his former team was in bad shape, and called on his team to pound the Browns on every down. By the time it was over, the Kansas City Chiefs had dominated the Cleveland Browns and shut them out 34–0.

It was quite an embarrassing loss for the Browns as they allowed two punts to be blocked and returned for touchdowns by the Chiefs' special teams unit. The blocked punts combined with two Nick Lowery field goals and two long Steve DeBerg touchdown passes to Robb Thomas and Emile Harry would cap off the scoring.

The Cleveland Browns continued to struggle in every facet of their game. Bernie Kosar got knocked out of the game after only completing eight passes for sixty-one yards. His backup Mike Pagel didn't fare much better as he tossed an interception and only threw for 132 yards. Eric Metcalf continued to play historically bad as he ran for negative four yards on three carries. The rookie Leroy Hoard had an interesting outing as he ran for a total of forty yards, but had one run of forty-two yards. His one carry of forty-two yards was just what the doctored ordered to cover up for his other ten carries that resulted in negative two yards total.

The Cleveland Browns were already in serious danger of losing the season before Halloween as their record was at 1–3 when they traveled to Denver for a Monday night showdown on national television against the great John Elway and the Denver Broncos. All the signs pointed to a Denver blowout with the way things had been going, but the Browns showed the heart of a champion one more time and gave the Broncos all they could handle in what turned out to be an instant classic.

John Elway kicked off the scoring with a beautiful thirteen yard touchdown scramble as he perfectly eluded the Browns' linebackers and defensive lineman rushing at him to bolt into the end zone before they could even realize Elway left the pocket! The Denver crowd went absolutely wild as Elway did what made him so good yet again. The Browns were able to answer back as Metcalf finally got back on track with a nice five yard touchdown run, however, the extra point was missed and the score was 7–6 Denver on top heading into the second quarter of play.

A few minutes into the second quarter, the Browns would answer a David Treadwell twenty yard field goal with a forty-three yard scoring strike from Bernie Kosar to his favorite target Webster Slaughter. Denver answered back with a scoring strike of their own when running back Bobby Humphrey scored on a nineteen yard rush to put Denver ahead 17–13. The special team's woes for the Cleveland Browns continued when they got their next punt blocked out of the end zone for a Denver Broncos safety. This increased the Denver Broncos lead to 19–13 heading into the locker rooms at halftime.

Despite everything that had gone wrong in the first half, the Cleveland Browns were still only down six points. They kept battling and re-claimed the lead on a Bernie Kosar to Kevin Mack eleven yard touchdown pass to put the Browns ahead 20–19 to close out the third quarter. The Broncos wouldn't stay down long, however, and jumped back in front with a sixteen yard wide receiver reverse touchdown run by Mark Jackson. It was shaping up to be a classic as the Denver Broncos now led 26–20.

The Broncos added a twenty-five yard field goal by David Treadwell to advance by nine points at 29–20. It was time for the Browns to put their foot on the gas of a fast-paced comeback. Bernie Kosar got right to work and connected with Brian Brennan on a twenty-four yard strike to cut into the lead at 29–27. The Browns finally overcame Denver. This time, it was Kosar leading a game-winning drive that was capped off in the closing seconds with a thirty yard field goal by Jerry Kauric that gave the Browns a long-awaited win against the Denver Broncos.

The Cleveland Browns had done what they could not do for so long beforehand—they had beaten the Denver Broncos, and it occurred at Denver's Mile High Stadium. Rookie tailback Leroy Hoard ran for only nine yards on seven carries while Eric Metcalf produced fourteen yards on five carries, but it didn't matter that they couldn't run the ball, they still beat Denver and it felt great! Bernie Kosar also looked good as he tossed 318 yards and three touchdowns. Perhaps this was it, the win to turn around the season. Maybe the jinx of Denver had finally been lifted, and the Browns could use the momentum to roll towards another playoff run.

All such hope and solid momentum would prove to be a mirage as the Cleveland Browns followed the emotional win with eight straight losses. Suddenly and painfully, the season and dynasty were both over. So was the head coaching career of Leon "Bud" Carson. Art Modell fired him following a 42–0 loss to the Buffalo Bills, a game in which Carson had the utter gull to bench Bernie Kosar in favor of backup quarterback Mike Pagel. The interim head coach was Jim Shofner who didn't fair well either. Under Shofner, the Browns only won one more time, a 13–10 home victory of the Atlanta Falcons.

The 1990 season turned out to be a nightmare for the Cleveland Browns and their loyal fans. To the surprise of many, after losing some key players in the off-season, they played terribly all year long. They finished with a dreadful 3–13 record. Kosar had his worst full season as a pro by only throwing for 2,562 yards and ten touchdowns. Kosar also missed two games due to injury and was benched in a third. It was a miserable year that everyone was happy to see end. The 1990 Cleveland Browns surrendered 462 points, the most points of any NFL team in the 1990s. Their −234 point differential is the third-worst total of any team in the 1990s.

The Cleveland Browns' running game that was supposed to feature the two-headed monster of Leroy Hoard and Eric Metcalf never truly did transpire. It failed to reach even the mildest of expectations. Second year speed back Eric Metcalf rushed for only 248 yards on just eighty carries. The eighty carries was stunning as it averaged out to only five carries a game. He managed a little bit better catching balls out of the backfield as he pulled in fifty-seven balls for 452 yards and a touchdown. Because the Browns were often losing in games, Metcalf did have plenty of chances to return kickoffs, which he did very well. Metcalf returned fifty-two kicks for a total of 1,052 yards. He was also able to take two of the kicks all the way back for a touchdown. This element of Metcalf's game would continue to improve as his career went on.

Rookie running back Leroy Hoard had a brutal first year in which nothing seemed to go right for the young back. He only received fifty-eight carries for a pedestrian 149 yards and three touchdowns. He played in fourteen of the sixteen games, and fumbled the ball six times in those fifty-eight carries. The hopes and hype for Hoard were high, and the Browns' brass still felt that he could play well despite the rough first season.

With both Hoard and Metcalf struggling for reps and yards, the Browns had to rely on veteran tailback Kevin Mack. The once one thousand yard rusher performed admirably in his role as he took 158 carries and converted them into 702 yards. The problem Mack had was ball security as he turned the ball over six times, which was by far and away a career high for him.

The inconsistent play at quarterback from Bernie Kosar effected the normally dangerous receiving corps as not a single receiver reached the sixty catch mark. Webster Slaughter led the wide outs with fifty-nine catches for 847 yards and four touchdowns. Brian Brennan pulled down forty-five catches for 568 yards and two touchdowns. Reggie Langhorne had forty-five catches for 585 yards and two touchdowns. The receiving core only having eight touchdowns all year, which is only one every two games, spelled doom for the entire team. It was clear that they were not clicking with the Jim Shofner offense strategy.

The dismal 1990 season was also the last in the excellent career of future Hall of Famer Ozzie Newsome. He played his entire thirteen season career with the Cleveland Browns and would go down as the greatest tight end in team history, and one of the best in NFL history. With the exception of 1987 during the players strike, Newsome played in every single game of every other season. His 198 career games played for the Cleveland Browns remains as one of the highest marks in team history. He finished his career with 662 catches for 7,980 yards and forty-seven touchdowns. In all those seasons and with all those catches, he only fumbled the ball three times. That is a remarkable number that few will ever be able to match. Ozzie Newsome made three pro bowls in 1981, 1984, and 1985. He was named to the 1980s All Decade team, and also voted in the NFL Hall of Fame in 1999. It was a shame that such a brilliant career had to end on such a low note. Ozzie Newsome would remain with the team after retirement, however, as he took a position in the front office starting the next season.

Felix Wright gives his thoughts on why it went south so quickly, including "Bud" Carson being fired by Art Modell:

> *"We had too many players holding out for better contracts, which is a management issue. Management needs to take care of their ballplayers, there shouldn't be any. If we have a team that has been to the playoffs five years in a row, those players are going to be looking to get taken care of and you need to negotiate with them. So Bud came back in the 1990 season without being fully loaded with all of his talented ball players. We started off not very good, and he ended up getting fired over the deal...which reverts back to management...if they would have conducted*

their business better, Bud would have still been there for several more years. It was disappointing, and the end of our run at that particular time. The following year is when I decided to leave for Minnesota."

The off-season presented many questions as more players would leave in free agency and the Cleveland Browns were once again in need of a new head coach. The run of "Bud" Carson lasted all of twenty-five regular season games and two playoff games. He was the scapegoat that Modell needed to blame the losing on, even though many in the media and also fans felt it was a series of lousy front office moves that truly hurt the Browns in 1990.

Art Modell decided to hire Bill Belichick as the new head coach of the Cleveland Browns. Belichick was the former defensive coordinator of the Super Bowl Champion New York Giants. Belichick was credited with devising the plan that won the Giants the Super Bowl championship over the high-powered offensive attack of the Buffalo Bills.

Bill Belichick was born into a family of football coaching pedigree. His father Steve was an assistant coach at the United States Naval Academy as the young Belichick grew up in Annapolis, Maryland. Growing up, he excelled at both football and lacrosse, playing both through high school at Annapolis High School until graduating in 1970. He remained around both games when he went to college for one year at Phillips Academy before transferring a year later to attend Wesleyan University in Middletown, Connecticut. He continued to play both sports before graduating in 1975 with a degree in economics.

It was after college that Belichick began one of the greatest coaching runs in NFL History as seen by many current peers, former players, and national media. It all began in 1975 when he took a minimum wage job working as Baltimore Colts' head coach Ted Marchibroda's special assistant. Belichick was rumored to only have been paid twenty-five dollars a week; if so, it didn't matter because he was on the professional level near the game that he loved and had in his blood.

The next stop for the eager Belichick was in Detroit, as he took over the role of special assistant to the special teams coach for the Lions. He did so well in that role that after only a year he was promoted to tight ends and wide receivers coach for the 1977 season in Detroit. After two years in Detroit, he spent one brief season with the Denver Broncos as their assistant special teams coach and defensive assistant. Following his stints in Baltimore, Detroit and Denver, he would take the job that would change his life and coaching future forever.

Bill Belichick joined the coaching staff of the New York Giants in 1979 as a special teams and defensive assistant on the staff led by head coach Ray Perkins. It was the perfect fit for Belichick as he remained in New York for the next twelve seasons in various roles. In 1983, Bill Parcells came in as the new head coach, replacing Perkins, and it was a match made in heaven for the two Bills.

While coaching under Bill Parcells, Belichick was able to learn from one of the best coaches in the game, and was influential in both of the New York Giants' Super Bowl wins at the end of the 1986 and 1990 seasons. The latter was the more impressive victory as Belichick's defensive scheme stopped the highest powered offense in football, the Buffalo Bills, and helped his offense get enough time with the ball to win the game. The Giants won on a last second missed field goal by Buffalo Bills' kicker Scott Norwood, but it was Belichick's wonderful scheme that held them to only nineteen points in the win.

Upon arriving in Cleveland, Bill Belichick rubbed a lot of veteran players the wrong way quickly. Reggie Langhorne expresses his initial dealings and feelings about Belichick, but also looking back at it years later he has a different opinion than he used to:

> *"At that time, I thought of Belichick as a jerk, I thought that he was a young head coach who had great ideas but shoved them down our throat. He wanted us to run the system strictly his way. As time has gone on, he and I have been able to make amends with each other for everything that went on during that time. I have come to respect the way he is as a coach and how he coaches games. However, it needs to be understood that most of the guys who were on my team in 1991 were veterans, and maybe he thought that too many of us had too much power as leaders of the team and he decided he needed to weed some of us out.*
>
> *He went on to do what he wanted with his career as he went on to become a Super Bowl champion. Although many of us left the*

team and still played well elsewhere...myself with the Colts...at the time, we did not see eye-to-eye. I held out of training camp after they acquired Michael Jackson in the draft...Belichick wanted him to start over me...I eventually ended up suing the team because of things that transpired. Everything that took place early on between me and Belichick was off-key from the beginning of our relationship. But like I've said, I have come to respect what he was trying to do and made amends with everything. I have grown up a lot over the last 15–20 years, which has helped me respect him as a coach and a man, and I wish I had the chance to play for him again."

Second year back at the time, Leroy Hoard gives his thoughts on the transition of coaches:

"A lot of the older guys had a problem with the coaching switch to Belichick. They had been in a system and suddenly it was different. Back then, coaches would even be smoking on the sidelines... things were just different, and these signaled changes were set to occur. The whole NFL was switching over to a new image and brand. There was more OTA's and workouts. Bill was there to make everyone have to earn it again. I don't fault him for that, it was hard work. You had to prove that you wanted to be on that team. It weeded the people out who weren't committed to it. Bill needed to know that everyone was on the same page, and guys weren't riding out the glory days of their contracts. So we promptly got a lot younger, we worked a lot harder. We worked a lot harder because he wanted to see who was committed to that process. That is how we started off...it was tough! If you were going to be a part of that team, you were going to have to earn it. The guys that made it through felt a certain sense of accomplishment, and the guys who couldn't, blamed it on the coaching style of Belichick."

Veteran wide receiver Brian Brennan gives his insight on playing for Bill Belichick during his last season in Cleveland and the coach's first season:

"Bill Belichick was a hard- nosed, no nonsense kind of coach. He was very detail-oriented. He had a somewhat, maybe, dry personality. I think the players at first respected his resume, they got to know him...and then in Bill's mind, the team was a little older

than what he wanted so he began to make switches. The changes he made were very un-popular with the fans, media and players. He held to his guns and the team changed under his watch. I remember the team under him was always well prepared. He instilled us with the goal to win every game! As time went on over the years, he showed that he was a good coach."

Leroy Hoard explains how much Kosar helped his game and why the addition of Belichick as coach sometimes led to a clash between Kosar and the new head coach, meaning that both had their own ways of doing things:

"In my rookie year, I excelled at pass protecting and that led to expanded playing time in the Belichick system. If you can't pass protect, you can't get on the field. We ran a passing play and I was doing my best to block for Kosar until he threw the ball away. I thought I had done a good job until Kosar ran over to me and put his finger in my chest. He was upset because his method was when he was scrambling...he didn't want me to block, but rather for me to get open to catch a pass from him. So I started doing exactly that. I started catching those little dink passes and they really started to add up. We always timed those plays up well. Bernie was one of the smartest football players I have ever played with. He was really good at making adjustments on the fly as the games went on. He could make large adjustments during a series, or even a two-a-day drill. He could tell his teammates what to do all at once.

It led to conflict with Belichick because Bill wanted more structure. This was his first coaching job and he needed to build structure while Bernie was just trying to win games. It wasn't that Bill wasn't trying to win games...he was trying to win them for the next ten years. Things moved slowly, and as competitors we just wanted to win!

Belichick would call a play, and Kosar would change it while we were still in the huddle. He was the smartest guy I have ever played with that understood what his talent and what his skill set were. He understood what adjustments he needed to make during a play to accommodate what his strengths and weaknesses were in accordance to everyone else in the offense and put them on the same page.

> *Playing with Kosar, I learned about how to run several different routes against various linebackers in the secondary. Learning those things, such as how to pick up blitzes, it helped extend my career as I got older. Those things became important, and playing with him helped me develop that skill set. I was able to play a lot longer because of things I learned about defense, playing with Bernie."*

The most important and immediate task for Bill Belichick would be handling the roster of aging veterans, and also talent leaving while bringing in the better talent through the Draft and free agency. He would need to work closely with Executive Vice President of Football Operations Ernie Accorsi and Director of Pro Personnel Michael Lombardi. One of the most pressing needs was safety as one of the Browns most reliable starters, Felix Wright, had left in free agency to play for the Minnesota Vikings. Wright was a leader on the defense, and his departure left a huge gap for the Browns to fill.

Bill Belichick would have a heavy influence on the defense and he wanted to make sure his new defensive coordinator Nick Saban was ready and equipped with qualified players. Nick Saban never played professional football but he did have nearly twenty years of coaching experience before arriving in Cleveland. He served as a defensive assistant at Kent State, Syracuse, West Virginia, Ohio State, Navy, Michigan State, and most recently Toledo at the college level. He did have one year as a defensive backs coach on the pro level while coaching for the Houston Oilers.

Bill Belichick and Nick Saban would have the luxury of the Draft's second overall pick as the Cleveland Browns' horrendous record from the year before allowed the high draft selection. More good news for the Browns was that this year's draft was loaded with several defensive threats. In fact, there was any number of highly skilled defensive players that the Browns would have the chance to pick with their selection. The Dallas Cowboys owned the first choice and elected to take defensive tackle out of Miami, Russell Maryland.

There were three names that jumped off the board for the Cleveland Browns that would all help the secondary upon arrival. The first was cornerback Bruce Pickens out of Nebraska. The second was cornerback Todd Lyght from Notre Dame. The Browns, however, passed on both Lyght and Pickens, instead opting to select Eric Turner, a hard-hitting safety out of UCLA.

Eric Turner stood six feet one inches tall and weighed in at 208 pounds, but he hit like a man twice his size. He was quick and strong, and would provide an immediate impact on the defensive side of the ball. He was the highest choice for a defensive back since 1963 when the St. Louis Cardinals selected Jerry Stovall. The Browns were so excited to get Turner that they wasted no time signing him to a multi-year deal. They signed him for a four-year, six million dollar contract, which included a $3.15 million signing bonus, making the first-year compensation a record for a National Football League rookie.

Their next order of business was to address the gaping hole on the offensive line. Veteran lineman Cody Risien had retired after the 1989 season, and they struggled in 1990 to fill his void. Risien was the anchor of the offensive line. Upon arriving in Cleveland for the 1979 season, Risien eventually would block for four, one thousand yard rushers. He was a part of five AFC Central Division titles and was selected to two Pro Bowls. His presence was sorely missed during the 1990 season, and the Browns knew that if they were to get a running game established again they would need to draft a suitable replacement.

With their second round pick, they drafted Ed King out of Auburn. King only spent three years in Cleveland and was never able to move past Tony Jones on the depth chart. It was another swing and miss for Michael Lombardi and Ernie Accorsi. They followed the King pick with two defensive linemen to strengthen the pass rush and run stopping attack when they chose James Jones out of Northern Iowa in the third round and Pio Sagapolutele from San Diego State in the fourth round.

They didn't own a pick in the fifth round, but when they got back to work in the sixth round, they selected wide receiver Michael Jackson out of Southern Mississippi. The Browns still had Webster Slaughter, Reggie Langhorne and Brian Brennan, but all three seemed to be close to leaving and the Browns knew that they needed to start picking up receivers to eventually replace departing superstars. Michael Jackson was a big receiver too, standing six feet four inches and weighing 195 pounds. He was tall, lanky, and fast!

Michael Jackson didn't always have dreams of playing football but a certain set of circumstances and irony would lead him to the National Football League after playing with Brett Favre during his college career. He explains his decision to play football and how playing wide receiver was not always his first choice:

Michael Jackson stretches out across the middle to catch a ball. Photo courtesy of Michael Jackson

"My original dream growing up was not that of a football career, but rather to be a police officer like my dad. He was the chief of police in the village in which I grew up. At that time, that is always what you wanted to be...whatever your dad was doing. It wasn't until I went off to college that the thought of being a pro football player even crossed my mind. In high school, I played quarterback and during that era there weren't a whole lot of black quarterbacks in the NFL. I went to the University of Southern Mississippi that already had someone to play quarterback, a young man named Brett Favre. It was because of this that I chose to learn the wide receiver position.

The possibility of playing in the NFL still didn't cross my mind until my senior year of college. I had been running track and people started talking...with my speed, size and height...that becoming a pro player was no longer a long shot. I suddenly started to realize that I had the confidence and skill set to become a professional athlete. I continued to work hard and even during my senior season the scouts that came in, were there to work Brett Favre out. We ran an option offense so he didn't throw the ball a whole lot. So I knew the opportunity wasn't going to be too grand. I had about four hundred or five hundred yards receiving and I knew I needed more than that to make it to the NFL.

With my speed again, I figured I could make an impression. There were a couple of guys the year before me that went to the league and that's all they talked about was the speed of the guys in the league. The receivers during my era were mainly short, and there I was with a height of six foot four inches and the speed to run a 4.23 forty yard dash. When the scouts came in to work Brett Favre out, I asked them if they were there to work me out as well, and they said, "no." So I withdrew from school in the spring of my senior season and moved down to Houston, Texas to work out and get in the eyes of the scouts and get an invite to the combine.

I ran for Kansas City, Tampa Bay, Cleveland, Dallas, and Houston. During that time, Houston had asked me not to run for anyone else because I had run a 4.29 forty for them. They told me they didn't think it was possible as tall as I was to be able to run that fast. They asked me to run the opposite direction because they thought it may have been wind-aided. I ran the opposite direction in a 4.31 in my Converse shoes, and that's what was so unbelievable. That is when I really started believing when Houston asked me not to run for anyone else, and they would take me outside of the draft. Then again, my competitive nature told me if they are willing to take me outside of the draft, then I have two weeks to run for other teams and possibly go into the draft.

I continued to work out for people. Nothing happened on the first day of the draft for me. So on the second day of the draft, that's when I got a call from the Cleveland Browns, but I thought it was a guy over at the camp just playing with me so I hung up on them.

That's when the call came back in again, and it was Ozzie Newsome with the Cleveland Browns and they were very interesting. That is when the reality really started to set in on me that I had a real opportunity. I knew nothing about it but was just taking a chance on whatever was going on. I listened to the call and was really excited about it, although skeptical if it was real. Then, when reality set in on me, I was excited at the fact it was actually going on. That is the true story of my arrival into Cleveland."

Like many others, Michael Jackson was a part of the guinea pig team that was assembled to be the first under new head coach Bill Belichick. Michael Jackson shares some of the memories of his first camp under Belichick:

"It was one week after the draft that I showed up for rookie camp wide-eyed and excited not knowing what to expect. Most people knew that I was new to the receiver position as well with only two years under my belt. From there, the story turned into a miraculous one based on the career I was able to have. It started out slow as most people didn't realize I had only been a receiver for a short while and not my whole life like most who played the position. I was so used to just throwing the ball, and now I was learning the nuisances about this new position. It wasn't as easy as it looked as I really was still fresh at being a wide receiver. I was determined to learn the position and make the team going into rookie camp. So instead of going against guys who weren't drafted at the top, I chose to challenge myself against guys like Eric Turner who were drafted number one. I went against guys like Frank Minnifield and Stephen Braggs. I wanted to challenge myself against the best right away. I wanted to go against their starters, and by doing that I started to learn a lot more and improve my game. That's how I was able to go from a receiver of only three years to someone considered one of the best on the team and a starter. This only happened because I pushed myself against the best."

The first year in the NFL can be tough, let alone coming to a team that despite having a first year head coach, and always having high expectations placed on them by the local media and especially the fans. The positive thing for Michael Jackson was that he was also coming to a team that had three veteran established receivers in Brian Brennan, Reggie Langhorne, and Webster Slaughter who could help him with the sometimes tough adjustment period of going from college football to the NFL. Michael Jackson explains how playing with guys like Brian Brennan and Reggie Langhorne helped him:

> *"The talent roster was so deep, I knew my competition was going to be strong and I had to bring my best on a daily basis. These guys were established veterans in the league. I knew I had to make big plays on the field in practice, and that's when I started to catch the eyes of the coaches. The coaches thought I was a work in progress with the skills and attributes that I had. I came out of training camp with the Maurice Bassett award, which is given to the rookie who has the most impressive camp. It was an impressive rookie class but I was bound and determined to make myself known. I was also bound and determined to make myself a staple in the fifty-three man roster. Every day in camp, I was determined to make a big play. I wanted to become a big play receiver...it became a motto of mine. One day, years later, I opened up a company under that "Big Play" name. So that was my mentality, and by the fourth game, I was a regular starter because of it. It was overwhelming as well because I was replacing the same guys I looked up to and learned from. They were my mentors and I was taking their spot. Players learn to deal with those types of things, unlike people in corporate America. Because of the strong relationships with teammates, we are able to learn from those types of situations. We remain friends...in fact, I still talk with Reggie Langhorne. These are things I had to learn to balance. Everything became a learning experience for me as a young athlete at the time. I was from the southern part of the country and was learning to adapt as well. This was something brand new to me, but I knew that I also had to do my job in order to stay with the team."*

With his strong work ethic and desire to get better every time out on the field, Michael Jackson quickly became a teammate others could mold themselves after and also count on. Michael Jackson goes on to explain what it was like to become a team leader so quickly:

"I started to get comfortable in the system once I became a starter. Now I had to worry about the fan base and media members. Those are all learning curves that have to happen with the young athletes. We played in a city where football was like the Grand Ole Opry in Nashville. That was the passion of the fans and media in Cleveland. Once you finally realize that, then a lot more weight is added to your shoulders. Now, you can't socialize too much because if you lose, it looks worse. If you have a good game, you have to learn how to handle that as well. Those are things you are constantly learning and you have to also appease the people paying your bills, which are the fans. I was very appreciative of the fans, although sometimes they don't understand how much because you could lose your cool. It's a hell of a learning curve."

Another key addition to the team in 1991 was tight end Brian Kinchen. He came to Cleveland after spending three seasons on the Miami Dolphins in a limited role. Kinchen describes the circumstances that brought him to Cleveland:

"I had taken a free agent contract to be with the team. I just had my second child and bought a brand new house when Coach Belichick called me in week three. He asked me if I could long snap, because they needed a long snapper. I didn't get to the team until Thursday of that week, and spent all day long snapping as an interview / tryout attempt. That very first week ended up coming down to a last second field goal in which I had a pressure-packed snap to make. I was lucky enough that it went off without a hitch, and we were able to make the kick and win the game. Had that not of occurred, I'm positive I would have been cut and replaced after the game. It was the first step in earning the trust of the coaching staff and the team. Coach Belichick was very adamant about me learning how to snap both long and short, and not getting hurt."

Brian Kinchen goes on to describe his relationship with Bill Belichick:

"He was very old school and still is. He pays strict attention to detail and is one of the hardest working coaches in the NFL. He's loyal if you work hard for him. I have to give him credit because even though he's hard and tough, he keeps his word. I am grateful to him because he gave me a chance to be a starter

in the NFL. As much I as didn't want to like the man, he gave me everything I ever wanted in the NFL during my career as I ended up playing for him later in my career as he coached me in New England. I kind of call him my NFL stepfather. I ended up spending six of my NFL years with him. I won a NFL championship with him in New England, so it's hard to have negative feelings towards the man.

Brian Kinchen was excited to catch balls from Bernie Kosar, saying:

"During my career, I was able to catch the ball from Dan Marino, Bernie Kosar and Tom Brady, so in that way I was blessed. He was a legend in Cleveland and you just knew it from the way the fans and media responded to him and adored him. He was seen as Cleveland's kid...he was Cleveland's quarterback."

The switches didn't end with just offense and defense as new special teams Coach Scott O'Brien would also have to deal with departures. Both of the prior season's kickers had departed Cleveland months before. Punter Bryan Wagner left for New England while place kicker Jerry Kauric retired from football after only playing one season in the NFL.

Arriving from New England to take over the punter position was Brian Hansen. He was a veteran of seven NFL seasons. He was drafted in 1984 by the New Orleans Saints and played most of his career with them. The prior season he was with the Patriots, so the departure of Wagner to New England and the arrival of Hansen was almost viewed as a trade to some.

Brian Hansen grew up in Sioux Falls and admitted that he was actually a Minnesota Vikings fan as a youth. His father was influential in his life and between him and his siblings, sports always played a role in his day-to-day routine. Hansen was very gracious when speaking about his youth and the path that led him to the NFL:

"Getting into sports was very natural for me...and my father and brothers were all big Minnesota Viking fans, so we were all plugged into the NFL weekly. We did have other teams that we watched but the Vikings were so close to where we were in Iowa that it was natural for us to pull for them. My dad was a

multi-sports athlete in high school and it just kind of came natural to me as well. I remember playing football games with my brothers in the backyard with a bunch of kids from the neighborhood. My dad really was the one who installed the love of sports into me. I remember playing catch with him and my brothers... no matter what the season was, we had a ball for that sport and used it to play catch with my dad.

Hansen took a liking to several players while growing up a Minnesota Vikings fan:

"Being a Vikings fan, I had several players on the team that I really liked. I enjoyed watching them as they were known as the purple people eaters and went to four Super Bowls as I was a kid. I really liked players like Carl Eller, Alan Page, Chuck Foreman, and Fran Tarkenton. Those guys were my boyhood idols because they were on my favorite team."

Brian Hansen took his love of sports to the next level upon reaching high school as he participated on the varsity level:

"In high school...at West Sioux High School in Hawarden, Iowa, I played football my first two years in school but then stopped right before my junior year because I didn't care too much for the coach, and was discouraged and didn't want to play for him. Football had become a passion for me because it was something I had been working on all year round so even though I sat out my junior year, I eventually came back my senior year. I really missed it that year I was gone and really wanted to come back and play. That's when I started punting. I had gone to a University of South Dakota versus North Dakota State game and saw two of the best punters in college football playing that day, and they were putting on a punting exhibition which encouraged my interest in punting. I started practicing punting more on my own after that in my backyard, and just kind of gravitated towards punting. I did play other positions my senior year however, such as tight end as well as wide receiver. But I really wasn't big enough to be a wide receiver or tight end so I just stuck with the punting. It worked out because I got a small scholarship from the University of Sioux Falls in South Dakota. I played tight end and punted for them as well until my senior year when I got injured. Because of the injury, I couldn't play tight end anymore so I just punted."

Hansen was not concerned with joining a losing team or a team in rebuilding mode such as the Cleveland Browns was heading into 1991; it was something he had been used to dealing with. Hansen explains why he was used to the losing before he arrived in Cleveland:

> *"I've never experienced championships or even winning teams, so the losing wasn't very new to me. It is kind of my reality. Getting drafted was beyond anything I had ever expected. I remember the night before I got drafted, I was talking to the Cowboys who were going to sign me because we didn't think I would be drafted. I had fully intended to play for the Cowboys had I not then been drafted by the New Orleans Saints. So despite going to a losing team in the Saints, then the Browns, it was pretty exciting just to be drafted and getting to play in the NFL. Going into New Orleans, I knew that they had never even had a winning season... and didn't have one up until 1987, my third year in the league with them. For us and the fans, a winning season seemed like we had just won the Super Bowl. It was a fun thing to be a part of because we had gone through so many years of mediocrity, so to go to a winning season was a pretty neat thing."*

The Cleveland Browns' organization had been known as one of the most prominent franchises in all of sports before Hansen arrived, but he insists that he knew very little of the passionate fan base and history of winning before arriving in Cleveland:

> *"I wasn't very familiar with Cleveland before signing with the team. I think we played there once or twice, and I remember the locker rooms and stadium not being very nice. That didn't help my perception of the Cleveland Browns because it was based on that. I guess I didn't know what to expect of the franchise...but based on the expectations I had about the team, the city, and the fans would eventually change in a positive way because I saw what a great city it was to play for. The fans of Cleveland embrace their team and it was a neat environment as a player to be a part of. The fans were so very loyal and faithful as the community embraced us...more so than other places I was at, which made it a neat thing to be a part of."*

Not only was Brian Hansen quickly impressed by the passionate fans in Cleveland, but the Cleveland Browns had just built new training facilities that helped him to adjust quicker:

> *"I had just been in New Orleans and New England, and neither one had all that impressive of a training camp facility. The Browns had this brand new, multi-million dollar state-of-the-art, as good as it gets facility. It was what I thought the NFL should be like. Coming from the Patriots, I was used to practicing at the actual stadium we played our home games in. The Saints had this old building that was in a very old and run down part of town. So to see Cleveland had such nice things going on, I was excited to be there. It was a neat place with great people! My perception of Cleveland prior to that was not nearly as high based on limited exposure and knowledge. It was great to see the city and how it had developed."*

Brian Hansen was able to get a first-hand view at the new coach and his ways as the team was headed into such a large period of transition:

> *"Bill Belichick has come a long way from his first year of coaching with the Browns. He's one of those guys who knew the X's and O's but didn't know how to deal with people. He was lacking in that department, and it was obvious when you look at the way he dealt with the media. He was just a tough guy to figure out. He was spirited, focused, and driven but with a head coach you have to have that intangible quality that you have to be able to motivate and talk to your players, and that is something he clearly lacked at that time. We had some pretty bad seasons after he came to the team. I didn't think at that point that he was head coaching material and never thought he would turn out to be what he is now. He has had incredible success, but back then he was a tough guy to get to know, and I think that was just his personality. I think he knew football very well but at that time he was an interesting guy to play for."*

Brian Hansen goes on to explain why Belichick wasn't afraid to make personal changes even with players who were popular amongst teammates and fans,

> *"Coach Belichick has a great eye for talent, and for developing talent and putting the right people together to excel under his*

> *coaching philosophy. He knew talent so well that the transition of players was because he knew exactly what he was looking for in a player. He would look at a guy like Bernie Kosar and realize he wasn't the guy to get me where I needed to go. He didn't have the style and philosophy that fit into the Belichick coaching mode.*
>
> *He was the kind of guy who wasn't afraid to make those kinds of changes even though those guys had been successful in the past. Bill kind of prided himself on having a plan in position, and knew what he needed to make it work. He wasn't afraid of making the decisions needed to get him where he needed to go. I don't know if it's a pride thing for him, but the success is due to the system he has in place and no player is bigger than the system...and that is what has led to his success."*

Brian Hansen made a couple of close friends on the team shortly after arriving in Cleveland:

> *"One of my closest friends on the team was Matt Stover, the place kicker. We formed and kept a close relationship over the years. We were very close by the nature of positions and I would hold the ball for him to kick. Brian Kinchen is in the mix as well as I still stay in contact with him. Stover and I still remain in close contact because we're very like-minded in our approach to football and also our faith. Matt was the one guy on the team along with Brian Kinchen who I was roommates with and spent a lot of time together with. Mall was a good friend and still is."*

Brian Hansen was not the only new kicker to arrive in town to begin the 1991 season. Jerry Kauric retired from football, after only playing one season, so the Cleveland Browns needed a new place kicker. Following Bill Belichick from the New York Giants was second-year kicker Matt Stover. He had been drafted the season before by the Giants, but never made it into a single game because of injury. He sat behind Matt Bahr while the Giants won the Super Bowl.

Matt Stover, born Joshua Stover, grew up in Texas where he idolized the Tom Landry-coached Dallas Cowboys. He looked up to Roger Staubach. In his words, "*How could you have a better idol than Roger Staubach?*" Stover played football growing up and excelled in his high school career at Lake Highlands High School in Dallas, Texas. Years later, a fellow Cleveland Browns place kicker Phil Dawson attended the same high school. In fact, Stover even coached Dawson at one point during high school. Stover graduated from Lake Highlands after he won All-District honors as both a wide receiver and kicker. He also showed how strong his leg were when during the 1985–86 season he kicked a fifty-three yard field goal.

Matt Stover continued to have success in college as he attended Louisiana Tech University. As a sophomore, facing Texas A&M, he once again showed off his power when he kicked a fifty-seven yard field goal, then a school record. By the time his college career was done, he had successfully converted sixty-four of eighty-eight field goal attempts. He left Louisiana Tech with 262 career total points and seven field goals of fifty yards or more. It was an impressive resume to bring to the Cleveland Browns, as for all intents and purposes, he was seen as a rookie with unlimited potential.

Stover was excited to come to Cleveland. He was following Belichick and believed that he could make a difference on the team's roster. Stover shares his excitement, saying:

> *"I had known of the hype behind the Dog Pound, and also knew Matt Bahr from my one season with him in New York. I remember the Kardiac Kids of the 1980s along with Bernie Kosar. I knew I was coming to a team that had a lot of great veterans on it. You had Mike Johnson, Clay Matthews, Bernie Kosar, Kevin Mack, Eric Metcalf, and all these great players. It was very exciting to have the opportunity to play with them.*
>
> *The general manager at the time was Ernie Accorsi, and he was a great guy along with Michael Lombardi. It was a great opportunity for me...and of course, Bill Belichick was the defensive coordinator from the New York Giants the prior year, so I knew him. Cleveland was a great football town to be a part of, and it ended up being awesome for me and my wife as we really enjoyed our time in Cleveland."*

With new players on both sides of the ball, new place kickers, new punters, and new coaches, the Cleveland Browns would encounter a lot of growing pains in the 1991 season. They sensed it would be an uphill climb but as usual, the Browns' fans were hungry for a winner and were willing to support whatever player was placed on the field in front of them. The fans hoped that maybe the 1990 season was a mere hiccup, and that things would get back to their normal ways in 1991.

The season kicked off at home against the visiting Dallas Cowboys led by head coach Jimmy Johnson. The Cowboys had seen some very thin years the past seasons after trading away their stud running back Herschel Walker prior to the 1989 season to the Minnesota Vikings for a slew of draft picks. While the move may have provided some very lean win totals for the Cowboys, it turned out to be one of the greatest trades in professional sports history.

The Dallas Cowboys only won one game in 1989 under rookie quarterback Troy Aikman and newly appointed head coach Jimmy Johnson. They improved in 1991 with seven wins because of key draft picks acquired in the trade. Players like Emmitt Smith and Michael Irvin began to become influential playmakers and put the Cowboys in the spotlight. Heading into the home opener, the Browns knew how much the Cowboys had improved in two seasons, and fully realized that they would have a tough test on their hands.

Things started off well enough for the Cleveland Browns as they led 7–3 after the first quarter following a one yard Kevin Mack touchdown rumble. It was in the second quarter that the Dallas Cowboys began to ruin the head-coaching debut of Bill Belichick with an explosive seventeen point second quarter. Troy Aikman hooked up with tight end Jay Novacek and Michael Irvin for touchdown passes. The Cowboys tacked on a Ken Willis twenty-five yard field goal and took a commanding 20–7 lead into halftime. The Browns battled back with a sixty-two yard touchdown to Webster Slaughter. The third quarter ended 20–14 in favor of the Cowboys and that would be the closest it would get. The Cowboys added two more field goals by Ken Willis in the fourth quarter, earning their 26–14 victory over the Browns. The Cowboys had handed Bill Belichick a loss to start off his head-coaching career.

The Cleveland Browns' defense struggled to contain Emmitt Smith, as any teams would in his career, and allowed Smith to rush for 112 yards on thirty-two carries. Troy Aikman torched the Browns' secondary for 274 yards and two touchdowns. The Browns' defense would have to tighten up as the season went on if they were going to have any chance at improving upon their game.

The Browns' offense continued to be the bigger story as they remained one-dimensional, and again couldn't get the rushing attack off the ground. Bernie Kosar did his part by throwing for 249 yards and a touchdown. The running game was of no help as the Browns' leading rusher was with thirteen yards on only three carries. Joe Morris, a veteran that Bill Belichick brought with him from New York, went for two yards on three carries. The veteran Kevin Mack ran for twelve yards on a game high seven carries. This was not the best opening week for the Cleveland Browns.

The Browns would travel to New England the following week to take on the Patriots. The Browns invaded Foxboro Stadium with the intention of beating up on the lowly Patriots, and erasing the bad memories of the prior week. And, they did just that. The Browns' defense stepped it up and shut out the Patriots' offense. The New England Patriots never scored, and the Cleveland Browns won with seemingly ease 20–0. The Browns defense picked off quarterback Tom Hodson twice, and limited him to only ninety-five passing yards.

The Cleveland Browns found a running game on the legs of second-year back Leroy Hoard. He was not active the prior week against the Cowboys, but the young Hoard made the most of his touches in this contest. Hoard did what he prided himself on, and took a Bernie Kosar pass in for a touchdown from seven yards out. Later in the game, it was Kosar connecting with Michael Jackson on a beautiful sixty-five yard touchdown pass. Matt Stover booted two field goals, and the Browns handed Bill Belichick his first victory as head coach.

There was very little drama in the Cleveland Browns' first two games of the 1991 season; however, the third game would be packed with it. Week three brought the cross-state divisional rival Cincinnati Bengals to town to take on the Browns. It was a close contest and a defensive battle the whole day as the Browns failed to score a touchdown, while the Bengals only scored one. Heading into the closing seconds of the game, it was the Cincinnati Bengals on top 13–11. The Browns had kicked three field goals with Matt Stover and scored on a safety when James Jones tackled Bengals' running back in his own end zone.

Down by two points late in the fourth quarter, Bernie Kosar led the Cleveland Browns on a last second drive in the hopes of getting the young Matt Stover into field goal range for one last shot to win the game. Kosar and the boys did just enough to get to within Stover's range at forty-five yards. As the packed crowd suspensefully held their breath, Stover booted it right down the middle and gave the Browns a 14–13 win, and their second straight to start the Bill Belichick era.

This was the first game winner of Matt Stover's NFL career. It was a sweet feeling for Stover after having to spend the 1990 season watching from the sidelines in New York. Nearly twenty-five years later, Matt Stover reflects back on the moment:

> *"It was amazing because it was only my third game, and it was an awesome opportunity. I had many more to kick after that so I just needed to stay humble...and knowing that our team was doing well enough to keep winning divisional games. I went on to miss field goals that season as well, so I had a lot of lessons to learn. Humility was a good part of my game and it gave me the ability to stay grounded."*

Matt Stover goes on to explain a very unique and wonderful thing that happened to him shortly after that game, courtesy of the opposing coach Sam Wyche:

> *"One really amazing thing about that kick was that a few days letter, I received a letter from opposing head coach Sam Wyche saying how he hated to see the kick go through, but how he always respected a great play and he told me congratulations. I was a new young player and he knew he would be playing against me a lot of years so it was a lot of respect given to me from coach Sam."*

Despite their win, the Cleveland Browns once again failed to get anything going on the ground. Eric Metcalf continued to be a one-year wonder as he rushed for a pitiful seven yards on six carries. Leroy Hoard was held to twelve yards on three carries. Kevin Mack once again led them with thirty-seven yards on ten carries. The multitude of running backs was simply not working.

The following week, Belichick would get his chance to take on his former team, the New York Giants in New York. It was another defensive battle as the Giants combined a Rodney Hampton touchdown run with two Matt Bahr field goals to lead 13–0 at halftime. The Browns answered with a Matt Stover thirty yard field goal conversion in the third quarter combined with a fourth-quarter Bernie Kosar to Kevin Mack touchdown pass to cut the lead to 13–10. That would end up being the final score and the New York Giants hung up to beat Bill Belichick and the Cleveland Browns.

The Browns would try to put together some answers over the week, and come out fresh against the New York Jets in their next game. The Jets would not allow it, however, as they jumped all over the Browns and led 14–0 at halftime. The Browns showed some heart and fought back to tie the game with a touchdown run by Kevin Mack and a touchdown pass to Leroy Hoard in the third quarter. This week, however, it was the Browns losing by a field goal as Jets place kicker Pat Leahy's twenty-eight yard field goal late in the game secured it for the Jets and sent the Browns record to 2–3.

Bernie Kosar was held in check against the New York Jets only throwing for 133 yards and a touchdown pass to Leroy Hoard. For Hoard, he was starting to find his notch catching balls out of the backfield. Eric Metcalf had four carries for twenty-seven yards. The receiving core also had its struggles as Reggie Langhorne and Brian Brennan were held to one catch each for minimal yardage.

At 2–3, the Cleveland Browns looked to even things up the following week against the Redskins as they had to travel to Washington. The game started off close as the Browns used a bit of trickery and went for a fake field goal that saw punter Brian Hansen connect on an eleven yard touchdown pass to Webster Slaughter. Washington Redskins' quarterback Mark Rypien tossed a first-quarter touchdown pass himself to keep the game tied after one quarter of action. The second quarter rightfully belonged to Washington as Earnest Byner and Gerald Riggs both had rushing touchdowns to give the Redskins a 21–7 lead at halftime. Things went from bad to worse in the second half with Washington touchdown runs from Ricky Ervins of twelve and sixty-five yards along with a one yard Gerald Riggs touchdown. By the end of the game, the Cleveland Browns had been profoundly defeated 42–17.

The Cleveland Browns then traveled to San Diego, California trying to rebound from a three game skid. Bernie Kosar had one of the best games of his season as he tossed for 297 yards and two touchdowns to Leroy Hoard. The Browns also cashed in on a Joe Morris one yard touchdown run. Their defense was a bit shaky again, however, and after four quarters of regulation football, the game was tied 24-24 heading into overtime.

The overtime period would not last long as it lived up to its motto of 'sudden death'. Cleveland Browns' linebacker David Brandon picked off a John Friesz and returned it thirty yards to pay dirt to give the Browns a thrilling 30-24 overtime win. It was a huge win for the Browns as it broke their three-game losing streak, and brought them to within one game of .500.

Back at home the following week, the Cleveland Browns found a way to keep their winning ways alive going against the Pittsburgh Steelers. It was another low-scoring affair, but another Leroy Hoard touchdown catch combined with a one yard touchdown run from Kevin Mack was enough to give them a 17-14 victory. Kosar remained consistent as he threw for 179 yards and a touchdown with zero interceptions. Eric Metcalf had his role continue to decrease as he only saw one carry for twelve yards. Leroy Hoard also only saw one carry on the day, in which he took for two yards in the win. The Browns had managed to bounce back from their three-game losing streak to win two straight and climb back to .500 at 4-4 at the middle point of the season.

Things weren't looking too bad for Bill Belichick as his first eight games of an NFL coach went better than he could have hoped for. To be .500 this far into your first season was an accomplishment in itself. The good vibes wouldn't last long, however, as the Browns dropped their next three games in a row. It was a brutal stretch that witnessed losses to the Bengals in Cincinnati 23-21, followed by a loss to the Philadelphia Eagles at home 32-30, and then another road loss to the Houston Oilers 28-24. All three games were winnable, but the Browns just couldn't seem to pull them out. They lost all three games by a total of only eight points.

The rough patch reduced the Browns to 4-7 on the season, and pretty much ended any chance at a playoff run. Despite their poor record, Belichick would not allow his team to give up on the season. They had a game at home against the Kansas City Chiefs and were determined to get a win against their former coach Marty

Schottenheimer. They had lost one and tied one in their prior two match-ups against Schottenheimer, and were anxious to get the win for their new coach Belichick. It was as if a win with their new coach would help them feel better about no longer having Schottenheimer on the sidelines.

The Cleveland Browns were able to kick things into high gear after a slow first quarter that ended scoreless. They began the second quarter running on all cylinders and earned the game's first points on a one yard Leroy Hoard touchdown run. Matt Stover would chip in with a thirty-four yard field goal before the half, and the Browns led 10–0 at the break. Their offense was playing well both through the air and on the ground for one of the first times all season. The defense was able to step up as well and picked off the Kansas City Chiefs' quarterback twice.

Things continued to go well in the third quarter for the Browns when Leroy Hoard caught a screen pass from Bernie Kosar and took it seventy-one yards for a touchdown. Hoard was continuing to show his skill for pass-catching and being a go-to target for Kosar in any situation. The big play by Hoard gave the Browns a comfortable 17–0 lead. The Chiefs would make a valiant late comeback, but in the end it was not enough, and the Cleveland Browns secured a 20–15 win.

While Bernie Kosar didn't have one of his better games, he did enough to get the job done. He tossed for 170 yards and a touchdown, despite having the two interceptions, which was unusual for the normally precise Kosar. Hoard had his best game as a pro as he ran for sixty-one yards on only six carries, and caught two balls for seventy-eight yards and a touchdown. Reggie Langhorne's efforts contributed with five catches for fifty yards in the win.

The Cleveland Browns looked to stay on the winning side of things the following week as they traveled to Indianapolis to take on the Colts. The Colts were the worst team in the league and on their way to a 1–15 season. The Browns were licking their chops all week long at the perspective match-up, and for good reason.

The game was never a close one. The Cleveland Browns jumped out to an early lead and never looked back. They went into the second quarter up 3–0, and exploded for twenty-eight more points to take a 31–0 halftime lead. Kevin Mack caught a three yard touchdown pass from Kosar and then followed it up on the next series with an impressive fifty-one yard touchdown run. Leroy Hoard scored on a two yard touchdown of his own. It was capped off when the defense decided to get in on the act as linebacker James Jones picked off a Jeff George pass and returned it twenty yards for a touchdown. Neither team scored in the entire second half. The Cleveland Browns won 31–0, improving their record to 6–7.

For the defense, it was their second shut-out of the season. They intercepted quarterback Jeff George two times, and held him to one hundred yards passing. The rushing defense was also good as they didn't allow future Hall of Fame running back Eric Dickerson to reach the end zone. The offense looked better as well. Leroy Hoard continued to prove how good of a pass-catcher he was by catching six balls for seventy-four yards. He only had two rushes for two yards and a touchdown. It was becoming clear that when Hoard was in the backfield that the chance of Kosar passing the ball was higher. That was a good and bad thing because even though it was effective at times, the defense was soon able to predict what the play call was when Hoard was lined up in the backfield.

The revolving running back carousal continued during the Colts game as Joe Morris received the bulk of the carries this time, rushing for sixty-eight yards on nineteen carries. Kevin Mack had ten less carries than Morris but still rushed for sixty-nine yards and scored twice. Mack was having a good season, despite the constant switching of who would receive the majority of the carries each game. Kosar went eighteen for twenty-three for 189 yards and a touchdown. He returned to his accurate ways and did not throw an interception.

Thirteen games into the season, the Cleveland Browns were a respectable 6–7. They had a rookie head coach and a team mixed with unproven young talent and aging veteran talent. All things considered, it could have been a lot worse. They weren't completely eliminated from the playoffs if only they could find a way to win the rest of their games. It was a long shot, but just to be in that position was a great improvement from the prior season and showed just how good of a coaching job Belichick was doing.

The Denver Broncos arrived in Cleveland the following week, and put an end to any Cinderella playoff dreams for the Cleveland Browns and their fans. It looked good for awhile as the Browns' defense did their best to hold John Elway in check. It was tied at halftime 7-7 as John Elway had a touchdown pass to Vance Johnson for the lone Denver score. The Browns' one trip to the end zone came on a three yard Kevin Mack touchdown run. With the game tied, heading into the fourth quarter, the Browns were still very much in the thick of things as the balance hung in doubt.

The Broncos were finally able to put the Browns away for good. Midway through the fourth quarter, it was John Elway hitting Vance Johnson on a six yard touchdown pass. It was followed a few minutes later by a thirty-seven yard David Treadwell field goal that put the game out of reach. The final score was 17-7, and the Cleveland Browns were eliminated from any chance of making the playoffs.

The Browns offense once again struggled to adapt to the Bill Belichick scheme. They only converted nine first downs all game, and Bernie Kosar often looked confused and slow. Kosar was restricted all game and only threw for 110 yards, zero touchdowns, and was picked off once as well. Leroy Hoard had three carries for eleven yards. Joe Morris didn't fair too much better as he only had two carries for three yards. Kevin Mack once again took the bulk of the carries as he ran for eighty-seven yards on fourteen carries. It wasn't nearly as rough for the Browns to pull off the upset as Browns' fans once again saw their beloved team get beat by John Elway and the Denver Broncos. Elway threw for 221 yards and two touchdowns in the win. The Browns showed a lot of heart and promise by competing all game. Nevertheless, the Denver Broncos were a superior team that season, and finished with a record of 12–4.

The home finale would be the next week against divisional opponent, the Houston Oilers. Despite being out of the playoff hunt, the Browns came out sharp and hungry. Leroy Hoard continued to take Bernie Kosar passes in for scores as he connected on an eight yard touchdown pass with Kosar in the first quarter. The Oilers would respond with a seven yard touchdown pass from Warren Moon to Ernest Givins. Bernie Kosar responded to the call of a shootout with Moon as he hit Brian Brennan for an eight yard touchdown pass. The Houston Oilers responded with a twenty-seven yard Al Del Greco field goal before the half, cutting into the Browns' lead and making it a 14–10 game at the half.

The third quarter was a defensive battle as each team failed to score. As the fourth quarter began, the Browns' fans could sense that their team was trying too hard not too lose, instead of trying to win. Sure enough, that strategy would fail once again as the Oilers would eventually score on a two yard touchdown pass from Warren Moon to Haywood Jeffires. The Cleveland Browns lost 17–14, and several players were upset with the very conservative nature of the play-calling as they failed to score a single point in the second half.

Bernie Kosar started the game red hot, and finished with 258 yards and two touchdowns. He had most of the yards and both touchdown passes before halftime. The running game was unable to do much as Kevin Mack was held to seventy-five yards and Leroy Hoard seventeen yards. Leroy Hoard did catch seven more balls for seventy yards and a score. The Browns could not stop Warren Moon, as he went for 254 yards and two touchdowns. In the end, it was one the Cleveland Browns let get away.

The final game of the season went the way of most them before it—strong defense and lack of offense. Bill Belichick was building the strong defense he wanted, but the offense continued to suffer. The game was held at Three Rivers Stadium in Pittsburgh, Pennsylvania as the Cleveland Browns took on the Steelers. The first half of the game was lethargic and didn't produce much action in the way of scoring for either team. The halftime score was 3–3 after Matt Stover and Gary Anderson exchanged field goals.

The Pittsburgh Steelers gained momentum in the second half with a long touchdown pass of sixty-five yards from Bubby Brister to Dwight Stone. Shortly after, the Steelers would score again when defensive back Richard Shelton intercepted a fourth quarter Bernie Kosar pass and returned it fifty-seven yards for a touchdown. Kosar would connect with Michael Jackson on a twenty-seven yard scoring strike before the night was over. It was a nice way for Kosar and Jackson to cap the season, but it was too late as the Browns lost

17–10 and finished the season with a 6–10 record. Good enough for third in the division.

Bernie Kosar managed to throw for 335 yards and a touchdown in the loss. The running game showed one last gasp of incompetence with another less than stellar effort. Leroy Hoard had seventeen yards on five carries. Kevin Mack ran the ball eight times for twenty-three yards, and Joe Morris had twenty-seven yards on twelve carries.

Bernie Kosar didn't allow the coaching switch to affect his game too much just yet, as he had a solid bounce-back campaign from the 1990 nightmare season. Kosar finished with 3,487 yards and eighteen touchdowns while only throwing nine interceptions. The team was making wholesale changes but Bernie Kosar continued to shine and be a favorite in fans' hearts. The problem for Kosar remained his ever decreasing mobility. Bernie Kosar was sacked forty-one times, losing 232 yards in the 1991 season; he also ran the ball twenty-six times for only seventy-four yards. It was a growing concern that Bill Belichick could not continue to ignore.

The offense scored 293 points, which was the sixteenth highest scoring offense in the league, or the twelfth lowest, depending on how fans wanted to look at it. The defense allowed 298 points, for which was fourteenth best out of twenty-eight teams. They only gave up five more points that then were able to score, a building block for the future.

For the third consecutive season, the Cleveland Browns' running game failed to produce a thousand yard rusher. Kevin Mack started eleven games running for 726 yards on 197 carries and scored eight touchdowns. He cleaned up his ball control problems from the prior season and only put the ball on the ground once. After Mack, there was a large drop-off when it came to consistent run producers. The veteran free agent pickup Joe Morris didn't do much, running for 289 yards on ninety-three carries, scoring twice. It didn't help that Eric Metcalf was hurt for a large portion of the season. He only started three games and ran for 107 yards on thirty carries. Leroy Hoard played in all sixteen games, rushing for 154 on only thirty-seven carries. He earned his salary by catching balls out of the backfield; in fact, he caught forty-eight passes for 721 yards and eleven touchdowns.

The year 1991 would be the final season for all three of Bernie Kosar's favorite targets as Brian Brennan, Webster Slaughter, and Reggie Langhorne all left the team following that season. It was clear that they were not going to fit into the new Bill Belichick system. Reggie Langhorne had thirty-nine catches for 505 yards and two touchdowns. Webster Slaughter caught sixty-four passes for 906 yards and three touchdowns. Brian Brennan finished with thirty-one catches for 325 yards and one touchdown.

With the three veteran receivers set to depart, Michael Jackson would have to step up from his rookie season. Jackson went for 268 yards on seventeen catches and scored twice. Jackson did play in all sixteen regular season games, which was also a good sign for him.

The new place kicker had a good first season as a pro with the Browns. Matt Stover was accurate consistently as he connected on sixteen of twenty-two field goals. He was also two of two from fifty yards plus. Brian Hansen averaged over forty-two yards a punt, so both facets of their kicking game seemed to be working out.

The AFC Central was won by the Houston Oilers with an 11–5 record. The Buffalo Bills wound up winning the AFC championship to earn the right to return to the Super Bowl. The NFC representative, the Washington Redskins, were too much to handle for the Bills, and the Redskins won the Super Bowl 37–24. One point of interest was that Earnest Byner, the one-time goat of the 1987 Championship game, was on the Washington Redskins' roster and earned a Super Bowl ring.

Fans were anxious to see what Bill Belichick could do with his second off-season, in the hopes of bringing in an influx of young talent to replace several veterans who continued to leave. As mentioned before, Kosar's top three wide receivers left town via free agency. Brian Brennan departed for Cincinnati, Reggie Langhorne went to play for the Indianapolis Colts, and Webster Slaughter signed with the Houston Oilers. This left a huge gap at receiver that the Browns would need to make their top priority in the off-season to be addressed.

One of the main problems during the 1991 season was that Belichick refused to hire an offensive coordinator, insisting that he could do it himself. This led him to butt heads with Bernie Kosar several times and didn't make much sense because his prior experience was on the defensive side of the ball. With the gaping hole at receiver, Belichick needed his second-year receiver Michael Jackson to step it up as the number one target for Kosar. Also, they needed Lawyer Tillman to reach his potential as he was entering his fourth season with the team. They brought in another fourth-year receiver, Shawn Collins; he came from the Atlanta Falcons. They would hope to bring in a steady fourth receiver courtesy of the NFL Draft. They already had Hoard and Metcalf who could both catch balls and perform well with them out of the backfield.

The NFL Draft was even more crucial this year as they needed to make sure they could fill the holes, and also provide threats on both sides of the ball. Coach Belichick was determined to get the roster just the way he wanted it with players that would fit his system. Belichick was not worried about hurting feelings by cutting popular players; he wanted things his way, and was hell bent on making it happen.

The Cleveland Browns would be picking ninth in the upcoming Draft and wanted to explore all options with the pick. It was a rather unique draft because the Colts held both the first and second overall picks. It was the first time since 1958 that one team held the first two overall picks. It was also the final NFL Draft featuring twelve rounds of selections; the league would reduce the rounds to eight the following season, and then the current format of seven the year after that.

The Indianapolis Colts went defense on both of their picks, drafting defensive end Steve Emtman out of Washington and linebacker Quentin Coryatt from Texas A&M. The Los Angeles Rams went defense with their pick as well and selected Sean Gilbert, a defensive end out of Pittsburgh. The Washington Redskins took Heisman Trophy winner Desmond Howard out of Michigan with the fourth pick. Howard was the first receiver off the board and would go on to become a NFL bust. He was one in a long line of Heisman winners to be a bust in the NFL. The Browns dodged a bullet by not even having the chance to draft him. The Green Bay Packers went defense with the fifth pick and took cornerback Terrell Buckley out of Florida State. Buckley would go on to be a lockdown corner for many years, and was high on the Browns' board. The Cincinnati Bengals took the first quarterback of the draft, David Klinger, out of Houston. The Miami Dolphins followed by taking another dangerous cornerback, Troy Vincent, from Wisconsin. The Atlanta Falcons took offensive lineman Bob Whitfield out of Stanford with the following pick, which left the Browns with almost a full board of receivers to choose from.

The Browns had plenty of options with the number nine pick. Several talented receivers were still on the board. There was Carl Pickens from Tennessee, Jimmy Smith from Jackson State, Courtney Hawkins from Michigan State, and Robert Brooks from South Carolina. Surely, with so many receiving threats available, the Browns would clearly take one of them...wouldn't they?

The answer was a resounding 'no', as Belichick insisted on picking another running back with their top choice. They had Eric Metcalf, Leroy Hoard, and Kevin Mack—all three who had proven they could be reliable starting running backs if used the right way. However, Belichick still wasn't sold on any of them. He knew they needed more touchdowns from that position, and this left him with no choice other than to select the man synonymous with the word "touchdown". With their first pick, the Browns selected "Touchdown" Tommy Vardell out of Stanford.

Tommy Vardell was one of the best running backs to ever graduate from Stanford University. Not only was he successful on the field but also brilliant in the classroom. He was a smart kid, and the Browns knew that he would keep his nose clean, work hard, and mold himself into the Belichick philosophy. Vardell had a great career in college as he rushed for 1,843 yards, scored thirty-seven touchdowns, and never fumbled the ball in his entire college career. His legacy will forever be remembered as Stanford Cardinal because he ranks second in Stanford football history for most touchdowns and third for most rushing yards. For seventeen seasons, he held the record for most rushing yards in a season for Stanford with 1,084 yards in 1991. The rushing record was eventually broken by Toby Gerhart in 2008.

The nickname of "Touchdown" came from his incredible ability to score. In his junior season, he only had 120 carries, but managed to score fourteen times on those rushes. That is in an incredible average of a touchdown every nine attempts with the ball. It was during his junior year that Vardell was given the nickname

"Touchdown Tommy" by then Stanford head coach Denny Green after scoring four touchdowns against their rival Notre Dame. Things kept going well in his senior year. Despite only playing in eleven games, he carried the ball 226 times for 1,084 yards, and scored twenty touchdowns.

His nose for the end zone and incredible ability to keep the ball secure and never fumble it, made him too good of an option for the Browns not to pick up. Vardell was a powerful downhill runner and would complement Hoard, Mack, and Metcalf perfectly. Vardell describes his running style coming out of college:

> *"I was a downhill runner that had a good sense of angles and leverage, and who could exploit weaknesses in defenses. I could find pockets where the integrity of the defense would be compromised, and I would attack it aggressively. This is what I did at Stanford. Much of my time while playing at Stanford, I was used like Mike Alstott. They would line me up in the tailback position and fed me the ball over and over again."*

It seemed as though the skills of Vardell would be a sure thing and a big hit in the NFL. Sadly, however, the Browns found a way to screw it up as Vardell explains:

> *"We ran a much different offense in Cleveland that had the big backs as single backs running belly plays and rotating with one another, and then a different set of players came in on third down. It was a tough situation for everyone. I needed to be given the ball more than a few times a game. I only hit the fourteen carry mark five times in my career in Cleveland. I think I averaged four or five carries a game. On the surface, it looked exciting, but I think all of the backs at the time would agree that it was very difficult to get into any sort of rhythm with the "running back by committee" approach. Again, going to the Browns, I had a vision of getting the ball twenty plus times a game, where I could run plays downhill, stretch the defense, and pound the ball over and over.*
>
> *I did not love the plays we ran. Our core plays required our big backs to roll laterally and read, rather than just step and accelerate. I always felt it took away from the power of our backs. It was a different style that I (and others) had to learn. This might have been the perfect scheme for other backs—and maybe even the*

right scheme for the pros in general—but it was counterintuitive to me to dance and read. We also got very predictable with what plays we were running with which personnel. I can remember playing the Saints and Sam Mills (their middle linebacker) was calling out every play and who was getting the ball during the course of our game. It was pretty crazy."

Despite how his time in Cleveland would end up turning out, Vardell was full of vigor and excitement when first hearing the news that he was drafted by the Browns, and would be coming to Cleveland to start his NFL career:

"I had lots of excitement when I found out I was going to Cleveland. I wanted to pound the ball in the snow, and had visions of getting the ball twenty plus times a game and wearing people out by the third or fourth quarter. I was especially excited about the fan base because the Cleveland fans didn't just show up on Sunday, they had brown and orange in their blood all week long. In Cleveland, the fan engagement never stops...it's twenty-four across all activities, sporting, family, and business alike during all seasons. With other teams, the stadium might be packed, and the cheers might be loud, but when the game ends, the fans trickle back to their lives, hanging their fan gear in their dark closets, only to be worn again the next game they opt to attend. And by Monday morning, the game is already distant memory.

In Cleveland, and in the spring time for that matter, the Cleveland businesswoman dons her professional suit and high heels for her important meetings of the day, and then she throws her satin brown and orange Browns' jacket on top. And this is not only accommodated for, but it is expected. The fact is that the Cleveland Browns are in the DNA of every minute part of Cleveland life, and because of this, the fan base is relentlessly loyal and mercilessly devoted to the team.

I wanted to be a part of that, and gave every ounce of myself in my immersion into the city and the team. I was an all-season participant, living there year round so that I could experience the Browns' richness . I wanted to be woven into the history of the Browns as somebody that was upstanding, a team player, and punished people on the field—just like some of the historical Browns had done. I gave my left knee for it."

At the time, both the fans and Vardell believed that he would be the featured back; if so, he could have been one of the best to ever wear a Cleveland Browns' uniform. Unfortunately, the Browns and Belichick never used him the right way, and stuck with a sometimes annoying and mostly non-effective four-back rotation. The move also annoyed fans because the team needed a receiver badly, and after ignoring the need in free agency, they thought for sure it would be a priority in the draft.

In the second round of the Draft, the Cleveland Browns knew they had to address the need at receiver before things got worse, and more players came off the board. The only problem was that they picked late in the second round, number fifty-two overall, and the pickings would be slim. With that being the case, they settled on Patrick Rowe. Even the most die-hard of Cleveland Browns' fans might have a tough time remembering Rowe, and for good reason...he only played one season in his entire NFL career. He caught three balls for the Browns that year, totaling thirty-seven yards. He was six foot one inches tall out of San Diego State, and he should have been good. But as injuries and luck would have it, it never panned out. He only played in five games, and out of the three balls he caught, he fumbled one of them.

The Browns had the luxury of two third-round picks and addressed their defensive needs with them. They selected Bill Johnson, a defensive tackle out of Michigan State; however, he never amounted to much in his NFL career. They used their second pick in the third round on linebacker Glen Dixon from South Carolina—another draft miss that never made an impact for the Browns at the NFL level.

The Draft misses would have a serious effect on the Cleveland Browns for several seasons to follow. Another problem was that they didn't have picks in either the fourth or fifth rounds. Once the Browns had the chance to pick again in the sixth round, the level of offensive threats had been picked clean. They had to settle on Rico Smith, a wide receiver from Colorado. Much like Patrick Rowe, Smith would fail to have any impact in his rookie season. He played in ten games, but only caught five balls for sixty-four yards and didn't reach the end zone on any of those five catches.

Things continued to fall apart after the Smith pick, as the Browns proceeded to select six more players who combined to play one career game. Those players were George Williams, Tim Hill, Marcus Love, Augustin Olobia, Keithen McCant, and Tim Simpson. Tim Simpson was the only one of the bunch to play in one career NFL game. The Browns had one more pick in that draft and used it to take Selwyn Jones, a defensive back out of Colorado State. He only played one season for the Browns, but he did have three interceptions in that season. From there, he played three more years, one with the New Orleans Saints, and two with the Seattle Seahawks.

One of the worst NFL Drafts in Cleveland Browns' history resulted in two receivers who combined for less than ten catches. A group of players who never saw a single play in an NFL game, and a running back who could have been great if not completely screwed up by having to take part in a multi back rotation. Many fans and Cleveland media point to this NFL Draft as one of the worst moments of Bill Belichick's stint in Cleveland.

Apparently, the Browns felt as though only having one reliable starting receiver would be enough to make things work. They figured to pass the ball often to running backs such as Leroy Hoard and Eric Metcalf to more than make up for the gaping hole at the wide receiver position. To their credit, it did work for a little while at least, as Leroy Hoard had twenty-six catches for 310 yards and a touchdown. Eric Metcalf caught forty-seven balls for 614 yards and five touchdowns. Combined, they managed to do the job of one actual wide receiver. With the draft producing slim results, they began looking elsewhere to fill other holes such as undrafted free agents and aging veterans who were still available.

One new addition to the Cleveland Browns in 1992 would be rookie free agent Ed Sutter, from Northwestern State University, a defensive specialist brought in to help solidify the defense and special teams. Ed Sutter gives his thoughts about coming to play for the Cleveland Browns:

> *"I'm from the Midwest and have always considered myself a blue collar hard-working person. I recall when Northwestern played OSU at Cleveland Stadium in 1991, my senior year. As we arrived in Cleveland for the game, the city felt exactly what football*

was all about. A big old stadium, Browns' signs, shirts, banners all over the place, American flags hanging on several houses, downtown smokestacks, the river and a slight mist coming down on a cool October day. I was signed by Minnesota out of college. In pre-season, we played the Browns and I fell in love with the stadium and the city again. Luckily, two weeks later, the Vikings released me and it was the Browns who called and signed me. I was absolutely thrilled."

Ed Sutter was excited at the chance to play for Bill Belichick and had kind words to say about his former coach:

"Bill is a very loyal person, and was great to people he trusted and who he could rely on. He made a few mistakes in Cleveland that I'm sure he would admit to, but unfortunately, the city grew impatient. I knew through watching him work, that he was the most detailed, hard-working coach that I had and would ever play for. Bill would take guys sometimes that other teams would not take a chance on, but he knew exactly what they could do, and how he could plug them into his system to help it work."

With the suddenly injury-prone Bernie Kosar continuing to age and playing behind a shaky offense line, the Cleveland Browns knew they would need a comparable replacement ready to come in for Bernie when he got hurt. The Browns' brain trust, namely Bill Belichick, wasn't sold on Kosar to begin with, and was always looking for a possible replacement if need be. That year's search led them to acquiring former Chicago Bears starting quarterback Mike Tomczak.

Mike Tomczak was no stranger to replacing a beloved veteran as he had done it in Chicago when he took over for Jim McMahon, a Super Bowl winning quarterback and crowd favorite. Fans from Cleveland already knew of him from his time as the starting quarterback for the Ohio State Buckeyes. He had been named Illinois High School Player of the Year while playing at Thornton Fractional North High School in Calumet City where he was coached by his father, Ron Tomczak. This led to him being awarded an athletic scholarship to Ohio State University. He proved to be a winner at Ohio State, and led the Buckeyes to a couple of Big Ten Championships.

Despite his success in both high school and college, Tomczak went undrafted out of college and signed as an original free agent with the Chicago Bears. While playing with the Bears his rookie season, he didn't see much playing time but was lucky enough to be a part of the Super Bowl winning team. When he eventually took over for McMahon, things went well. He won his first ten starts at quarterback, which set an NFL record.

While starting in Chicago, he proved to be the man for the job as he led them back to the playoffs in 1988. He also showed that he could play in bad weather as he was the starting quarterback for Chicago in the infamous "Fog Bowl" playoff game against the Philadelphia Eagles. The Chicago Bears won the game, earning them a trip to the NFC Championship Game.

Mike Tomzczak would eventually fall out of favor in Chicago and sign with the Green Bay Packers. This was before the epic starting streak of Brett Favre began, which actually allowed him a chance to play while in Green Bay. He started in seven games, totaling eleven touchdown passes of his 128 completions and nine interceptions. Some in the Green Bay media and other media members around the NFL pegged him to be the next starting quarterback going forward in Green Bay. As luck would have it, he began a lengthy contract hold-out. The Green Bay Packers weren't interested in playing contract games with Tomczak, and chose to cut him loose instead.

It was a move that would payoff for Green Bay as they opted instead, to trade with the Atlanta Falcons for a young man by the name of Brett Favre, and let him battle it out with Don Majowksi for the starting role. Favre became the Green Bay Packers' starting quarterback in the fourth game of the 1992 season, stepping in for injured quarterback Don Majkowski, and started every game through the 2007 season. One can only wonder what would have happened if Tomczak had not have held out for more money—if the legend of Brett Favre may have ever happened. Among just a few of his records include, most career passing yards, most career pass completions, most career pass attempts, most career interceptions thrown, most consecutive starts by a player, most career victories as a starting quarterback and for a few years, he held the most touchdown passes in a career as well.

As the Green Bay Packers chose to go with the future Hall of Fame quarterback instead of paying Mike Tomczak, the Cleveland Browns decided that Tomczak was the man for the job. In the strong chance of Kosar with his diminishing skills going down with an injury, they knew that Tomczak would be ready when called upon. Keep in mind why this is so noteworthy, the Cleveland Browns could have traded for Brett Favre but chose not to.

With the very limited amount of valuable additions, the Browns were set to take the field for year two of the Bill Belichick reign in Cleveland. Despite their lack of fire power, they did double their win total the previous season, and was hopeful of improving in the new season.

The chances of having a strong start to the season should have been good, as their week one opponent were the lowly Indianapolis Colts. Remember, the Colts only won a single game the prior season, and should have been an easy test to begin the season. The game was in Indianapolis, but the Browns were still favored to win. Instead of the walk through to victory that the Browns' fans hoped for, it was the Indianapolis Colts starting the Browns' season off with another loss.

The Cleveland Browns' lack of offense and weapons to score were on full display as they only managed to score three points all game. The Colts weren't much better, but a first-quarter touchdown rush by Rodney Culver combined with a fourth quarter twenty-six yard touchdown catch by former Browns' player Reggie Langhorne, were more than enough points to shut the Browns down.

The Browns struggled to move the ball all day, and were held to just thirteen first downs. Bernie Kosar had one of his worst opening days as a professional. Kosar threw for 175 yards on fifteen completed passes, but didn't connect on any touchdown passes, and did throw two interceptions. One of the biggest problems for Kosar continued to be poor offense line play. The Browns' offensive line allowed a sickening eleven sacks, including four by former Browns' player Chip Banks. The two rookie top picks also placed Kosar flat on his back several times. Quentin Coryatt had two sacks and Steve Emtman had one.

Only two Browns' receivers caught passes as Michael Jackson pulled in three catches for forty-nine yards. Little known receiver Jamie Holland also had two catches for twenty-seven yards. Back-up tight end Pete Holohan helped out with four catches for thirty yards. They were counting on Eric Metcalf and Leroy Hoard to be effective pass catchers out of the backfield that day, and it simply didn't happen. Eric Metcalf only had one catch for eleven yards while Leroy Hoard only had one catch for ten yards. The day for the Browns' first round pick, "Touchdown" Tommy Vardell wasn't much better as he only ran for twenty-six yards on nine carries. Punter Brian Hansen got his work in, punting it eight times for an average of 46.9 yards per attempt. Matt Stover had a mixed day as he made a field goal but also missed one.

As bad as the offense looked, the defense actually looked much better and improved. They held Colts quarterback Mark Herrmann to 177 yards, and Vince Newsome picked off a pass. They also had a sack by Anthony Pleasant. The defense held starting tailback Rodney Culver to fifty-two yards on nineteen carries. Not a bad first week for the defense despite the offense's struggles.

Things wouldn't get much easier for the Browns the following week as the high-powered offensive attack of Dan Marino and the Miami Dolphins rolled into Cleveland for the home opener. It was a Monday Night game on national television, and Bill Belichick did not want to be embarrassed as he was just in week one.

Nevertheless, by the end of the first quarter, the game was headed for a Miami Dolphin blowout as they led 14–0 after two quick scores. Dan Marino completed a twenty-five yard touchdown pass to Mark Duper to get things rolling, followed by a seven yard Mark Higgs touchdown run. The game went into halftime with the same score 14–0.

Down two touchdowns to start the second half, the Browns were in need of points, and quickly. They got some off the foot of reliable place kicker Matt Stover who connected from twenty-eight yards out to cut the Dolphin lead to 14–3. Miami Dolphins place kicker Pete Stoyanovich would respond with a twenty-two yard field goal, and close out the third quarter with a 17–3 lead.

Pete Stoyanovich opened up the fourth quarter with a thirty-two yard field goal, and the Dolphins expanded their lead to

20–3 with just under a quarter left to play. Down seventeen points late in the game, the Browns finally decided to wake up and started doing some scoring of their own. Kosar hit Michael Jackson in the end zone from six yards out and gave the Browns their first touchdown of the season. A little bit later, it was linebacker David Brandon returning a Mark Higgs fumble thirty-two yards for another Browns' touchdown. And, just like that...the Cleveland Browns were only down 20–17 with all the momentum on their side. Things kept rolling. The next time the Browns got the ball back, Kosar connected with tight end Mark Bavaro for a three yard touchdown to give the Browns their first lead of the 1992 season.

The packed house at Cleveland Municipal Stadium was roaring as they saw their team rally back from the brink of another embarrassing loss, to take the lead with only a few minutes left to go. All of this was occurring in front of a nationally televised audience. Sadly, for the Browns and their loyal fans though, Dan Marino had just enough time to lead yet another one of his epic comeback drives, capped off by a Mark Higgs one yard touchdown run to give the Miami Dolphins a 27–23 win, and hand the Browns their second loss of the season.

The Cleveland Browns were in a slump, and had waited until the fourth quarter to start doing anything, but when they did they were firing on all cylinders. Bernie Kosar finished with 230 yards with two touchdowns and no interceptions—a drastic improvement from week one as the biggest key was his offensive line allowing him to stay on his feet. They only gave up two sacks all game long. It was important for anything the Browns hoped to accomplish that Kosar would have time to throw and go through all of his needed check-downs.

Rookie running back Tommy Vardell had a nice night, rushing the ball sixteen times for eighty-four yards. He also caught two balls for twenty-nine yards. It was a strong night for the rookie running back on the national stage. Leroy Hoard continued his early struggles, however, with only two carries for zero yards. Eric Metcalf didn't fare much better on the ground as he ran for sixteen yards on two carries. Metcalf did, however, have a productive night catching the ball as he caught four balls for fifty-nine yards.

Michael Jackson continued to step into his role as number one receiver by snagging five passes for ninety-eight yards and a touchdown, including a sixty yard bomb from Kosar. Veteran tight end Mark Bavaro contributed his part with four catches for thiety-seven yards and a touchdown. As long as Kosar was lacking a number two and three receiver, he would continue to need good play out of his tight ends.

Dan Marino had his way with the Browns' secondary by throwing for 322 yards and a touchdown, including the game-winning drive when the Browns couldn't come up with any way to stop him as he marched the Miami Dolphins down the field for the go ahead score. The Browns' pass rush faired a little better as they were able to sack Marino three times. Rob Burnett, Ernie Logan, and Clay Matthews all recorded sacks against the future first ballot Hall of Famer.

As impressive as their comeback was to watch, it wasn't enough to get a win and the Browns started the season 0-2 for the first time since 1984. They then traveled cross country to take on the Los Angeles Raiders. They would have to do so without starting quarterback Bernie Kosar. It was discovered that he had incurred an injury during the Miami Dolphins game, and would not be able to play against the Raiders. The true shocker was that they wouldn't be going with the experienced backup quarterback Mike Tomczak, but rather Todd Philcox.

Todd Philcox went undrafted in the 1990 NFL Draft, as he was coming out of Syracuse University. He signed with the Cincinnati Bengals as an undrafted free agent and only threw two passes in his only season with the Bengals. The Browns took a flyer on him in 1991, and he played in four games that season, throwing eight passes, and completing four. Not feeling that Tomczak was ready yet, it was Philcox's time to shine in Los Angeles.

As luck would have it for Todd Philcox and the Cleveland Browns, he wouldn't have to do much as the game quickly turned into the Eric Metcalf show. Early in the first quarter, it was Metcalf taking a screen pass and rushing it in for a four yard scoring strike to give the Browns a 7-0 lead. A few possessions later, it was Metcalf again, this time taking a handoff and scoring from six yards out to put the Browns ahead 14-0. The Raiders used the next two quarters to pull within one point at 14–13. Once again, Metcalf took over the game. Metcalf took another dump off pass from Philcox, and ran sixty-nine yards for the touchdown. A few minutes later, Metcalf did it again—this time, scoring from sixty-three yards out on a screen pass. The Raiders could not stop the speed of Metcalf, and the Browns picked up their first victory with a 28–16 win on the strength of four Eric Metcalf touchdowns.

The box score for this contest wouldn't come close to telling you how things actually went. Technically, the Browns only earned seven first downs. They had two huge plays from Metcalf that led to quick scoring drives in which first downs weren't even needed. Todd Philcox only completed ten passes all day, but they went for two hundred yards; again, because of the breakaway speed and big play capability of Eric Metcalf. The four touchdown day was a career high for Metcalf as he caught five balls for an incredible 177 yards. He ran the ball four times for ten yards, but scored a touchdown on one of those carries.

The big plays by Eric Metcalf were desperately needed because the rest of the offense combined to do very little. Tommy Vardell and Leroy Hoard combined for twelve carries and four total yards. Leroy Hoard did have two catches for ten yards. Back-up tight end Pete Holohan had three catches for sixteen yards and that was it for the offense in Los Angeles. Thank goodness for Eric Metcalf's inspiration and skilled play, or the Browns would have been 0–3 , instead of 1–2.

The Browns' secondary was once again shredded, this time for 395 yards by Los Angeles' starting quarterback Todd Marinovich. They did manage to pick him off three times, which kept the Raiders out of the end zone several times. The rushing defense also held strong as they kept legendary running back Marcus Allen at bay, only allowing him to scamper for fifty-two yards. After the game, it was discovered that Todd Philcox had broke his thumb, so they would have no choice but to go with Mike Tomczak until Kosar was ready to return.

Week four, back home in Cleveland, brought in their familiar rival, the Denver Broncos. This time, however, the game produced little to no drama, and the Broncos won in boring fashion, 12–0. It was a game that saw zero touchdowns, and all the points came on four field goals by Broncos' place kicker David Treadwell. The Mike Tomczak debut went poorly, as he completed nine of nineteen passes for seventy-five yards and two interceptions. Tomzcak was not the only one to throw interceptions that day as Matt Stover tried to convert a botched field goal attempt into a pass that was also intercepted. Any thoughts that Belichick might have had about having Tomczak replace Kosar going forward did not get off to a good start.

Apparently, Bill Belichick thought instead of riding the hot hand of Eric Metcalf, he would use this game to give Leroy Hoard the bulk of the work. Hoard had ten carries for seventy-one yards along with four catches for fifty-four yards, it was a good night for Hoard. Metcalf had eight carries but was held to only twenty-one yards in those attempts. What was very puzzling was that the Browns only chose to throw the ball to Metcalf three times, which he was able to turn into only eleven yards. It was a far cry from the effort they made the prior week to get him the ball. Vardell saw six carries for fourteen yards. After only four games, things were not going well in Browns' town.

One positive note was that the Browns' secondary improved and did not allow John Elway to pick them apart. The Browns' defense held Elway to 157 yards and zero touchdowns. They did, however, allow Denver running backs Reggie Rivers, Gaston Green, and Greg Lewis combined to rush for 157 yards. They would need to tighten up that hole in the defensive line going forward as it was obvious they would not be getting much help from their offense, and points would be at a premium.

At 1–3, and now on their third quarterback of the season, the Browns were in desperation mode and needed to do anything possible to keep the season afloat as their hated rivals, the Pittsburgh Steelers, invaded Cleveland Municipal Stadium for week six of the NFL season. The Browns had a much-needed "bye week" after the Denver debacle, and needed the Steelers game to get back on track.

Not discounting the Pittsburgh Steelers, but the Cleveland Browns' team was heading towards a lighter spot in their schedule, and needed to take advantage of some winnable match-ups. They did just that in their contest against the Steelers. Mike Tomczak was steady all day and completed ten of seventeen passes for 171 yards and one touchdown. That touchdown came in the fourth quarter on a forty-seven yard beautiful strike to Michael Jackson to help secure the game, 17–9.

The Browns' defense stepped it up big and didn't allow the Steelers' offense to cross the goal line all game, instead holding them to three Gary Anderson field goals. Speaking of field goals, it was Matt Stover once again coming through when called upon, and hitting a clutch fifty-one yard field goal of his own earlier in the game. The Jackson touchdown and Stover field goal was complimented by a one yard Kevin Mack touchdown rumble.

The Kevin Mack touchdown came as a surprise since they hadn't been using him much. Mack emerged from the bench, and ran the ball twelve times for thirty-two yards and the touchdown. Tommy Vardell was limited to three carries for seven yards. Leroy Hoard never saw the field, but Eric Metcalf did get seven attempts for forty-nine yards. Metcalf also caught three balls for forty-eight yards. Most importantly, perhaps, was the Browns' defense holding All Pro running back Barry Foster to eighty-four yards on twenty-four carries; it was an average less than four yards per carry. They also kept Foster out of the end zone, which was just as impressive due to his skills. It was a win that the Browns sorely needed and were grateful to have.

The Green Bay Packers visited Cleveland Municipal Stadium the next week, and Mike Tomczak would get the chance to show his former team that they made a mistake by letting him go. The first half was a quiet and uneventful one as the only scoring came off of a Matt Stover twenty-six yard field goal. The score remained 3–0 until the early third quarter when Green Bay kicker Chris Jacke connected on a forty-four yard kick to tie the game. The Browns would answer with a one yard Kevin Mack touchdown rumble to take a 10–3 lead into the fourth quarter. The Green Bay Packers wasted no time answering right back with another Chris Jacke field goal, this time from thirty-seven yards to cut the lead to 10–6. The Browns didn't flinch and just kept with the game plan of black and blue football. It worked to perfection as Kevin Mack once again bulldozed his way into the end zone for a five yard touchdown run. This was enough to put the Browns ahead for good as they won their second straight game by a score of 17-9. This win also allowed them to pull even on the season at 3-3.

Mike Tomzcak had a very modest thirteen of twenty-one pass completions for 158 yards and zero touchdowns or interceptions. His opposing quarterback Brett Favre went twenty of thirty-three for 223 yards with zero touchdowns and zero interceptions. One impressive thing that Tomczak was able to do was spread the ball out amongst several targets. Michael Jackson had four catches, Eric Metcalf had three catches, starting tight end Scott Galbreath had two catches while Ron Wolfley, Mark Bavaro, Shawn Collins, and Lawyer Tillman each had a catch. Mike Tomczak wasn't exactly lighting the world on fire, but he was getting the job done and not turning the ball over. It was also a complete win as the Browns' run defense played great, holding Green Bay Packers' starting running back Vince Workman to only thirty yards on just ten carries.

As for the running back situation, much to the chagrin of several players, it continued to be anyone's guess from week to week as to who would be their feature back. The Green Bay game saw Kevin Mack receive the bulk of the carries as he took nineteen handoffs for seventy-five yards for two touchdowns. Eric Metcalf was limited to four carries for twenty-one yards while Tommy Vardell had nine rushes for thirty-eight yards. Leroy Hoard had two carries for seven yards.

With a record of 3-3, the Cleveland Browns were on the cusp of turning things around and putting together a solid season. They traveled to New England to take on the re-building New England Patriots team. It was a Matt Stover's kicking showcase early and often as the first three scores of the game came on field goals from Matt Stover of twenty-nine, twenty-eight, and twenty-one yards. The Patriots showed serious fight as they came roaring back with three straight scores of their own. A Hugh Millen to Kevin Turner nineteen yard touchdown pass combined with a Hugh Millen to Ben Coates two yard touchdown pass, and a Charlie Bauman thirty yard field goal gave the Patriots a 17-9 lead on the Browns entering the fourth quarter.

Despite the rally, the Cleveland Browns took a deep breath and got back to work themselves with a clutch performance on both sides of the ball in the fourth quarter. They struck quickly with a thirty-two yard Matt Stover field goal, his fourth of the contest to cut the New England lead to 17–12. A little bit later on, with time running down, Mike Tomczak connected with tight end Scott Galbraith for a touchdown to give the Browns a much-welcomed 19–17 road victory.

Mike Tomczak was again, not spectacular, but he was steady enough to get them the win. He tossed for 186 yards, one touchdown, and most importantly did not turn the ball over. The Browns now had a winning record at 4–3, and Mike Tomczak had put them in a winning frame of mind. Leroy Hoard didn't receive any carries, but he did catch one ball out of the backfield that he took for eleven yards. Kevin Mack received sixteen carries for thirty-eight yards.

It was the rookie Tommy Vardell who would shine on this particular day, as he received a career high seventeen carries for eighty yards. Vardell's effort combined with Michael Jackson catching three balls for thirty yards was sufficient offense to put the Patriots away. Instead of having one or two really talented players, the Browns continued to base their success on a group of semi-talented players doing their best to work together for the common goal of winning. And, it appeared to be working well.

The Browns' defense was very good that day as well, holding the Patriots' leading rusher Jon Vaughn to only thirty-four yards. Hugh Millen did have modest success against the Browns' secondary, however, as he tossed two touchdown passes and threw for 194 yards with zero interceptions. The defensive line also did a good job getting pressure on Millen, sacking him four times.

The Cleveland Browns were suddenly red hot, winners of three straight and improving by the week. They were 4–3, and Mike Tomczak was now 3–1 as the starting quarterback since taking over for the injured Bernie Kosar and Todd Philcox in week four. The Browns' were riding high and feeling good about themselves for a short time, that is...until they were given a cruel dose of reality the following week in Cincinnati at Riverfront Stadium.

Things looked bright for the Browns as they drew first blood on a first quarter thirty-nine yard field goal by Matt Stover. The Browns took the lead 3–0, however, it would be the Bengals who scored the game's next twenty-seven points. The Bengals scored on three Boomer Esiason touchdown passes to Craig Thompson,

Rodney Holman, and Tim McGee. They combined the three touchdown passes with two Jim Breech field goals to build their 27–3 lead. The Browns would score late, on a fourth quarter thirty yard touchdown pass from Tomczak to Michael Jackson, but it was far too little too late as the Browns lost 30–10. Towards the end of the route, the Browns let seldom-used fourth string quarterback Brad Goebel even get some action, as he went two for three in garbage time.

Mike Tomzcak had a serviceable game as he connected on sixteen of twenty-eight passes for 252 yards, including a forty-two yard strike to Lawyer Tillman at one point. Tomzcak also went the entire game without throwing a single interception. The problem was that their offense, once again, became one-dimensional as they had to rely solely on the passing game. Their rushing game was stuck in mud all day and couldn't get anything going against the stout Cincinnati defense. Kevin Mack had eleven carries but only rushed for thirty yards. Eric Metcalf was held to minus one yard on five carries. Tommy Vardell touted the rock five times but only accumulated eleven yards for his efforts. Leroy Hoard had his number called three times, and racked up twelve yards. As Tommy Vardell had previously said, "the running back by committee was not working and the play-calling started to become extremely predictable."

The Browns' rushing defense did well, as they held the Bengals' top rusher Harold Green to fifty-eight yards. Their secondary encountered issues, however, and allowed Boomer Esiason to throw for 192 yards and the three touchdowns. The pass rush failed to get any heat on Boomer and he was never sacked.

Midway through the 1992 season, the Browns were 4–4, which is a lot better than many people would have figured them to be after the horrible off-season. Given the fact that they were on their third starting quarterback of the season combined with the fact that hadn't had a single one hundred yard rusher, a break-even record was something to be proud of. For the second straight season, Bill Belichick actually had fans and local media thinking playoffs as they entered the second half of the season.

The second half of the season kicked off in Houston, Texas with a highly anticipated match-up against the high-powered offensive run and shoot attack of Warren Moon and the Houston Oilers. It was a packed house of excited and rowdy fans that filled up the Astrodome that Sunday to watch these division rivals go head-to-head on the field. The Browns, still reeling from the prior week's blowout loss to the Cincinnati Bengals, were out for blood. The team was determined to play much more physical on both sides of the ball than they did the prior week. They knew that all three phases of their game would have to be working in sync to get past the Oilers on their home field in the Astrodome.

Motivated to win, the Cleveland Browns got off to a hot start, and used their momentum to score in each of the first three quarters to build a 17–0 lead heading into the fourth quarter. Matt Stover had hit a forty-four yard field goal in the first quarter, followed by a forty-six yard Mike Tomczak to Leroy Hoard touchdown pass in the second quarter. Leroy Hoard continued to showcase how good he could be catching passes out of the backfield and taking off down the field with them. In the third quarter, it was safety Stephen Moore snuffing out the promising Oilers drive when he recovered a fumble and took it seventy-three yards for a Browns' touchdown.

The Browns eventually knocked Warren Moon from the game, and the Oilers turned to backup quarterback Cody Carlson to try and get a late rally going. It didn't take Carlson long to find former Cleveland Browns' wide receiver, now Oiler, Webster Slaughter for a twelveyard touchdown pass. He was the second former Cleveland Brown to score on them that season after the Langhorne touchdown opening week against the Colts. The Browns would answer the Oilers touchdown with one of their own when Mike Tomczak connected with tight end Mark Bavaro for a seventeen yard touchdown pass later in the fourth quarter to put the game away for good.

The Houston Oilers would eventually score one more time before the game was over on a Cody Carlson eighteen yard touchdown pass to Earnest Givins. But it was simply not enough as the Browns hung on to win the game 24–14. The win helped improve their record to 5–4, and also secured a crucial road division game victory in a tough place to play.

Mike Tomczak was, once again, steady but not great. He contributed enough to win and that is all Belichick was looking for from his starter. Tomczak threw for 219 yards and two touchdowns, and he didn't throw any interceptions. His precision passing and ball safety style was endearing him to the heart of Belichick and guaranteeing him more snaps behind center.

While the Browns' passing game was doing better than expected, their running game remained inconsistent and non-effective. Kevin Mack had thirteen carries for only thirty-nine yards. Eric Metcalf only had seven carries for twenty-one yards, and Vardell had five carries for thirty-one yards. Leroy Hoard did not receive a handoff but did catch two passes for sixty-eight yards, including the forty-six yard touchdown. Their defense didn't record a sack but Eric Turner did intercept a Cody Carlson pass.

The Cleveland Browns were a very pleasant surprise this season at 5–4, and with Bernie Kosar ready to come back and play any week, the decision for Bill Belichick was getting tougher. Would he stick with Tomczak, or would he go back to Kosar who had yet to win a game that season? The Browns returned home the following week to face the San Diego Chargers, and were hoping to keep the winning momentum going.

The Cleveland Browns' game against the San Diego Chargers turned out to be a low-scoring, lack of action nail biter that would come down to the final moments of the game. The Chargers drew first blood in the first quarter with a twenty-six yard touchdown pass from Stan Humphries to Shawn Jefferson. The Browns responded with a thirty-six yard field goal later in the half. Both teams went to the locker room with the Chargers up 7–3.

The fans in attendance, hoping to see more action after an uneventful first half, were let down as neither team managed to score a single point in the third quarter. Both teams finally began to hustle and got things moving in the final quarter as Mike Tomczak came up big with a beautiful twenty-four yard touchdown pass to his number one threat Michael Jackson. A few minutes later, Matt Stover added on a field goal and the Browns took the lead 13–7 late in the fourth quarter.

The Cleveland Browns were so close to winning their second straight game and improving their record to 6–4. Their defense just needed to hold the Chargers one more time, and then let their offense run out the clock. With excitement in the air, things were looking good as the defense had been able to contain the Bolts' offense all day. Their top receiver Anthony Miller had been held to six catches for sixty-five yards, and the Browns just needed to hold the high-octane receiver at bay a little longer to pull off the victory. Regrettably, for the Browns' secondary, they could not hold on. Stan Humphries threw a bullet down the field to connect with Anthony Miller for a forty-five yard touchdown, and secured a San Diego Chargers' victory.

Needless to say, it was a heart-breaking loss for the Browns. They were so close to winning and had played such good defense all game until the last second collapse. The Browns' secondary was able to bend all game until finally breaking when it mattered most. Humphries finished with 234 yards and those two big touchdowns. The Browns could not get a pass rush on him and he was only sacked once. Frank Minnifield did have an interception as well; however, it simply wasn't enough.

It was the same old story for the Cleveland Browns' offense—a non-existent running game, which left the passing game to try and do all the work. Tomczak had his best game of the year, throwing for 322 yards but was picked off twice. Lawyer Tillman, who up until that point, had not lived up to his draft billing from years prior, stepped it up and caught eight passes for 148 yards. It was the best game of his career but came in a loss. Michael Jackson chipped in with four catches for eighty-four yards.

The Cleveland Browns' number one pick—the ninth overall in the Draft—the man they called "Touchdown", had one carry all game for minus one yard. Their top pick from two years prior, Leroy Hoard didn't receive a single handoff. He did, however, run the one catch he had for twenty-five yards. Strategic weapons were starting to appear in the form of the young backs, but it was apparent that Bill Belichick simply didn't know how to use them effectively. The Browns had three young and talented running backs but continued to give the bulk of the carries to the veteran Kevin Mack who had seventeen more for only thirty-five yards.

With as many wins as losses ten games into the season, the Browns knew they had something good in the works; they just needed to figure out how to use it to make that final playoff push before it was too late. They were coming off a heart-breaking loss to the San Diego Chargers as they traveled up north to Minnesota to take on the Vikings in the Metrodome. They would need to pull themselves together, and find a way to progress forward as a team.

This would be the week, however, that the magic of Mike Tomczak appeared to finally run out as he got off to an awful start. Tomczak completed fifteen passes, but only for fifty-four yards and two of them were picked off by the Vikings. Tomczak didn't throw any touchdowns and was pulled in the second half and replaced by Todd Philcox. Bernie Kosar still wasn't healthy enough to play, but this outing of Tomczak may have been just the motivation he needed to put the final tabs on his rehab.

The Minnesota Vikings' secondary keyed in on Philcox as well. He didn't fare too much better than Tomczak. Philcox was held to three of seven passings for only seventeen yards and was also picked off. The Browns' defense also gave both Vikings quarterbacks Rich Gannon and Sean Salisbury fits all day, and the game remained close. The Browns were actually up late in this one again, as they held a 13–10 lead late in the fourth quarter. It was then that Minnesota defensive back Audrey McMillian picked off a Todd Philcox pass and returned it twenty-five yards for the game-winning touchdown. Back-to-back weeks, the Browns were on the verge of victory, and in back-to-back weeks, they had their hearts broken. Instead of being 7–4 and contending for a division title, they were 5–6 and searching for lost pieces of their heart and soul.

The boys in orange and brown would return home the following week, and welcome in the monsters of the midway, the Chicago Bears. Mike Tomczak had played pretty decent while going 4–4 in his role as starting quarterback. Kosar was healthy, and rather than staying with Tomzcak or going back to Philcox, Bill Belichick was willing to put everyone's favorite son, Bernie Kosar, back in the starting quarterback role. Some in the media felt as though Belichick might have lost the teams and fan's support if he didn't go back to a healthy Bernie Kosar despite the team's success without him. Bernie Kosar would win this battle, but in the long run, Coach Belichick would win the war.

Chapter Six

Diminishing Skills

On Sunday, November 29, 1992, Bernie Kosar could not suit up quick enough to get back on the field and lead his team against the visiting Chicago Bears. Always the competitor, Kosar hated having to sit out the prior nine weeks, and was chomping at the bits to return to the action on the field. He wanted to show Coach Belichick and everyone else that he could still play despite being out so long. He also wanted to make up for the poor first two weeks of the season that he had before the injury. There's nothing worse than a poor start at the beginning of a new season, especially when you then have almost three months to sit on the bench and think about it.

The Cleveland Browns had gone 5-4 in his absence with two different starting quarterbacks winning games. One thing in favor of Kosar was that Mike Tomczak was mediocre in his absence. Tomczak went 4-4 with seven touchdowns, and seven interceptions. He wasn't overly good, but at the same time he wasn't that bad either. Had the Browns managed to find a way to hold onto wins against both the Minnesota Vikings and San Diego Chargers and stood at 7-4 instead of 5-6, there is a strong possibility that Tomzcak would have kept his lead position, and a healthy Kosar would have remained on the bench a bit longer.

Feeling good, Bernie Kosar was aiming to send a message to the coaching staff, the local media, and the Browns' fan base that he still had something left in the tank, and his early season struggles were merely a fluke. The Chicago Bears were bad that year, and were coming to Cleveland at a perfect time for Kosar and the reeling Browns. The Bears were having quarterback troubles of their own, and had to turn to little known quarterback Peter Tom Willis in the hopes of getting their own season turned around.

The game started off well for the Cleveland Browns when linebacker David Brandon picked off a Peter Tom Willis pass and returned it for a ninety-two yard touchdown. The Browns then added two Matt Stover field goals in the second quarter advancing their lead to 13–0 despite another slow start from Bernie Kosar. The Chicago Bears were able to answer back before halftime when Neal Anderson took a Willis dump-off pass thirty yards for a touchdown.

At halftime, the Browns were winning due to their strong defensive play, good place kicking, and a steady running game. Not much was being asked of Kosar, and he delivered even less. Eric Metcalf had his biggest play of the season in the third quarter when he took a Chris Gardocki punt seventy-five yards for a touchdown. The Bears would answer right back with a sixty-eight yard touchdown pass from Willis to Tommy Waddle but they would never get any closer. The Browns added a late Kevin Mack one yard touchdown rush to put the game away late.

After two straight fourth-quarter collapses, the Cleveland Browns' defense came back with a passionate effort and was the driving force in their 27–14 win. With Bernie Kosar having one of the most lackluster days of his career, only throwing for fifty-nine yards and zero touchdowns, the defense needed to step up and they did exactly that. They blitzed and sacked Peter Tom Willis all game long, racking up seven sacks on the day. Rob Burnett recorded 2.5 sacks, and Steven Moore had two sacks. Everson Walls had an interception to go along with the David Brandon pickoff. The Browns' run defense also looked good as they held the Bears' rushing attack to only seventy-three yards on nineteen carries. The great defense and special teams' effort was more than enough to make up for the lousy play of Kosar. It felt good for the Browns to get their first win of the season in a game that Kosar started; it was just a shame that he had nothing to do with it.

The Browns' running game saw six different players get a chance at running the ball. They even tried a wide receiver reverse that saw Lawyer Tillman take it for fifteen yards. Kevin Mack once again received the bulk of the carries as he touted the rock twenty times for fifty-three yards. Eric Metcalf only had five carries, but was able to gain forty-five yards on those carries including a sixteen yard dash. Tommy Vardell was held to fifteen yards on six carries.

The running game continued to be a dilemma that the young Coach Belichick was light years away from solving.

The Cincinnati Bengals were on their way into Cleveland Municipal Stadium to take on a suddenly rejuvenated Cleveland Browns' team. For the second straight week, the Browns took a lead into halftime, and for the second straight week, Bernie Kosar had nothing to do with it. The Browns once again used a stellar defensive effort and modest running game to build their 13–7 halftime lead. The thirteen points came on two Matt Stover field goals, and a seven yard Kevin Mack touchdown rush.

The Browns decided to end all doubt in the third quarter, and had one of their rare offensive breakouts of the season. Bernie Kosar threw a screen pass to Eric Metcalf who took it in for a thirty-five yard touchdown. A few minutes after that, Kosar hooked up with Michael Jackson on a forty-five yard bomb for another touchdown. It was Kosar's first breakout performance of the season, and it couldn't have come at a better time. Mike Johnson would recover a Bengal fumble in the end zone and put the Browns ahead by a score of 34–7 late in the third quarter. The Bengals managed to score on a couple of touchdown passes from David Klinger and then Donald Hollas to Jeff Query before it was over, but in the end it was the Browns emerging victoriously by a score of 37–21.

It was a great win for the Cleveland Browns that came at a perfect time. It improved their record to 7–6, and was an indication that the playoffs was still within their grasp. It was a home win and more importantly a win in their division. Bernie Kosar finally snapped out of his season-long slump with two touchdowns and 232 yard effort. It looked as though the Browns would be hitting their stride, and at the absolute perfect time to do so. They had a healthy quarterback regaining his confidence, a solid defense shutting down offenses on a weekly basis, and three games to go in the regular season. To the utter surprise of everyone involved, however, the Cleveland Browns would not win again that season.

The 1992 season ended on a three-game losing streak for the Browns as their offensive struggles that they dealt with most of the year finally caught up to them and they couldn't overcome it. They simply could not score as they were held to fourteen points, and under all three of their final games. In fact, on the sixteen-game season, they only managed to score more than fourteen points in eight of those games. Out of those eight games, they won seven of them. It was clear that if Bill Belichick would just hire an offensive coordinator and get out of his own way, the Cleveland Browns could have been a damn good team with a very good record. Instead, they ruined what was a good defensive season with lackluster offense.

The three-game tailspin included a 24–14 loss in Detroit against the Lions that saw Kosar throw two interceptions and gain most of his passing yards (276) when the Lions were already in prevent mode protecting the late lead. They then lost 17–14 to the Houston Oilers at home the following week, officially knocking them from playoff contention and also eliminating any chance they had at a winning season. The Houston loss saw them squander a 14–3 fourth quarter lead as Bernie Kosar tossed three more interceptions. The season would end in Pittsburgh with a 23–13 loss to the Steelers. Kosar left the game early after going five of seven for forty-one yards. Tomczak came in relief of Kosar, and tossed 141 yards and one touchdown. The once-promising season ended at 7–9 with one final defeat at the hands of their rivals.

Bernie Kosar's 1992 season was riddled with injuries, allowing him to only play in seven games. Kosar threw for a career low 1,160 yards and eight touchdowns while throwing seven interceptions, and getting sacked twenty-one times in only seven games. At the age of twenty-nine, Kosar had the body of a thirty-nine year-old and the year of beatings was starting to add up to the point where they could no longer be ignored.

The Cleveland Browns as a team continued to improve and win seven games, one more than the prior season. The problem for Kosar was that the team went 2–5 in the games he started, while they went 4–4 in the games started by backup Mike Tomczak, and 1–0 in the game started by third string quarterback Todd Philcox. This was the first real sign that Bill Belichick may have been considering a long-term change at quarterback. If it wasn't Mike Tomzcak to replace Kosar, it was going to be someone; Belichick just had to find that man. Despite missing the nine games, this would be the last season that Bernie Kosar spent the entire season on the Cleveland Browns' Roster.

The real shame of the lack of offensive firepower throughout the season was that the Browns' defense did enough most weeks to put them in position to win, with the exception of a few late fourth quarter collapses. The three that hurt the most were the losses to the Miami Dolphins, San Diego Chargers, and Minnesota Vikings, all of which were within their grasp until the very end.

With the late season collapse, the local media was quick to come down hard on the Cleveland Browns. Michael Jackson shares how he dealt with it:

> *"The* Plain Dealer *and I did not have the greatest relationship because I was a very outspoken individual when it came to my person. When something was said about me, I was going to have a response. At the time, I was a young player and didn't realize that some of these things you just have to swallow. Because of my commitment to my group, I felt like when something was said about the receivers, that affected me. So, of course, I had to defend the whole group and myself, and the media made it seem like Belichick and I had a horrible relationship."*

Michael Jackson disagrees with the *Plain Dealers'* portrayal of him and explains his true feelings for his coach:

> *"I loved the way Bill Belichick handled things internally. He would come to you directly and let you know what was on his mind and what he thought. He allowed you to give him your response and feelings. He gave you the ability to speak your mind, and I was one of those people who didn't mind speaking it publicly or personally. To set the record straight concerning the relationship between Belichick and myself, we had a great relationship.*
>
> *He was an honorable man who told you the way that it was. That's where people tend to misunderstand the way that it was because the media would tend to write it a different way in order to create controversy. The longest running program in the world is the news media, and it never has anything good to say. It's the same thing with the written press as well, as no good news sells papers so they have to spin it to paint a picture to the fans. It was when the veteran receiving core was being broken up, Tony with*

> *the* Plain Dealer *held me responsible which is crazy because I don't make those decisions. When you're a sportswriter, you can't be a fan of a player. They were supposed to remain impartial and didn't. "*

Before entering the off-season, the Cleveland Browns needed to look back and examine every detail to see where the areas of need where, and what they could do to build on their existing strengths. They only allowed 275 points all season; the problem was that they only scored 272. It was an average of only scoring seventeen points a week, which was much lower than the league average. It was bad enough that it was the twentieth lowest of twenty-eight teams. An immediate glaring need was once again the lack of depth and firepower at the wide receiver position.

Michael Jackson did well in his first season as the main target despite having to re-adjust his timing and rhythm with three different quarterbacks throughout the course of the year. Jackson played in all sixteen games and started fourteen of them. He caught forty-seven balls for 755 yards and seven touchdowns. It was good enough for the team high in each category. Jackson also showed a great set of hands as he didn't commit one fumble all season. He showed that he could be a big play receiver as well, as he averaged over sixteen yards per catch. Michael Jackson had been asked to step up and fill the role as number one receiver after the departures of Reggie Langhorne, Brian Brennan, and Webster Slaughter and he did exactly that. The Browns would expect more from him as the season went on as they knew he possessed All Pro talent.

It was a swift drop-off from Michael Jackson to their second receiver Lawyer Tillman who only had twenty-five catches for 498 yards and one fumble. One of the very discouraging things about Tillman was that he did not have a single touchdown, fumbled the ball once, and was only able to start nine games. He missed five games due to injury, and continued to fail to live up to the expectations they had when they drafted him.

The Browns had to rely on the play of their tight ends each week because of the lack of production coming out of the wide receiver position. Veteran Super Bowl winning tight end Mark Bavaro did his best to fill that role as he contributed twenty-five catches for 315 yards and two touchdowns. Despite being a veteran on his last legs, Belichick knew he could count on Bavaro for leadership and durability. Bavaro had been a part of two Super Bowl wins with Belichick in New York with the Giants. Bavaro proved Belichick's faith in him to be correct as he suited up and played in all sixteen games.

Mark Bavaro was really the only threat they had that year at tight end as their two other tight ends did very little of anything. Scott Galbraith played in fourteen games, starting two, and catching four balls for sixty-three yards. Pete Holohan played in nine games, starting one, and had twenty catches for 170 yards. With the impending retirement of Bavaro, they would need Brian Kinchen to move from the special teams unit as the long snapper, and start focusing his efforts at tight end.

The two rookie receivers drafted by the Browns, Rico Smith and Patrick Rowe, were both a gigantic bust. Patrick Rowe never saw the field because of injury. The other rookie, Rico Smith, had a dismal season, playing in ten games, starting one, and only caught five balls for sixty-four yards. Shawn Collins also did little to help as he was held to three catches for thirty-one yards. Not exactly what the Browns had in mind when they signed him as a free agent. Jamie Holland was limited to two catches for twenty-seven yards. The hole at receiver was large and glaring, and would need to be addressed if the Browns were ever to turn the corner.

Their running game also remained a mystery. Despite having three young, hungry and talented running backs, they insisted on giving the veteran Kevin Mack most of the carries. Kevin Mack had 169 carries for 543 yards and six touchdowns. He also showed great ball security as he only fumbled it once in the 169 touches.

The highly touted and talented rookie, Tommy "Touchdown" Vardell, never truly got the chance to show what he could do. He played in fourteen of sixteen games, only starting ten of them. He was limited to ninety-nine carries for 369 yards. Vardell also showed his athleticism and ability to do whatever was called upon him as he caught thirteen balls for 128 yards. In a bit of irony, the man they called "Touchdown" failed to score a single touchdown all season. Of course, it wasn't his fault because the team never used him the way they should have, and he was unable to establish the rhythm he needed to get into week-in and week-out.

Eric Metcalf, once a dual purpose threat, was limited to merely a sometimes pass-catching threat out of the backfield. Metcalf only received seventy-three carries for 301 yards and one touchdown. His biggest problem was holding onto the ball as he fumbled it six times throughout the course of the season. Putting the ball on the ground is a quick way to get in the doghouse of Bill Belichick, or any head coach for that matter. Metcalf did do an excellent job receiving, however, as he caught forty-seven balls for 614 yards and five touchdowns. Four of his six touchdowns came in week three against the Raiders. He did have a seventh, however, as it was a punt return for seventy-five yards against the Chicago Bears.

Leroy Hoard had the same issues that Tommy Vardell did—limited carries and no rhythm established. He only received fifty-four carries all season, and ran for 236 yards with those chances. Like Metcalf, he was able to make his difference by catching passes out of the backfield. Hoard caught twenty-six passes for 310 yards and one touchdown. Just like Metcalf, however, he had the same problem of coughing up the ball and put it on the turf three times throughout the season.

The Nick Saban-coached defense really stepped up their games and it showed in the team's overall numbers and performance. Only once did they allow a team to score thirty points on them. Only five times did they allow a team to score more than twenty points on them. There was eleven times in which a team failed to score twenty points on them, and twice in which they held a team under ten points. With a defense like that, they should have only lost a handful of games, instead of nine. The Browns' defense did score three of the team's thirty touchdowns. The defense ranked tenth overall in the entire NFL. They only allowed eighty-six first downs all season, which is exactly one more than the offense was able to convert.

Clay Matthews and Rob Burnett both led the team in sacks with nine sacks apiece. Michael Dean Perry wasn't far behind as he had eight and a half sacks himself. James Jones and Anthony Pleasant both had four sacks and helped established a strong pass rush against any offensive line. Anchoring the defensive secondary with three interceptions was Vince Newsome. Outside of him, there wasn't much production other than Everson Walls and Frank Minnifield with two interceptions a piece.

Matt Stover maintained another consistent season as he hit twenty-one of twenty-eight field goals, including one from fifty plus yards. The Browns did not score many touchdowns, but Stover did convert twenty-nine of thirty extra point tries. Brian Hansen continued to get plenty of practice booting the ball with seventy-four punts, averaging forty-one yards a punt, and he even had a punt travel seventy-three yards, which was a career long.

Heading into the off-season, the Cleveland Browns were once again optimistic as they had improved their win total by one game from the prior season, and appeared to be moving into the right direction. They continued to have key departures such as Frank Minnifield, who decided to retire after the season. Other veteran All Pros such as Clay Matthews were also starting to wind down as this would be their final season with the team. Their defensive was starting to take on a much different look than the one they had during their earlier playoff years.

The new starting defensive backfield consisted of Everson Walls and Terry Taylor at cornerback, with Randy Hilliard and Najee Mustafaa as the nickel backs. The starting safeties were now Eric Turner and Stevon Moore. Veterans Mike Johnson, Clay Matthews, and David Brandon came back for another year terrorizing opposing quarterbacks from the linebacker position. They would have some added help that season as the Browns went out and signed veteran linebacker Pepper Johnson. He had been a part of two Super Bowl winning teams in New York as a member of the Giants, so Belichick knew he could trust and rely on him.

Another key addition was defensive lineman Jerry Ball. They traded their upcoming third round Draft pick to the Detroit Lions for Ball. He was a mountain of a man who lined up at six foot one and weighed in at 330 pounds. He had spent the first six years of his career with the Detroit Lions. He averaged three plus sacks per season, but had nine in the 1989 season for the Lions. His strength wasn't getting quarterbacks to the ground, but rather stopping the run—one of the few elements of the Browns' defense they struggled with. The plan was to line up Jerry Ball next to Michael Dean

Perry. It was a combination known to the Cleveland Browns' fans as "Rush & Crush."

Joining Jerry Ball and Michael Dean Perry on the defensive line would be Browns' veteran defensive ends Anthony Pleasant and Rob Burnett. It was a solid line with a good core of veterans that knew the exact system Belichick and Saban chose to run. They were counted on heavily to create turnovers and get quick stops so the struggling offense would have time and decent field position to improve.

The defensive unit wasn't the only one signing additions to help the team. It was also that off-season in which the Browns would make a move that would forever rock the foundation of the team for many years to come. They went out and signed veteran free agent quarterback Vinny Testaverde. Even though Tomczak hadn't worked out the way Belichick hoped, he still wasn't sold on Bernie Kosar as the man going forward, and this move proved it.

Testaverde was an excellent college quarterback at the University of Miami. He took over for Bernie Kosar when Kosar graduated. He filled Kosar's shoes very well as a senior in 1986, as he was a consensus first-team All-American and won the Heisman Trophy, on his way to becoming the Hurricanes' all-time leader in career touchdown passes with forty-eight. His career at college was so good that he eventually was inducted into the University of Miami Sports Hall of Fame in 1998. On May 7, 2013, Testaverde was also inducted into the College Football Hall of Fame. His time at Miami only had one major dark note as he threw five interceptions in the 1987 Fiesta Bowl, a 14–10 loss in a game where they were heavily favored. The poor performance not only cost Miami the game, but also the National Championship.

Testaverde was the first overall draft pick of the Tampa Bay Buccaneers in the 1987 NFL Draft. The following year, Testaverde became the Bucs' starting quarterback, with a 47.6% completion rate for 3,240 yards and thirteen touchdowns, and thirty-five interceptions. His numbers were horrible and many fans took to blaming his poor performance on his noted color blindness. He was a giant bust as the number one pick; nevertheless, the Tampa Bay Buccaneers tried everything they could to stick with Testaverde as long as they could because of how high they drafted him. He spent four more seasons with Tampa, throwing a total of seventy-nine touchdowns and 112 interceptions. He only threw for 3,000+ yards twice during that span.

Vinny Testaverde left Tampa Bay after the 1992 season, and signed with the Cleveland Browns as a free agent. At the time, no one really thought much of the move other than he would be a veteran backup for the often injured Kosar.

Testaverde couldn't take the job away from Kosar in pre-season, nor did anyone believe it would be an open competition to do so. No one that is, except for Coach Bill Belichick, who made it clear to anyone who would listen inside of the organization that it was only a matter of time before Kosar was out, and Testaverde was in.

The running game would feature three returning young tailbacks—Eric Metcalf, Tommy Vardell, and Leroy Hoard. Kevin Mack was still on the roster, but only received ten carries and only played in four games; thus, it was clear that it was time for Mack to pass the torch. With those three backs carrying the bulk of the load, there wouldn't be any more excuses, and the three of them would have to step up their game when given the chance.

The hole at receiver continued to be glaring, but this year the Browns knew that it couldn't be ignored any longer. They went out and found a perfect second receiver to go along with Michael Jackson in the starting lineup. This was another key move also because Mark Carrier had spent his first five seasons in Tampa Bay with Vinny Testaverde. This was another subtle sign that the end for Bernie Kosar was forthcoming.

Much like Michael Jackson, Mark Carrier was a large, fast, physical receiver who could break the bump-and-run coverage for a big play. Carrier was also known to have soft hands and could catch anything thrown his way. He was selected by the Tampa Bay Buccaneers in the third round of the 1987 NFL Draft and was 57th overall selection out of Nicholls State University. In college, he was named first-team Associated Press All-American and first-team Kodak All-American by the American Football Coaches Association (AFCA) in 1986. He finished his football career at Nicholls as the all-time receiving leader in receptions (142), yards (2709), yards per catch (20.4) and one hundred yard games (11).

Mark Carrier also knew a thing or two about winning. Despite his lack of playoff experience in Tampa Bay, his college days brought a lot of victories. He helped Nicholls State reach the Division 1AA National Championships eventually losing to Georgia Southern in the Quarterfinals, the eventual National Champions. Years later, he was voted into the Nicholls State University Hall of Fame, forever leaving his mark on the college. He also showed his loyalty and commitment to finishing something when he returned to Nicholls State after his NFL career ended, and achieved his degree.

While in Tampa Bay, he earned a 1989 Pro Bowl selection as he caught career-high eighty-six receptions for 1,422 yards and nine touchdowns that season for the Buccaneers. He followed it with another solid 1990 season where he caught forty-nine balls for 813 yards and four touchdowns. He also had just under seven hundred yards the following two seasons, and would be the perfect complement to Michael Jackson. The other quality about Mark Carrier was that he had the ability to stay healthy; only once in his career did he not play all sixteen games in a season.

The Cleveland Browns' coaching staff would mainly remain intact, as Belichick once again refused to hire an offensive coordinator. Nick Saban would remain on staff to head up the defensive unit. Scott O'Brien would oversee the special teams, which also didn't have any major changes. It was the same group of men kicking and returning. One major change was long snapper Brian Kinchen beating out Scott Galbreath for the full-time starting tight end job, so the young and enthusiastic Kinchen would have double duty.

With help on both sides of the ball acquired in free agency and via trades, the Browns were slowly starting to become stronger in all areas. The upcoming NFL Draft was still very important, however, as they needed to fill holes on the aging offensive line. They had improved in many areas, but they still needed to sure up that line. The once stalwarts of the line were now gone, those men being Mike Baab, Dan Fike, Paul Farren, and Cody Riesen. Dan Fike was the last to leave, and the original participants of the once great line were now all gone.

The Cleveland Browns could have gone several different ways in the draft; they still needed wide receiving threats despite the addition of Carrier; they were still very thin at that position. They were originally slated to pick eleventh in the first round, but made a trade with the Denver Broncos swapping first round picks. The Broncos would give the Browns their pick, which was the fourteenth. The Broncos also gave the Browns their third round pick, which was good because the Browns had traded their original third round pick to the Detroit Lions for Jerry Ball.

Any hopes of Belichick picking a young quarterback to mold into his system in case both Kosar and Testaverde didn't work out flew off the board early when the top two picks were quarterbacks. Drew Bledsoe went number one overall to the New England Patriots, and Rick Mirer went second to the Seattle Seahawks. They were already pretty loaded at running back, and that was a good thing because the two best backs in the draft were gone by the time the Browns got to pick as well. Jerome Bettis was selected by the Los Angeles Rams, and Garrison Hearst went to the Phoenix Cardinals.

The Browns were in good shape to draft a wide receiver if they chose to do so, as only one had been drafted in front of them when Curtis Conway went seventh to the Chicago Bears. Still on the board at wide receiver were OJ McDuffie from Penn State, Sean Dawkins out of California, Kevin Williams out of Miami, Florida, or Qadry Ismail from Syracuse. Any one of them would have been a great addition to the team in an area where they sorely needed it. Instead, they drafted a center in Steve Everitt from the University of Michigan.

As noted earlier, the Browns' O-Line had been shaky the prior seasons as the veterans were leaving, and the most important position on the line is the center. He is responsible for making the calls and reading the defense, especially with less-than-experienced quarterbacks. Now, clearly that would-n't be needed with Bernie Kosar, but this was another subtle sign that Belichick was starting to think a change long-term at quarterback very soon. Steve Everitt would be a key player with whoever they ended up going with.

Everitt would join starting guards Houston Hoover and Rob Dahl on the line alongside of tackles Gene Williams and Tony Jones. They would have to gel quickly if the team was to have any success moving the ball both on the ground and in the air. Tony Jones had already given some very good years at tackle after being drafted by the Browns in 1988. Everitt would mesh well with Jones and the others, and prove to be a solid draft pick.

The Browns went defense with their second pick and selected defensive end Dan Footman from Florida State. They stuck with defense when they drafted linebacker Mike Caldwell in the third round with the pick they acquired in the trade from Denver. They didn't own a pick in the fourth round, and used their fifth pick to select Herman Arvie, a tackle from Gramling State. They used their sixth and seventh round picks on linebackers, selecting Rich McKenzie from Penn State and Travis Hill from Nebraska. They had six total draft picks and used none of them on skill position players. Skill position players refer to Quarterbacks, Wide Receivers, Running Backs, Cornerbacks, Tight Ends and Safeties. They could have used help in all of those areas with the exception of running back. Steve Everitt would pan out with the first pick, while the others never contributed much.

The beginning of the 1993 season could not have started any better for Bernie Kosar and the Cleveland Browns. They began the year with a convincing opening day win at home against the Cincinnati Bengals by a score of 27-14. Kosar was efficient as he went eighteen for thirty with one touchdown and 214 yards with no interceptions. Second year running back Tommy Vardell led the team in rushing with sixteen carries for sixty yards. Eric Metcalf continued to excel by catching passes out of the backfield and underneath the zone coverage as he took in nine balls for sixty yards. In his first game as a Cleveland Browns player, Mark Carrier caught three balls for seventy-nine yards.

They showed the incredible ability to come back from a double-digit deficit early in the game as they were down 14-0 to the Bengals after the first quarter. With the home crowd cheering them on and the 'never say die' attitude that Kosar instilled in his teammates, the Cleveland Browns conducted a furious fourteen point rally in the second quarter to tie the game by halftime. The rally consisted of a fourteen yard touchdown pass to Michael Jackson and a one yard touchdown rumble from Tommy Vardell, the first touchdown of his pro career. They secured the game in the second half on two Matt Stover field goals and a 'highlight reel worthy' twenty-two yard fumble return for a touchdown to put the Browns ahead 27–14.

The Browns' defense had a great game as they picked off David Klinger two times as well as sacked him six times, including two from Michael Dean Perry. The "Rush & Crush" combination of Jerry Ball and Michael Dean Perry was already paying off! The defense also showed much improvement with defending their running game as they held Cincinnati's top rusher Derrick Fenner to only forty-one yards.

The Cleveland Browns followed their week one win with a thrilling home win over the powerhouse San Francisco 49ers with the entire nation watching on *Monday Night Football* for week two. Kosar went seventeen for thirty-two with 186 yards and one touchdown in the 23–13 win. The 49ers were one of the best teams in football and considered a heavy favorite to return to the NFC title game against the Dallas Cowboys, which they ended up doing. This was a huge upset for the Browns and a giant confidence builder. The win came on the strength of a seventeen point second quarter that saw a seventeen yard touchdown pass to Michael Jackson—it was part of a one hundred yard night for Jackson. The Browns even showed some creativity when Coach Belichick inserted defensive lineman James Jones in the game on the goal line to score a one yard touchdown rumble. The defense had another big night as they intercepted Future Hall of Fame quarterback Steve Young three times. Jerry Ball also had his first sack as a Cleveland Brown. Matt Stover continued to show his improving skills as he converted three field goals.

Things were looking great for Bernie Kosar and the Cleveland Browns. However, everything changed week three in Los Angeles, California. The Cleveland Browns traveled cross country to play Jeff Hostetler and the Los Angeles Raiders as part of the showcase game on NBC Football. Things got off to a horrible start for the Browns as the Raiders jumped out to a lead and held it throughout the majority of the game. Late in the fourth quarter, the Los Angeles Raiders led 16–3 over the sluggish Cleveland Browns. Kosar was struggling badly when Belichick did the unthinkable and pulled him from the game. Kosar was eight for seventeen with zero touchdowns and three interceptions. It should be noted here that the Browns were working on a short week and had to travel cross country for the game. Nonetheless, Coach Belichick was not looking to hear excuses from any of his players, and saw this as his first and golden opportunity to make the switch he knew was coming all along.

Bernie Kosar was pulled from the game and replaced with backup quarterback and former college teammate, Vinny Testaverde. This came as quite a shock because Kosar was a hometown boy that fans loved. He was one of the most popular players to ever wear the Brown and Orange. Despite his erratic play in the Raiders game, Kosar had been a consistent star in his nearly ten-year career. He led the Cleveland Browns to the playoffs five times and three AFC Championship games. This was a gutsy and unpopular move for Coach Belichick to pull off.

Vinny Testaverde jumped at the chance to get in the game for the struggling Kosar, and did not waste his golden opportunity to impress. He worked his magic and led the Browns on a roaring comeback, complete with a touchdown pass to Lawyer Tillman and a touchdown run from Eric Metcalf. They tacked on a safety and won the game 19–16, improving their record to 3–0. Testaverde went ten of twenty-two for 159 yards with a touchdown in relief of Kosar. The game was also notable for Tommy Vardell as he rushed for over one hundred yards for the first time in his professional career. Eric Metcalf and Leroy Hoard combined for nine carries, which totaled minus six yards. Vardell was beginning to separate himself from the pack.

Kosar did not lose his starting job, but the leash for him got a lot shorter after the Testaverde come-from-behind win. The following week, the Browns traveled to Indianapolis to play the Colts where once again Kosar got off to a cold start. He didn't get much of a chance to get started as Belichick pulled him after only throwing eight passes; he completed four of them for fifty-three yards.

Vinny Testaverde once again came in and provided a quick spark off the bench. He led the Browns on a touchdown drive, capped off with a ten yard touchdown pass to tight end Brian Kinchen. He went on to complete nine of sixteen passes for 127 yards in one half of play. It wasn't enough, however, as the Indianapolis Colts won 23–10, handing the Browns their first loss in the process. It also didn't help matters that they had no rushing attack as their top rusher, Vardell, was held to only forty yards on eleven carries. The offensive line began to show cracks as well, as they let up four sacks and the fumble in the end zone that led to a Colts' touchdown.

A full-blown quarterback controversy was in the works, and second-year tailback Tommy Vardell knew that he could not get involved. He explains why, as a player, you have to keep focused and not get attached to a certain teammate, as difficult as that may be at times:

> *"As a young player, what happens with personnel is often surprising and not understood. I can remember this in training camp my rookie year. There were guys during camp that were released that I thought were really good, and guys that made the team that I thought weren't so good. I don't believe all decisions are based on 'who is the best player at the position'. There are politics, pride, and power plays in football just like in business. As such, when personnel changes happened in front of me, I treated it more like changing scenery more than something that could impact me significantly. It sounds calloused and even selfish, but as a player you don't really get deeply attached to anyone, because that person could be gone the next day. You become a devoted teammate, but you don't let your roots anchor in to people so much that if they are removed this upends your game. This is probably a product of free agency, where players are constantly changing teams, and teams are changing players. I love the days when you committed to a team and a city and no one left—and everyone was loyal to one another, and all were in it together. Now, players are commodities, plug ins to meet a need and when the parts wear out they're replaced. This is the business, so when the quarterback controversy was happening, I think most of the players kept their noses down, did not get too involved, and played their game."*

Tight end Brian Kinchen gives his insight on the developing situation going on with the team at the time:

> *"When Vinny came in, you can understand why a change may have been in the works as he was just a big, tall, strong quarterback. You always kind of knew that the coaches wanted their own*

guy. When Bernie got benched, we still thought it was only going to be a couple of games. We didn't think it was going to last. We just thought that with the pressure of the media and fans that it was only a matter of time before Bernie was going to be back in the saddle again."

The 1993 season was a bit different whereas it featured two bye weeks instead of one like normal, which gave the Cleveland Browns a chance to catch their breath. It also gave Coach Belichick an extra week to think about possibly benching Bernie Kosar for Vinny Testaverde as the first of two bye weeks came after the loss to the Colts. Belichick refused to pull the trigger on a quarterback switch during the bye week, and chose to stick with Bernie Kosar as they returned home to face Dan Marino and the Miami Dolphins.

The first half proved to be a wild one that saw the Future Hall of Fame quarterback Dan Marino get knocked out of the game, and also shut down for the season. Kosar looked strong early as he went fifteen for nineteen for eighty-two yards and a touchdown pass to Michael Jackson. The Browns also tacked on a late second-half touchdown when Najee Mustafaa picked off a Scott Mitchell pass and returned it seventy-four yards for a touchdown.

The Browns led 14–10 at halftime and things looked like they were going to return to normal for Cleveland at the quarterback position. However, the Miami Dolphins scored two quick touchdowns in the third quarter to take a 24–14 lead, and Kosar was once again promptly pulled from the game in favor of Testaverde. This was the first time that Coach Belichick pulled this move in front of a hometown crowd. Needless to say, the crowd was not in favor of the move, and voiced their displeasure with Coach Belichick.

However, Belichick's strategic move didn't work this week as the Browns failed to score and lost 24–14. Testaverde went six for thirteen only throwing for forty-four yards and one interception. Once again, the Browns didn't receive any help from their starting backfield as Vardell was held in check for seventeen yards on six carries. Eric Metcalf wasn't any better with seven carries for thirty-six yards. The juggling of quarterbacks was simply not working, and it would force Belichick to make a decision and stick with it. He shocked many when he decided to sit Kosar and name Testaverde as the starter for the rest of the season. The Browns had a 3–2 record thus far, however, Belichick had seen enough of Kosar behind center.

Vinny Testaverde quickly rewarded Coach Belichick's faith in him the following week as they visited the Cincinnati Bengals at Riverfront Stadium. Testaverde was red hot and connected on three big first-half touchdown passes to Tommy Vardell, Randy Baldwin, and Brian Kinchen. The Browns went on to win and Testaverde finished the game with 127 yards and the three touchdown tosses. The switch to Testaverde was the spark that the entire team needed, and it showed as they played better in every area of the team. Tommy Vardell rushed for ninety-eight yards, his second highest career total. The defense even played better as they sacked David Klinger and Jay Schroeder a combined four times. The twenty-eight points was the highest amount scored by the Browns to that point in the season as well. The move to swap quarterbacks looked brilliant in week one of trying it for Belichick.

The Cleveland Browns remained hot the following week as their hated rivals the Pittsburgh Steelers came to Municipal Stadium. Vinny Testaverde started the scoring with a sixty-two yard touchdown pass to Michael Jackson. Eric Metcalf later followed with a ninety-one yard punt return for a touchdown, and the Browns were up 14–0 midway through the second quarter. Pittsburgh responded with their all pro tailback Barry Foster who scored on two rushing touchdowns to tie the game heading into halftime.

Vinny Testaverde continued to excel and threw for another touchdown pass to Ron Wolfley to put the Browns back in the lead. Three Gary Anderson field goals gave the Steelers back the lead heading into the final minutes of the game. It was then that Testaverde got knocked out of the game with an injury. He was nine for fourteen for 167 yards at that point with the two touchdowns and zero interceptions.

With the Cleveland Browns down 23–21 to their bitter rivals and the beloved Bernie Kosar about to come off the bench and into the game, it almost seemed like a Hollywood script too good to be true. Eric Metcalf removed all the suspense and drama, however, as he returned the next Pittsburgh punt for a seventy-five yard touchdown to put the Browns back in the lead. The Steelers only punted to Eric Metcalf twice, but both times he burned them for a score, totaling 166 yards in the process. Everyone was ready for another epic Kosar comeback, but Metcalf took matters into his own hands giving the Browns a victorious 28–23 win. It moved the Browns to a division best 5–2 record, and once again everything seemed to be swaying right in Browns' town.

It was discovered later that evening that Testaverde's injury was serious, and he would be out for several weeks. This would give Kosar another chance to shine in the roll he had flourished at. For so many years prior, Cleveland Browns football meant Bernie Kosar at the helm, and now all that seemed in serious jeopardy, especially if he couldn't prove himself up to the task and worthy in the absence of Testaverde. Kosar knew that he would have to play well to once again earn the trust of Coach Belichick and Cleveland Browns' management team.

On Sunday, November 7, 1993, Bernie Kosar would lace up his cleats for the final time as a Cleveland Brown. Playoff nemesis John Elway and the Denver Broncos were set to visit Municipal Stadium on a cold afternoon in late fall. The contest was a blowout as Elway and the Broncos had their way with the Browns all game long. Late in the fourth quarter, the Broncos were crushing the Browns by a score of 29–7. Kosar knew the Browns were done, and may have even known his time was about to be done as well when he ignored the play call from the sidelines and decided to draw up his own play instead. He directed his team on the palm of his hand, and it resulted in a thirty-eight yard touchdown strike to Michael Jackson. Little did anyone know, but that would be the last pass Kosar would throw as a member of the Cleveland Browns' team.

When Bernie Kosar returned to the sidelines, Coach Belichick was livid that he had changed the play, never mind the fact that the game was long decided and it resulted in a score. Belichick was absolutely furious, and this would be the final act of defiance he would allow from his quarterback.

There have been many stories told about that play. Now, twenty years later, Michael Jackson clears up what actually happened in the huddle on that day, and how it was him and not Kosar that changed the play:

> *"I had already ran several dig and crossing routes that day already. At that point, the Broncos were teeing off on us. So when*

the play came in from the sidelines, we didn't change the play, but I told Bernie that I had been going in here all night with this play and they were killing me...I can't keep going down there... This time I'm going to take three steps in and if the safety comes up, I'm going to go behind him. If you throw it, I'll be there.

We had cohesiveness in the huddles because of the coolness of Bernie Kosar. We shared on the field what was happening and how it was happening, and Kosar was like a coach on the field. If something was there, he was willing to go to bat for it. To this day, he hasn't made mention of what really went down. He didn't change the play...it was called as it was sent in by the coach. I'm the only one on the whole play that changed the route. Bernie was aware of the fact that it was going to happen. Everyone was on the same page. If you look at the play, I was supposed to be running a dig route, which is coming in. Rico Smith was on the other side and supposed to run a post route to clear the safeties out. But we were doing that all game and the safeties were teeing off on us, so when I told Bernie I couldn't do it anymore, he understood. I told him I would take my three steps in to draw in the safeties, and then I was headed up the field.

If you look at the play...me and Rico both look like we're running post routes, but I ran a dig post. Bernie put the ball on the money and we were able to get six points. The problem was that Belichick thought Bernie changed the play in the huddle...and he didn't. Bernie called the play as it was, I just changed what I did. I was lucky Bernie didn't tell on me because I was still a young player and couldn't afford to get in trouble. I was one of the most productive players on the team but one of the lowest paid players on the team. I held my breath forever, I commend Bernie until this day for never telling on me."

Bernie Kosar finished the game with 226 yards, two touchdowns and zero interceptions; however, it was not enough to save his job. The very next day, the Cleveland Browns called a press conference to announce the release of the beloved quarterback. It was a shock to the fans, the community, the local and national media, and to his teammates who felt the tension in the locker room, but still never saw that move coming.

Leroy Hoard gives his reasons as to why the switch and eventual cut was made:

"Bernie was like a father. If there was an issue on that team, the voice of reason was Bernie. If Bill was working us too hard he would tell us to suck it up...or never hesitated to let us know we needed to do something differently. Very rarely if ever on any sports team in any sport, does a captain get cut in the middle of a season...put that in perspective, regardless of Bernie's production. You can have veterans get cut, but not your leader. Bernie's skill set was changing things on the fly and manipulating defenses without having a powerful arm. Bernie just kind of found a way to keep things going and put the team in the right spot to keep things successful. He was never a guy with a strong arm and great delivery or athletic great escape ability. He was everything but a regular quarterback...he was a blue collar guy who knew how to get things done.

Vinny Testaverde was different...he had a cannon, and was big and strong with mobility. He was closer to the prototypical quarterback. Bill comes in and sees Bernie throwing out routes and standard passes for a quarterback, but couldn't make the longer passes anymore. We needed someone with a stronger arm who could make the throws on more consistent passes because that would put our team in a better chance to win games. Bill didn't understand Bernie Kosar like we do...he didn't realize not to look at all the physical eye-catching stuff. But let's be honest, if you're a head coach and your job is on the line, do you feel comfortable with that...and if you don't, your career is on the line too...and you have to worry about the next five to six years. I'm not saying he had to make the change, but he had to look at all of his options. Now I don't know if this was Bill's exact thinking...I'm just trying to see how he came to that conclusion.

Because of Bernie, I was able to catch all those outlet passes, and now I was back to blocking. It affected all of us as our roles on the team changed as we went to a more of a conventional offense. Deep down, I hated to see it happen because I think we could have won with Bernie. But when you are a new coach and the players don't fit your system, your job is on the line as well. Although we all hated the decision, I can't say that any of us didn't understand it. A teammate's performance can affect your standing with the team...almost like Johnny Manziel going out partying.

A lot of us tried to understand that it is a business and tried not to make up reasons as to why it happened and just go from there. I'm still in contact with Bernie now...we're still friends and that will never change no matter where he played. It was brutal! Because we could never get over the hump and lost far too much... we made changes that worked against us sometimes. I just wish it didn't have to end that way."

Tommy Vardell gives his logic on why he thinks the Browns chose to make the move when they did and also how he felt about each quarterback:

"I think Bernie was cut because the Browns felt like they had to cut him. They figured that carrying a demoted Bernie Kosar through the season would lead to ongoing and continuous quarterback controversies, booing, and a general disruption that would be very difficult for the team and city to manage. Instead, what they got by cutting him was the same booing, and the same disruption that they would have had to manage with making the change at all. So the real hinge point in this is around whether or not Bernie was going to be the starter, not whether or not he was cut. The fallout from his demotion was going to be equal either way, in my opinion.

Vinny is one of the best athletes I have ever had the privilege of being around, and Bernie is one of the savviest athletes I have played with. With these traits, they both shine in different situations and under different circumstances. I loved playing with Bernie's improvisation skills and understanding of the game. I also loved knowing that I was going to get a tight spiral and an efficiently executed play with Vinny. At the point of choosing, I am grateful that I did not have this burden. From whatever perspective one sees the cut, I loved them both."

There was a public outcry from the Cleveland Browns' fans as they were livid upon hearing the news. Before they could even grasp the fact of the physical reasons as to why Kosar was cut, the financial ones immediately stood out. Bernie Kosar had just signed a seven-year, twenty-seven million dollar contract extension only five weeks prior. Although contracts are guaranteed for the first half of the season under the new basic agreement, players are paid by the game during the second half. Thus, the Cleveland Browns saved themselves a lot of money by cutting Kosar when they did.

Place kicker Matt Stover feels as though the move was shocking, but had no effect on the way he does his job and wouldn't have any effect on the way he prepared for it:

> *"Personally, my reaction as a kicker was that I had a job to be done, and that was a job that the coaches could easily evaluate. In fact, anyone in the country can determine how well I would do on a given day so I needed to stay focused and not let it bother me. I needed to continue to do my job the best I could.*
>
> *As far as being his teammate, I was shocked and didn't know the situation well. I think the decision to cut Bernie in the middle of the season was a mistake. If Belichick was that upset then he should have benched Bernie but not cut him. I think they wanted to make a clean start before that season even began and have Vinny start and be the head of the offense."*

Brian Hansen was punting with the team at the time and gives his insight on exactly what happened with the Kosar drama and why he felt it all went down the way that it did:

> *"The controversy hurts the way the team performs. Even when those types of things happen, you still have to focus on your own responsibilities and how you're supposed to perform. It does affect the overall chemistry of the team. Sometimes the changes can work out for the better, but sometimes they don't. There were players on the team who liked Bernie and hated to see him go. In the business we're in, it's just reality that when you're not producing the next guy behind you will take your job. When that happens, you have to get past it and move on for the betterment of the team. I couldn't worry about and it wasn't a factor for me. I didn't think much of it...and I was just surprised by it. It makes you realize that when someone at that level is released that no one is safe and that you need to play at a high level."*

Brian Hansen insists that the move did not divide the locker room and the main goal always remains winning:

"I realize that maybe the offense line felt something because they are a tight-nitched group, but I didn't have a preference. I felt bad for Bernie when he got benched then released but I wasn't going let it affect my play. I'm sure it wasn't a divided locker room despite a few of the players being close to Bernie and upset that he got cut. Maybe they let it affect their play, but no one vocalized they were upset in the locker room; we just concerned ourselves with playing.

I will say that it was a shock...and we didn't find out from the coaches, but we found out from the news. The team didn't even tell us about it. It wasn't Bill's style to tell us or consult us. Then after it was made, he didn't even address it. It's hard to say what the strategy and thinking was from the coaching staff as to the time and how they did it. They may have thought that they were paying a lot of money to Bernie and didn't feel like it was worth it. It didn't matter to them that he was a favorite son of the city. Emotion doesn't weigh in decisions like that...they wanted to make a clean break and move on into a different direction. They felt there was no need to prolong it and that's why they did it so swiftly. That's just the way he does things and operates so he just hauled off and pulled the trigger."

Tight end Brian Kinchen gives his thoughts on the shocking cut:

"It was a move to eliminate the growing distraction, but also for the coaching staff to prove they made the decisions and not the media or fans. It was a sign that no one was safe and could be cut at any time. It was a power move on behalf of Bill Belichick. It really was shocking because when we heard the rumors that it may happen, we still didn't believe it would ever be possible. We just really couldn't believe it...that it was a reality.

Bernie Kosar was a Cleveland Brown, thick and thin, and was supposed to be there. If he was a guy who could be sent down the road, then certainly anyone was possibly in danger of being cut. It was one of the more traumatic moments and ordeals of my career. We were just snake bit in the moments and the days in which that happened. He was a good guy and we enjoyed being around him because he didn't make life miserable. He was very kind hearted and it was difficult to see him go. We just couldn't wrap our heads around the move at all. Even if he isn't your guy, he is a leader and deserved to be a part of that football team. I think Belichick just decided that it would be better to do away with the distraction than have him around."

Even defensive players were shaken by the move at quarterback. Ed Sutter explains the mood and reasoning at the time:

"Bernie Kosar was a team leader and a great teammate. It was hard to see him go, and it obviously created a lot of controversy around the team and a lot of unrest around Cleveland. Vinny Testaverde was a great athlete and teammate as well. He was not the leader that Bernie Kosar was, and that may have hurt him a little at the start. He was very well respected, but the controversy over the Kosar situation made things very hard on Vinny and the rest of the team."

Cleveland Browns' fans were quite upset, and it showed when local sports-talk radio stations in Cleveland received about 150 faxes during a three-hour period after the news announcement, with an average of nine fans criticizing the Browns for every one fan who supported them. Local television stations showed season ticket-holders standing in line at Municipal Stadium, demanding their money back.

Bill Belichick was short and to the point when asked about the move at a news conference, saying, *"Basically, it came down to his production and a diminishing of his physical skills."* Art Modell, the Cleveland Browns' owner agreed with Belichick's assessment. Modell had just given Belichick a two-year contract extension, which signaled the beginning of the end for Kosar.

"I think he's been hurt so much," Modell said of Kosar, *"he has taken more punishment than any quarterback I have known in this league. He played a half against Miami last year with a broken ankle, something I have never seen in football."*

"The problems with our offense go a lot deeper than who the quarterback is," Kosar told a group of cheering fans at a dinner appearance the very night. Kosar went on to say, *"When you make a decision like this, certain things need to be said to justify it."*

Many felt that the true story was that Bill Belichick was a conservative former defensive coordinator, and preferred a ball-control offense featuring rushing and short passes. Kosar was a 'let it fly' kind of player who wanted the freedom to call his own plays. Earlier in the season, Belichick ordered Kosar to stop changing plays at the line of scrimmage. Then, after Kosar refused to listen, he benched him. Before the game, after studying the film, Kosar pointed out that the Broncos could probably be kept off balance by throwing the ball on second and third downs. Belichick chose to ignore Kosar, which only added fuel to the fire.

Reggie Langhorne, who was with the Indianapolis Colts at the time, was also shocked to hear about his former teammate:

> *"At the time, it did catch me by surprise. Belichick stated Bernie had diminishing skills and it is up to a coach to make those decisions based on what he wants done on the field. How he went about it with Bernie, I'm not a big fan of, but they make decisions and have to live by them. Belichick made his decisions and stood by them. Bernie was beloved in Cleveland. I love him as a brother, we came into the league together, we did a lot together, but we all have issues in our career that we wish were handled differently. Maybe Belichick can look back and wish he did it differently. I'm sure Bernie feels that he could have did some things differently to avoid being in that situation. It was one of those things that happened that made me scratch my head and say, wow, I can't believe that."*

Felix Wright also shares his feeling on the shock of Kosar being cut:

> *"I was a little surprised by it, I think the Coach was saying something like Bernie had diminishing skills. Bernie wasn't a real fast guy to begin with...he was a very smart guy...he understood football and what worked and what didn't work. I think everyone knew that he was a quarterback that needed protection because he was not a scrambler and someone who was going to run the ball. He was going to beat you with his arm and not his legs.*
>
> *I have to say that the "young" Belichick at the time, didn't really understand his personnel, it was his first head coaching assignment. Maybe he wanted to have that Michael Vick quarterback at that time, I'm not sure. Testaverde could do it all... he could run and pass, and get up the field with his legs when he needed to. So yeah, I was a little surprised by it...but anytime*

you have coaching staff changes, philosophies change and they want different things out of quarterbacks. For an athlete, that is frustrating because you have to deal with a new staff and re-learn everything...such as new terminology, and it can be very tough. It was... it is...and you have to adjust as a ballplayer...this is what happens in professional sports. It ended up working out well for Bernie as he won the Super Bowl later that same season with the Dallas Cowboys, which is pretty cool."

Kosar's favorite target at the time of being cut, Michael Jackson, gives his input on the situation:

"The fact that we changed the final play in the Denver game looked insubordinate to ownership and Coach Belichick. There already were some prior things going on with the organization that had caused troubles in the air, with Vinny already on the roster. I think it was a move that they were looking for the right moment to make, and they got the perfect opportunity to do so with the change of a play...or as it was seen by them, change of play incident against Denver.

I'm not sure, as I was just a player and not upstairs in the meetings to take part in that decision. I think when you factor in the transition of losing Bernie Kosar in 1993, that team fell apart because no one felt secure. Bernie Kosar was the Cleveland Browns at that time. If management was able to make a decision to rid themselves of Art Modell's son, then any one of us could go at any second...suddenly no one was untouchable from being cut. We used to look at it like everyone would be gone way before Bernie could ever go...but now he was gone just like that. Everyone was like, 'Oh, shoot, who's next?' It had the same magnitude of the team leaving town. It had the same effect on the players as the move did in 1995 on the fans. That's what happened to the rest of the 1993 season. It was a total disaster once Bernie Kosar was cut."

It was also seen as a shock because Vinny Testaverde would be out for several more weeks with a separated shoulder, and the move indicated that they thought third-string quarterback Todd Philcox could step in and do a better job than Bernie Kosar. The following week against Seattle, on the first play of the game, Philcox fumbled the ball; it was recovered by Seattle and was run in for a Seahawks touchdown. It was the fastest score in franchise history for Seattle. Philcox finished nine of twenty and passed for eighty-five yards with two interceptions. The Browns went on to get blown out 22–5.

The Cleveland Browns never recovered from the loss of Kosar, and only won once more in their next five games following the Seattle loss. They lost to the Houston Oilers, Atlanta Falcons, Houston again, and then the New England Patriots during that stretch. Their lone win came at home against the New Orleans Saints by a score of 17–13. It was Vinny Testaverde's first game back from injury.

As the Browns returned to the city of Los Angeles—the same city that started the whole controversy—to take on the Los Angeles Rams, it didn't have nearly the same feel or importance of the first time. It was the second to last game of the season whereas the Browns had a record of 6–8, and a lost team with no hope of making the playoffs. Despite the gloomy situation, Testaverde didn't let it affect his play on the field and had one of the best games of his career. The Browns routed the Rams by a score of 42–14 in a game that saw Testaverde complete twenty-one of twenty-three passes for 216 yards and two touchdowns.

Eric Metcalf, another player who seemed to step it up every time they played in Los Angeles did once again with fifty-six yards on the ground and fifty-seven through the air. It was a feel good win for a team that had been through hell that season. Mark Carrier also got in on the scoring with a fifty-seven yard punt return for a touchdown. Despite the drama of the season, Carrier was showing himself to be a great pickup.

They still had a chance to improve on their previous season's win total if they could just pull off one more victory the following and final week in Pittsburgh against the Steelers. The Browns were 7–8 and the win would also prevent a fourth straight losing season. The Steelers quickly crushed that dream as they beat the Browns with ease by a score of 16–9 in a game that saw the Browns fail to score a touchdown, instead having to rely on three Matt Stover field goals. The Browns finished 7–9, another losing season, and their fourth straight overall.

The Cleveland Browns team had looked great at certain points in the season and completely lost at other points. The offense did show improvement at times, but still lacked the consistency needed to win in the NFL. Vinny Testaverde finished with 1,791 yards and fourteen touchdowns. The leading rusher was Tommy Vardell who ran for 644 yards and three touchdowns. He also suffered three fumbles, something that he was not used to doing. Eric Metcalf had another streaky season of hot and cold periods that saw him rush for 611 yards on 129 carries with one touchdown. Metcalf also caught sixty-three balls for 539 yards and two touchdowns. Metcalf continued to show how versatile he was as he returned thirty-six punts for 464 yards and two touchdowns.

The free agent signing of Mark Carrier looked like a wise move as he caught forty-two for 746 yards and three touchdowns. Not bad for his first year with the Browns and having to go through three different starting quarterbacks. Fellow starting wide receiver Michael Jackson had his best season as a pro, catching forty-one balls for 756 yards and scoring eight touchdowns. The scoring improved from the prior season as they scored 304 points and their defense only allowed 307 points. Again, the points allowed were almost identical to the points scored, showing exactly how close they were to getting over the hump.

The addition of Jerry Ball didn't exactly do what they hoped as he only had three sacks and his counterpart Michael Dean Perry only had six. Jerry Ball would leave the team for the Los Angeles Raiders following the season. Anthony Pleasant led the team with eleven sacks, and Eric Turned led the Browns with five interceptions.

As for Bernie Kosar, he made the horrible ordeal work for his benefit by signing with the defending Super Bowl champion Dallas Cowboys. He would play behind all pro quarterback Troy Aikman and end up winning a Super Bowl later that same season. It was bittersweet for Kosar even though it wasn't with the team that drafted him and he grew up with, but in a way it was the gods of football making it up to one of the hardest working and smartest players to ever wear the brown and orange.

After the Super Bowl win, Kosar departed from Dallas and went on to play for the Miami Dolphins as a backup to legend Dan Marino. He saw limited action before retiring after the 1996 season. He finished his career with 23,301 yards and 124 touchdowns with only eighty-seven interceptions. He also finished with an excellent 59.3 completion ratio. He had fifteen fourth-quarter comebacks and seventeen game-winning drives, including seven come-from-behind game-winning drives in 1986 alone.

Few will dispute that he is one of the most beloved Cleveland Browns players in the history of the franchise. People still wear his jerseys to the games nearly twenty years after he played here. Since his departure, the Cleveland Browns have never again been steady at that position and have gone through twenty-three different starting quarterbacks.

The Cleveland Browns had written off Kosar, and would need to turn the corner quickly. With the distraction gone, Belichick was ready for his squad to take the next step. Starting in 1994, the Browns were poised and ready to do exactly that. Things were about to pick up, and wins were about to pile up.

Chapter Seven

Playoffs

Bill Belichick and the Cleveland Browns were on a mission heading into the 1994 season. They made a lot of bold moves during the first three years of his tenure, but didn't exactly win a lot of games. It was time for those moves to finally start paying off, and the fruit of their labor to show itself. The current roster compared to how it looked when he arrived was drastically different. With a few minor exceptions on each side of the ball, almost no one remained.

The team belonged to Belichick and his handprints were all over it at every position. He had his man behind center, and believed that he had gotten rid of all distractions. In this new 1994 season, it would be playoffs or bust. Anytime you get rid of one of the most popular players in team history, you better deliver with wins to follow such a risky move.

The pressure was on for Belichick to lead the Browns to the playoffs or else his days as a head coach in the NFL would be numbered. Art Modell was not a patient man. The fact that after three seasons under Bill Belichick's leadership and no playoff runs, it was surprising that he hadn't already made a switch at head coach, which was shocking to many fans and personnel around the NFL. Bill had refused to hire an offensive coordinator despite his background being in defense. It was time for Belichick to start producing wins, or update his resume and prepare to go back to being just a coordinator.

Some NFL insiders believed the reason why Belichick felt that he could do whatever he wanted, was because even if Modell fired him he would always have a place on any staff that Bill Parcells was currently the head coach of. Parcells was currently the head coach in New England, where he arrived in 1993 and took over one of the worst teams in the league. They drafted Drew Bledsoe and went from two wins to five wins in one season, and in the 1994 campaign would win ten games and reach the playoffs. So Belichick knew that he was playing with house money to some extent. He also knew not to make heavy promises when he took over after the 1990 season, informing management that it would take five years to completely turn around the Browns. By Belichick's math, they still had another year to get to the playoffs despite the growing unrest of the Cleveland Browns' fans.

Bill Belichick showed his first sign of maybe feeling the pressure, when he finally gave in and decided to hire an offensive coordinator before going into the off-season period of free agency and draft. Belichick promoted Steve Crosby from running backs coach to offensive coordinator. Crosby had been around the game of football since he was a young boy growing up in Kansas. He played college ball at Fort Hays State University, a little known college that Crosby would leave a big mark on by the time he was done playing there. He was an Associated Press Little All-American in 1973, two-time National Association of Intercollegiate Athletics All-District in 1972–1973, and a two-time All-Great Plains Athletic Conference selection in 1972–1973. By the time he graduated, he had compiled 2,780 rushing yards and twenty-seven touchdowns. He also showed his willingness to be a team player when he filled in for the quarterback and even the middle linebacker when both went down due to injury.

He was drafted by the New York Giants in the seventeenth round of the 1974 NFL Draft. It is hard to believe that the draft was ever that many rounds; in fact, Steve Crosby was one of the few players ever to be drafted that late and actually make an NFL roster. He played three seasons with the New York Giants before making the decision to retire.

After he retired from playing professional football, his first instinct was to finish college and earn a master's degree so he could become a high school teacher. Despite earning the degree, he never made it to teaching because he was offered the golden chance to be a scout for the Miami Dolphins. A chance to be a part of the staff working under Don Shula was simply too good for anyone to pass up. It turned out to be the best move he could make as he stayed in Miami through the 1983 season. He was a part of their Super Bowl team in 1982 that lost to the Washington Redskins.

While with the Miami Dolphins, he rose from being just a scout to becoming both the special teams coach and linebackers coach.

Steve Crosby departed Miami after the 1982 regular season to serve as the Atlanta Falcons running backs and quarterbacks coach for two seasons. From there, he arrived in Cleveland in 1985 and took over the role of running backs coach. It was a major success as the Browns boosted to onew thousand yard rushers that season, Earnest Byner and Kevin Mack. For unknown reasons, perhaps issues with Marty Schottenheimer, Crosby left Cleveland after one great season. He returned to the Atlanta Falcons in the same role he left, and remained for the next four seasons. He left Atlanta after the 1989 season and arrived in New England to become their special teams coach. After only one season there, he returned to Cleveland to be on Bill Belichick's staff as the running back coach. Things went well with him and the head coach and the connection he had with Belichick was strong enough that heading into the 1994 season, Belichick made the move that fans and local media never thought he would and promoted Crosby to offensive coordinator. One major reason for it was the interesting scheme that they had with using multiple running backs in each game plan. Despite it not being popular with the running backs, Belichick liked it and Crosby would be his main man.

Heading into the off-season, head coach Bill Belichick and Director of Player Personnel Michael Lombardi knew they had to be aggressive but also very intelligent with bringing in the exact right talent to mesh well with the current chemistry and philosophy of the team. They had a great mix of veteran and young talent, and knew that they were just a few tweaks away from becoming a serious playoff contender. They would work with defensive coordinator Nick Saban and new offensive coordinator Steve Crosby carefully to bring in just the right talent.

It would be the special team's coach Scott O'Brien that would have to first deal with a major switch of player personnel as starting punter Brian Hansen left Cleveland to play for the New York Jets. Hansen was not only a talented player on the field but also a locker room leader for his actions off the field as well. Despite leaving Cleveland, Hansen would always leave a mark of class on the team for his contributions while playing for the Browns.

Brian Hansen became a South Dakota State Director for Fellowship of Christian Athletes (FCA) in Sioux Falls, South Dakota after leaving the game. Hansen talks about his time in Cleveland and how God continued to move him in a positive direction after his time in the NFL was over:

> *"Partially due to the influence of our team chaplain (Tom Petersburg) and my teammates while being a member of the Cleveland Browns, my post-NFL experience led me to a position in full-time ministry with the Fellowship of Christian Athletes. I have been living in Sioux Falls, South Dakota for the past sixteen years and serving coaches and athletes across our state through the unique sports ministry we call FCA.*
>
> *I came to realize towards the end of my playing days what a blessing my years in Cleveland and in the league had been. Although there were no championship seasons, rather a pattern of playing for some of the worst teams in NFL history, I saw that football was a tool God uses in our life to test us, teach us, and develop us in our Faith. More than that, it's a model. As athletes, we understand what it means to be disciplined, committed, and passionate and to sacrifice for the cause...the very thing God desires in us living and serving Him. We do it for a short time in the games we play, but have a lifetime to carry those principles and disciplines on. If we miss that, we have nothing but fading memories of glory days and stories and stats that nobody wants to hear about.*
>
> *I was blessed also in my time in Cleveland by teammates like Matt Stover and Brian Kinchen who encouraged me in my true purpose in life. Guys that lived a life set apart from the ways of the NFL and the world. Their example at a key time in my life helped me grow as a father and husband, and in dealing with the challenges and pressure of the NFL.*
>
> *As I see the disturbing events of any given season that occur in the lives of players and darken the image of the NFL, I am encouraged to know God is working in and through coaches and athletes to impact the world for the cause of Christ. We live in a sports crazed world, but I'm confident God is in it and using it for a greater purpose than a pursuit of temporary victories and awards that will tarnish and fade away."*

The Cleveland Browns had to fill the gaping hole at punter and decided to reach out to a local talent, Tom Tupa. He had been in the league since 1989, spending three seasons with the Phoenix Cardinals and one season with the Indianapolis Colts. Tupa was from Northeast Ohio, attending high school at Brecksville-Broadview Heights. He played quarterback and punter for them, and led them to the State Championship game in his senior year. He also starred on the basketball court where he averaged 20.8 points per game.

Tupa went to college at Ohio State University where he sat behind former Cleveland Browns quarterback Mike Tomczak for three seasons while waiting for his chance to play. Tupa took over the starting quarterback job at Ohio State University in 1987, throwing for 2,252 yards, fifteen touchdowns and twelve interceptions. He had been punting the prior three seasons and did that year as well despite his new role as starting quarterback. He was selected as an All-American punter in his senior season, which was extra impressive considering he was splitting time at quarterback.

Friends on and off the field were Stover, Kinchen & Hansen.
Photo courtesy of Brian Kinchen

He was voted to the All Big Ten team that season as well. Tupa was a four-time football letterman and was also selected to play in the 1988 Hula Bowl All-Star game. This was actually his second stint with the Cleveland Browns as he was cut by the Browns right before the start of their 1993 season.

The Browns also decided to beef up their line backing core with the addition of Carl Banks. Veteran leader and defensive captain Clay Matthews had left in free agency and the Browns were quick to address that large need with Carl Banks. Bill Belichick had a positive history with Banks as he coached him during both Super Bowl winning seasons with the New York Giants. Banks was a standout in their Super Bowl XXI victory in which he recorded fourteen total tackles, including ten solo tackles. Banks was a member of the NFL's 1980s All-Decade Team because of his exceptional time with the Giants after being drafted by them in 1984. After leaving the Giants in 1992, Banks had one brief disappointing season with the Washington Redskins before they released him and he signed with the Browns. He was determined to perform like he did in his prime as he returned to play under his old coach and help Cleveland take the next step.

As Todd Philcox failed miserably in his attempt to backup Testaverde and Kosar in prior years, the Cleveland Browns knew they still needed to get that hole filled in case of another Testaverde injury. They brought in veteran backup and Super Bowl winning quarterback Mark Rypien from the Washington Redskins. This move was seen as a huge upgrade from Philcox as Rypien had encountered great success in his career while in Washington. Professional wrestler Bret 'the Hitman' Hart is one of the most notable athletes to come out of Calgary, Alberta, Canada but Mark Rypien can also lay stake to that claim. He was born in Canada but was quickly moved to the United States where his parents raised him in Spokane, Washington. He was a natural athlete and it showed when he got to high school and became a three-sport athlete. Rypien was also known for his accuracy as a deep passer. He excelled at football, basketball, and baseball at Shadle Park High School. He was also no stranger to winning championships as his basketball team won the 1981 Washington State Title.

Mark Rypien's college career at Washington State University did not go as planned as he encountered several knee injuries until the point in which he almost left the game. He was able to turn what was left of his college career around and perform well enough at the Senior Bowl to get a few NFL teams to take a closer look at him. He was eventually selected by the Washington Redskins in the sixth round of the 1986 NFL Draft. It didn't come with much fan fare as he was the 146th overall pick and the eighth quarterback selected. A few of the quarterbacks that went before him included Jim Everett, Chuck Long, Jack Trudeau, Bubby Brister, Hugh Millen, Robbie Bosco, and Doug Gaynor to name a few. Only one of them went on to have a decent NFL career.

Much like his college career, Rypien's pro career did not get off to a good start and was injury riddled as he spent his first two seasons on the injured reserve list. His team did win the Super Bowl at the end of the 1987 season. It wasn't until the 1989 season that Rypien finally got his chance to play full-time as the Redskins traded away Jay Schroeder and he was able to beat out the incumbent Doug Williams for the starting spot. Rypien immediately showed that he was worthy of the spot as he threw for 3,768 yards with twenty-two touchdowns. Two seasons later in 1991, he would have the best season of his career with 3,564 passing yards and twenty-eight touchdowns while only tossing eleven interceptions. He led the Washington Redskins to Super Bowl XXVI after recording a 14–2 regular season record. He played well in the big game and accumulated 292 passing yards and two touchdowns, leading his team to a 37–24 win over the Buffalo Bills. Rypien's performance earned him the Super Bowl MVP Award; he was the first foreign-born player to earn the honor.

The Redskins would make it back to the playoffs the following season with a win in their first round playoff game on the road in Minnesota against the Vikings only to meet with defeat the following week against the perennial Super Bowl favorites, the San Francisco 49ers. Rypien's numbers slipped a bit that season as well with 3,282 yards but only thirteen touchdowns and seventeen interceptions. Things got worse for Rypien the following season in 1993 under new head coach Richie Petitbon as his numbers continued to drop. His 1993 season only saw him start ten games and throw four touchdowns with ten interceptions; his career in Washington would soon be over.

Richie Petitbon didn't last as the head coach in Washington, and when new head coach Norv Turner took over, the writing was on the wall for Rypien. He participated in the off-season workouts but it wasn't long before Washington released him to put their re-building mode in full progress. The Browns brought in Rypien and didn't hesitate to sign him as their new backup.

With a new backup quarterback, a new punter, and a solid addition to the line backing core, the Browns were already having a strong off-season heading into the 1994 NFL Draft. Their two biggest holes remained the secondary and depth at the wide receiver position. They had two picks in the first round and would have a good chance at filling both of those holes.

The 1994 NFL Draft was highlighted early by future NFL Hall of Fame running back Marshal Faulk being selected second overall by the Indianapolis Colts. By the time the Browns were on the clock to make their selection, plenty of great options remained on the board. They used their selection to improve the secondary when they picked Antonio Langham, a cornerback from the University of Alabama.

Antonio Langham had a taste of championship while playing in Alabama as in 1992 the Crimson Tide were National Champions. As a junior in 1993, he was recognized as a consensus first-team All-American and would win the Jim Thorpe Award as the nation's top defensive back. His college career was not without controversy, however, as it came with a black eye when he caused the Crimson Tide to forfeit most of its 1993 season and suffer NCAA sanctions by signing with an agent during the previous off-season. Compounding the problem was that he signed and submitted an application to enter the 1993 NFL Draft, rendering him ineligible under NCAA rules, regardless of whether he had signed with an agent or not. In his defense, his coach Gene Stallings didn't do him any favors when he failed to inform both the Southeastern Conference and the NCAA of Langham's draft application, or to declare Langham ineligible as required by NCAA rules. The Cleveland Browns' front office looked past his checkered past, and focused on his Crimson Tide's team record for career interceptions with nineteen.

Antonio Langham went on to become a lockdown corner for the Cleveland Browns and a fan favorite in the process. With one hole filled in the first round, the Browns focused on filling their second one as well. Michael Jackson and Mark Carrier proved that they could be a viable one-two punch at wide receiver with Vinny Testaverde throwing them the ball. The Browns still needed that third guy to step up and looked to the draft for any impact options. They found one with their second pick in the first round, the 29th overall, when they selected Derrick Alexander out of Michigan University.

Derrick Alexander sat behind former Heisman Trophy award winner Desmond Howard in his first two seasons at Michigan before getting his chance to shine in his junior season when he became the Wolverines number one receiver. He relished the role of 'go to receiver' and in his junior and senior seasons he led the team in receptions and receiving yards. The Browns liked the fact that he could fill multiple roles when needed as well. He showed the ability to return kicks in college as he once returned a punt for seventy-nine yards, the longest punt return in Outback Bowl history, as well as the only punt returned for a touchdown. It was also his final college game, which made a great lasting impression for NFL teams scouting him. Derrick Alexander was also twice named to the All-Big Ten Conference team, and was honored as an All-American in 1992.

It was a great first round for the Cleveland Browns as they made two good picks as Langham was the top cornerback selected. Derrick Alexander was the fourth wide receiver off the board, however, the three men picked in front of him—Charles Johnson, Johnnie Morton, and Thomas Lewis never did much in the NFL. Thus, the Browns were viewed as getting the steal of the first round with the combo of Langham and Alexander. Although it should be mentioned that the Browns did pass up on wide receiver Isaac Bruce in the second round, and Bruce would go on to have a great NFL career far surpassing that of Alexander.

The Browns stayed aggressive on the defensive side of the ball as they used their third round draft pick on Romeo Bandison, a defensive tackle from the University of Oregon. They did not have a fourth round pick but selected Issac Booth with their fifth round pick, he was a defensive back from the University of California–Berkeley. They were looking to become deep at each position.

To the surprise of many fans and local media, a tormented soul returned to the Browns that season when Earnest Byner decided to return to Cleveland. Browns fans welcomed him back with open arms and had for the most part, forgave him for the untimely fumble in the 1987 season's AFC Championship Game against the Denver Broncos. More than five years had passed, and it was time for the old wound to finally heal.

Earnest Byner had done well for himself after he was traded from Cleveland to Washington prior to the 1989 season. He made the Pro Bowl in 1990 when he gained 1,219 yards rushing that season. The following season, Byner rushed for 1,048 yards and was a key part of their Super Bowl Championship. The football gods had awarded Byner with a Super Bowl ring in his time away from Cleveland, much like they did for Bernie Kosar. The addition of Byner wasn't seen as a move to help the team in many ways other than depth, however, Tommy Vardell would get hurt in 1994, only playing in five games so the move to acquire Byner ended up paying off.

The Browns had a great off-season; they made some key pickups, drafted well, and managed to avoid injury. The players were eager to put the dramatic 1993 season behind them, and start fresh in their pursuit of the playoffs. It had been four long seasons of losing records and missing the playoffs. This Browns team had the talent and the desire to make big things happen. Even if it was one year earlier than Belichick had promised, there was no denying that this Cleveland Browns team could make it happen.

The fans were also eager to put the past season of heartache and drama behind them, and showed their excitement for the season to kick off by driving four hours south. They traveled down Interstate 71 to invade Riverfront Stadium in Cincinnati to cheer on the Browns as they took on their cross-state rivals the Bengals. The fans from Cleveland were vocal and made their voices heard in support of their Browns in the Battle of Ohio.

The Cleveland Browns started strong with a nineteen yard Matt Stover field goal followed by a Vinny Testaverde eleven yard touchdown pass to Leroy Hoard in the first quarter. The Hoard touchdown would become even more important one play later as it set up the first two-point conversation in NFL history. The 1994 season was the first in which teams were allowed to go for two points, and Bill Belichick didn't waste any time trying it. Placeholder Tom Tupa took the snap and instead of placing the ball on the ground for the standard extra point kick, decided to pick the ball up and scramble out of the pocket and into the end zone for the two-point conversion. It was a great day for the Browns special teams coach Scott O'Brien as shortly after the two-point conversation, it was Randy Baldwin taking a kickoff eighty-five yards for a touchdown. Later in the second quarter, it was Eric Metcalf scoring on a ninety-two yard punt return. By halftime, the Browns were up 25–10 on the strength of their incredible special teams' play.

They hung onto the lead in the second half and won 28–20 despite a late twenty-four yard touchdown pass from David Klinger to Darnay Scott. Neither starting quarterback played all that well as both threw multiple interceptions. Vinny Testaverde did throw for 149 yards and a touchdown. Leroy Hoard was the main tailback as he received sixteen carries for ninety-two yards and did have the touchdown catch. The new addition to the defense, Carl Banks, had one sack. Rookie Antonio Langham played well and recorded his first career interception. For the second straight season, the Cleveland Browns had beaten the Cincinnati Bengals during week one and started off the season on a positive note.

That positive note wouldn't last, however, as the very next week they were beaten on their home field by the Pittsburgh Steelers. They had won the previous four seasons in a row at home against Pittsburgh, but that streak came to a crashing halt. The game had started well enough for the Browns as they used a one yard touchdown pass from Vinny Testaverde to Walter Reeves and a twenty-three yard field goal by Matt Stover to build an early 10–0 lead. It wouldn't last as Pittsburgh came roaring back on the strength of a Neil O'Donnell touchdown pass to Yancey Thigpen as well as a Barry Foster touchdown run. The Steelers led 14–10 at the half, and hung on to shut out the Browns in the second half to secure the 17–10 win. The game was a nightmare for Vinny Testaverde as he tossed four interceptions and was sacked twice. Three of his interceptions were brought in by Darren Perry. Their previous week's leading rusher Leroy Hoard was held to fifteen yards on just five carries.

Week three featured a 32–0 blowout win at home over the Arizona Cardinals in which Vinny ran for a touchdown and threw for two of them including an eighty-one yard strike to rookie Derrick Alexander. Eric Turner would pick off a Jay Schroeder pass late in the game and return it ninety-three yards for a touchdown. Rookie sensation Antonio Langham also had an interception in the big win. They followed up the win with a nail-biting victory the next week at Indianapolis 21–14 on the strength of three Testaverde touchdown passes. The Browns avenged the previous season's week four loss against the Colts and in the process moved to 3–1. All three passing touchdowns were made to running backs as Eric Metcalf scored from fifteen and fifty-seven yards, and Leroy Hoard scored from sixty-five yards to win the game in the fourth quarter. Eric Turner had another interception while Dan Footman recorded a sack.

The Cleveland Browns remained hot the next week as they trounced the New York Jets 27–7 in Cleveland. The Jets normal starting quarterback Boomer Esiason was injured before the game and replaced by backup Jack Trudeau. The Browns' stellar defense made sure the Jets were never cleared for takeoff as they kept them grounded all game. It was a rare strong performance out of their rushing game that gave the Browns the victory with touchdown rushes by Earnest Byner, Eric Metcalf, and Leroy Hoard. Eric Turner was once again the MVP of the defense with a sack and an interception.

Following a "bye week", the Cleveland Browns played on national television as the NFL was starting to experiment with *Thursday Night Football* on cable television. The Browns traveled to play the struggling Houston Oilers. In a low scoring 11–8 victory for the Browns, the key play came on a second quarter twenty-five yard touchdown pass from Vinny Testaverde to Mark Carrier to give the Browns the lead. They converted a two-point conversion and then a thirty-five yard Matt Stover field goal later in the quarter that gave them an 11–0 lead they would never surrender. Outside of the touchdown toss, Testaverde was met with struggles and threw two interceptions. Rookie Issac Booth had an interception for the Browns in the win as well. The win gave the Browns a 5–1 record and a four-game win streak as they headed home to take on the winless Bengals.

The Cleveland Browns returned home for round two of the 1994 Battle of Ohio. The Cincinnati Bengals looked strong early and sprung out to a 10–3 lead on the strength of a David Klinger to Tim McGee touchdown pass. The Browns would tie it on a Vinny Testaverde to Leroy Hoard touchdown pass. The Bengals responded with a field goal and took a 13–10 lead into halftime. It would be the closest the Bengals would come to securing their first victory that day because the Browns came out of the locker room to start the second half red hot and scored the final twenty-seven points of the game. Two Matt Stover field goals combined with a Travis fumble recovery for a touchdown and a seventy-three yard punt return for a touchdown by Eric Metcalf broke the game wide open. Leroy Hoard would tack on a late one yard touchdown run to cap everything off for the Browns who won 37–13 in dominant fashion.

Despite their blowout win, it wasn't all good news for the Cleveland Browns as Vinny Testaverde left the game late with injury. He had gone eight of eighteen with 103, a touchdown and an interception while he was in the game. His replacement, Mark Rypien came in and went only three of eleven for thirty-six yards. Rookie wide receiver Derrick Alexander had one of his better games as he caught three balls for fifty-eight yards. Once again, it was the defense and special teams of the Browns that took the game over, with the punt return touchdown and also the fumble returned for a score. They also recorded three sacks in the victory. One year removed from cutting Bernie Kosar, the Browns started the season 6–1; it was the best they had looked in almost a decade.

Because of the injury to Vinny Testaverde, both he and Mark Rypien would have to combine to lead the Browns to play in the house of horrors known as Mile High Stadium in Denver. Testaverde still wasn't one hundred percent healthy and only lasted long enough to throw fourteen passes. Rypien would relieve Testaverde but it wasn't enough. The wounds of three AFC title game losses were still very fresh for the Cleveland Browns and their fans, and this game didn't make things much better. Any chance of getting past their demons quickly flew out the window that day as Denver dominated from start to finish.

The Broncos scored on a first-half touchdown pass from John Elway to Jerry Evans along with a touchdown run from Leonard Russell to give the Broncos the 14–6 lead at the half. The Broncos kept it rolling through the second half on the strength of two Jason Elam field goals and a later John Elway to Glyn Milburn touchdown pass to put the game away. The Browns lost 26–14, for only their second loss of the season. Mark Rypien did his best as he threw for 210 yards on seventeen completions and a touchdown pass to Mark Carrier. Rypien also converted a two-point conversion pass to Derrick Alexander, but it simply wasn't enough to get past John Elway and the Denver Broncos.

The Cleveland Browns' defense had their only bad outing of the entire regular season. They could not figure out how to stop John Elway as he had his way with them all game long. Elway finished with 349 yards and two touchdowns on thirty completed passes. Elway also ran it twice for fourteen yards, including a beautiful twelve yard scamper for a first down. He picked apart the Browns' much improved secondary all day with eight pass completions to Glyn Milburn for seventy-six yards and a touchdown. He made sure not leave out his favorite target, Shannon Sharp, who pulled in nine passes for eighty-five yards. Anthony Miller joined in the fun with four catches and eighty-two yards.

Rather than mess with a dual quarterback issue, the Cleveland Browns decided to give Testaverde the following week off so he could fully heal from his injuries. They put their faith in Mark Rypien as they returned home to take on the vastly improved New England Patriots. The Patriots were quickly on the rise under head coach Bill Parcells, who was the mentor of Bill Belichick from their days in New York together. This was the first chance for the student (Belichick) to show his mentor (Parcells) that everything he taught him was not in vain, as he was eager to prove he belonged in the coveted fraternity and brotherhood of NFL head coaches.

The game itself was as expected between the two defensive-orientated coaches and it was saw very few points. The Cleveland Browns used two Matt Stover field goals combined with a one yard touchdown pass from Mark Rypien to Leroy Hoard to secure the 13–6 victory. Mark Rypien was serviceable with fourteen of twenty-eight pass attempts being completed for 164 yards and a touchdown with an interception as well. Leroy Hoard continued with his best season as he ran for 123 yards on twenty-one carries. Hoard also had the big touchdown catch.

The Browns defense bounced back from one of their worst efforts of the season with one of their best as they dominated the Drew Bledsoe-led Patriot offense. The Browns picked off Bledsoe four times and sacked him twice. The interceptions came from Eric Turner who had two more along with an interception from Tim Jacobs and Mike Caldwell. It was a big win for Belichick against his mentor, and more importantly the win, their seventh, matched their win total from the prior season.

The Browns remained on a roll the following week as they traveled to Philadelphia and beat the Eagles 26-7. For the second straight week, Rypien would get to start as Testaverde didn't dress for the game because of injury. Matt Stover had a huge game kicking four field goals. The Browns combined that with a Rypien to Carrier touchdown pass and Earnest Byner touchdown run to win easily. The Browns' defense had their second straight big week as they shut down Randall Cunningham and allowed zero touchdown passes with an interception. They also kept the Eagles starting running back Vaughn Hebron down to thirty-nine yards. The defense sacked Cunningham three times, twice from Michael Dean Perry. Again, Rypien was nothing great, but he did enough to get the job done with 158 yards and a touchdown. Leroy Hoard continued to rush the ball well with eighty-six more yards.

Vinny Testaverde would return to the starting lineup the following week as the Cleveland Browns traveled to Arrowhead Stadium to take on the Kansas City Chiefs. It was one of the toughest places in all of sports to travel to and obtain a victory. The Browns hung tough for as long as they could, with touchdown passes by both Vinny Testaverde and Mark Rypien to take a 13-10 lead into the fourth quarter. They had made a costly error earlier in the game when they failed in an attempt to convert a two-point conversion other than taking the standard one-point kick. The Chiefs tied it in the fourth quarter on a twenty-eight yard Lin Elliot field goal, and then won it a few minutes later on a Kimble Anders touchdown run.

The Cleveland Browns dropped to 7-3 with the 20-13 loss to the Kansas City Chiefs. They couldn't get too down on themselves considering that the Chiefs' comeback was led by one of the greatest quarterbacks in the history of the NFL, Joe Montana. The Chiefs were also led by former Browns head coach Marty Schottenheimer who seemed to have the Browns' number.

Nevertheless, at 7–3, the Cleveland Browns were still very much in the hunt for a division title as they returned home to face the visiting Houston Oilers. The Oilers had fired their head coach Buddy Ryan earlier in the season, and were now led by interim head coach Jeff Fisher. Little did anyone know, but Fisher would remain in that spot for the better half of the next seventeen seasons, even after the team moved to Tennessee and became the Titans in 1997. Jeff Fisher would lead the Titans to the Super Bowl in 1999, losing narrowly to the St. Louis Rams. He would win 142 career games as coach of the Titans during his long tenure.

Despite how well Jeff Fisher's career as an NFL head coach would turn out, things did not go well for him on this particular day. A healthy Vinny Testaverde got the call to start and played the entire game. And, he played well, tossing 199 yards and two touchdowns in a 34–10 win. Testaverde used both of his tight ends perfectly with the touchdowns being thrown to Brian Kinchen and Frank Hartley. Leroy Hoard continued to be the new go-to-guy out of the backfield with twenty-three more carries for 103 yards and two touchdowns. The Browns' defense continued to wreak havoc as well with four more sacks. The Browns were firing on all cylinders and it showed as they improved to 9–3 three fourths into the season.

The Cleveland Browns' momentum would come to a halt the next week, however, when they were upset by the visiting New York Giants. In Belichick's first game against his former team, the Browns came out flat and never got on track, resulting in a 16–13 loss. They remained in the game the whole time, however, and actually forced a tie game in the fourth quarter on a Leroy Hoard touchdown run. The Browns' defense also did their best to keep them in the game as Eric Turner had another interception, and they recorded four sacks, including two from Don Griffin. The Giants had the ball one last time and made it count with a Brad Daluiso thirty-three yard field goal to win it for the Giants. The lone bright spot for the Browns was the seven catch effort from Derrick

Alexander for 171 yards. It wasn't enough as the Browns dropped to 9–4 as they headed to Dallas to take on the highly talented and two-time defending Super Bowl Champion Dallas Cowboys.

The Dallas Cowboys were coming off of two straight Super Bowl championship wins and playing with a giant chip on their shoulder as most national pundits were not picking them to three-peat. Instead, a lot of press around the league felt that the San Francisco 49ers were the new favorites to win the NFC title. This was the same Dallas Cowboys team that handed Bill Belichick his first NFL head coaching loss in the first week of the 1991 season in Cleveland. The Cowboys had improved ten-fold since then, and now boasted a top five player at almost every position.

Troy Aikman held one of the most desirable positions in the country—playing quarterback for the Dallas Cowboys. After a rough rookie season in 1989 that saw him play in eleven games and throw eighteen interceptions with only eight touchdowns, Aikman began to drastically improve each season after that. By 1992, his fifth season in the league, he threw twenty-three touchdowns that year with only fourteen interceptions, leading the Cowboys to the Super Bowl. They blew out the Buffalo Bills in the Super Bowl by a score of 52–17 and Aikman earned MVP honors with four touchdowns and 273 yards. Aikman followed up the great 1992 season with a decent 1993 season that saw the Cowboys return to the Super Bowl, beating the Buffalo Bills once again. Aikman was one of the elite quarterbacks in the league and had the Cowboys looking strong again. Aikman would eventually earn Hall of Fame honors after his playing career was over because of his excellent play as a Cowboy.

Helping Aikman in the backfield was fellow future Hall of Famer Emmitt Smith who joined the Cowboys in the 1990 NFL Draft. Smith was widely regarded as the best running back in football and was always among the league leaders in touchdowns and rushing yards. He rushed for 937 yards in his rookie season, and then eleven straight one thousand yard rushing seasons following that. At that time of the game against the Browns in 1994, Smith was in the midst of a 1,484 yard, twenty-two touchdown season. He was sure to cause problems for the Browns' defense, even if they were incredibly improved since their last meeting in 1991.

Troy Aikman's main target that season, and pretty much every season he was in the pros, was flashy wide out Michael Irvin. The "playmaker" Irvin had always come up huge in the role of Aikman's go-to-guy. Irvin was drafted by the Dallas Cowboys in 1988 and would end up spending his entire career with the team. He may have had a wrap sheet a mile long off the field, but on the field Irvin was the best receiver on the field in almost any game he played in. He was in the middle of his fourth straight one thousand yard plus season, and was sure to provide match-up problems for the Browns' secondary. Coach Nick Saban would have to run double teams with Eric Turner and Antonio Langham doing their best to smother Irvin all game long.

No one could deny the talent that the Dallas Cowboys showcased on the field. Their lone weak spot, as many opponents and national media saw it, was their head coach Barry Switzer. He was in his first season as an NFL head coach and was replacing Jimmy Johnson, who had just led the Dallas Cowboys to back-to-back Super Bowl championships. A feat that was good enough for Johnson to be fired by Jerry Jones.

Barry Switzer came from the college ranks, as he was very successful while at the University of Oklahoma. In his first two seasons as head coach, he led the Sooners to unbeaten seasons. It was the beginning of thirteen straight winning seasons and six Orange Bowl victories in nine appearances. He also led the Sooners to a couple of Fiesta Bowls, winning one and losing one. He led the Sooners to three National Championships in 1974, 1975 and 1985.

He is viewed as one of the greatest coaches in college football history. The only problem was that this wasn't college football, and the pressure was on. He was doing well with the Cowboys as they were 11–2 heading into the Browns game. The problem was that one of those losses came against the San Francisco 49ers, a team that Jimmy Johnson never had a problem beating, thus leading to some fans already being upset with Switzer despite his great resume and very good start to the season.

The game was held on a Saturday in Dallas, Texas in front of a packed house at Cowboy Stadium. Nick Saban's defense would have their hands full as the Cowboy offense had been red hot coming into the game. The Cowboys' offense had scored an average of thirty-four plus points per game in their last three games with blowout victories over the Eagles, Redskins and Packers. The Browns would be a heavy underdog in this one as the Cowboys defense, led by coordinator Butch Davis, was also playing well.

The Cowboys came as ten and a half point favorites by the Vegas line. Regardless, the Browns would not be intimidated and were eager to shake off their bad loss from the prior week against the New York Giants. The Browns defense had held all but one team, Denver, to twenty points and under all season long, and was up for the challenge of trying to do it again.

The game got off to a hot start with both teams scoring quickly in the first quarter. The Cowboys drew first blood with a seven yard touchdown pass from Troy Aikman to Emmitt Smith. The Browns answered back with a two yard touchdown pass from Vinny Testaverde to his main target Michael Jackson to tie the game at seven apiece heading into the second quarter. The Browns' defense—which had been playing great all season and continued to as they held the Cowboys high-powered offense in check—shut them out in the second and third quarters. Meanwhile, Matt Stover was kicking everything possible through the uprights, and three field goals later the Browns led 16–7 midway through the fourth quarter. The Cowboys did their best to rally with a four yard touchdown run to cut the lead to 16–14. Matt Stover added another field goal and the Browns were clinging to a 19–14 lead in the final moments of the game. One last Cowboys drive was snuffed out with a dramatic and impressive Browns goal line stand to give the Browns the shocking 19–14 road victory.

The Cleveland Browns' defense had played amazing once again to seal the victory. They picked off Troy Aikman twice while forcing two fumbles. Don Griffin and Eric Turner were once again responsible for the big interceptions of Aikman; they had been both playing incredible all season long. Don Griffin also had a sack from Aikman along with one from Anthony Pleasant.

The Browns' offense didn't exactly light the league on fire, but they contributed enough to win on the strength of four Matt Stover field goals and ninety-nine rushing yards from Leroy Hoard. In his fourth season as head coach, it was by far the signature win for Bill Belichick that he so desperately needed and wanted. The

Browns were now 10–4 and headed back to the playoffs, with still two games left in the season to try and catch the Steelers for the division championship.

Tight end Brian Kinchen gives his reasons as to why the Cleveland Browns were able to excel that season:

> *"It was very exciting for me to make it into the playoffs and be able to contribute to the team. Vinny had a really good relationship with all players and that helped. He wasn't very stand-offish, he was a good leader and that helped our progress and trust level that season. The way he played that year helped with the entire team's confidence level. Bill did a great job coaching us, he worked us hard in camp and never took his foot off the gas pedal. Talent is great, but you need cohesiveness and unity to really win and become an actual team. I can't describe how important it is to really have success on Sundays by having everyone unite and get along from top to bottom...and that's the players and the coaches and everyone from top to bottom. They were a quality group of people who brought their lunch pal to work every day ready to work hard!"*

Ed Sutter gives his opinion on why the team did so well that season:

> *"We played great defense and special teams. We didn't have a lot of injuries, and once we got momentum, things kept rolling."*

Michael Jackson describes why the team was able to get back on track in 1994 and make the playoffs:

> *"After the terrible ending to 1993, it was a relief for it to be over...it was transition time with everyone invited back to camp. Bernie Kosar being cut the year before was kind of like a death. Everyone is sad when someone passes away until three weeks later and it's back to work as normal. People don't think of things with such extreme analogies, but that was the reality! We had to get back to work and back on course. So in 1994, everyone is working to fill those vacancies that have been left because now there are a lot of spots available for somebody to step up and become the man...become the face of the organization. So now, we had all kinds of players fighting to become the face of the organization because the prior face was now gone. I think that has*

a lot to do with the success of the 1994 season. Vinny Testaverde was rejuvenated because Derrick Alexander and myself had gone to him and spoken with him about many things on and off the field. We told him that we knew his history and all these different things, but to please give us an opportunity to make things happen on the field. We built and felt the confidence in Vinny, which is something that I don't think that the core of receivers had done prior to that. Prior to that season, I don't think Vinny had a core of receivers that built that type of confidence and trust in him. He was willing then, to make the throws that he probably wouldn't have in the past.

That is one thing the fans don't get to realize when it is happening and all of that. We became more of a team and a family. We did more things together in groups as groups. We were more involved with one another personally. When that happens...then you have people who will do things for you that they wouldn't normally do for you if you didn't have that cohesiveness. "

With everyone and everything clicking on full cylinders, the Cleveland Browns traveled to Pittsburgh, Pennsylvania to try and avenge a loss from earlier in the season. It wouldn't be easy as the Steelers were one of the best teams in the league that season, and knew a home win over the Browns would wrap up the division title for them. The Cleveland Browns would need to be on high alert.

The Pittsburgh Steelers were roaring to go and didn't waste any time jumping out to a 14–0 first quarter lead with a forty yard touchdown pass from Neil O'Donnell to Yancey Thigpen. Barry Foster also had a one yard touchdown run and the Browns were in trouble early on. They mustered a brief comeback in the second quarter when Vinny Testaverde hit Mark Carrier on a seventeen yard touchdown pass. The score would prove to be too little too late as the Steelers tacked on a late field goal and seized the game at 17-7.

It was another case of the Cleveland Browns' defense playing good enough to win, but not receiving nearly enough help from their anemic offense. Testaverde did manage to throw for 250 yards and a touchdown, but the two interceptions hurt him and the team.

With one game to go in regular season, the Cleveland Browns still had a lot to play for. Even though they were already in the playoffs at 10–5, this last win would guarantee them a first round home playoff game as the top non-divisional winning team. The good news was that they got to play that pivotal sixteenth game from the friendly confines of Cleveland Municipal Stadium against the Seattle Seahawks. This was huge because Seattle was used to playing in their Kingdome and did not fare well in outdoor stadiums. Plus, this game was scheduled for Christmas Eve, and it was very cold. The wind was whipping hard that day, blowing at thirteen miles per hour, making it feel much colder than it actually was. The Seahawks were 6–9, and for all intents and purposes, had nothing to play for. These factors alone helped the Browns become a 10.5 point favorite going into the game.

The Cleveland Browns had two primary missions that day—to win, and not get anyone hurt in the process. It was a tricky mix because they didn't want to go in soft but also knew that they couldn't afford any major injuries at this time. They needed to build a large enough lead so they could rest players late in the game, which is exactly what they ended up doing. They led 21–0 by halftime thanks in part to a Vinny Testaverde touchdown pass to Mark Carrier as well as a Testaverde quarterback sneak for a touchdown. Eric Metcalf contributed with six yard touchdown run and held the commanding lead going into the half.

In the third quarter, they picked up where they left off momentum-wise, answering a quick Seahawks field goal with a Testaverde to Derrick Alexander touchdown pass from three yards out to give the Browns a 28–3 lead. Coach Belichick pulled his starters and the Browns kept scoring, this time with a wide receiver reverse that saw Mark Carrier run it in the end zone from fourteen yards out. Carrier had quite the game with a touchdown catch and run. The Cleveland Browns rolled to a 35–9 victory and finished the season with an impressive 11–5 record.

Despite not playing much of the second half, Testaverde still looked strong. He finished with 228 yards and two touchdowns. Leroy had another good game in a strong season, running for seventy-four yards on twenty-four carries. Mark Carrier finished with ninety-eight yards on five catches, and one touchdown running and one touchdown passing. On defense, Eric Turner had one more interception in his best season as a professional.

It was a great regular season for the Belichick-led squad. They bounced back from a drama-filled season of disappointment to have a double-digit win season, and earn a first round home playoff game. The Nick Saban defense continued to excel as they had a season for the ages. They only allowed 204 points all season, an average of 12.8 points per game. That was incredible and went well with an offense that at times, had trouble scoring. The offense finished with 340 points, an average of 21.2 points per game. It was a healthy 136 point differential.

The Nick Saban-led defense only allowed a team to score more than twenty points just once. They held opponents to under ten points, six different times. They had one shutout, and twice didn't allow a team to score a touchdown. Eric Turner had the best season with nine interceptions, leading the team by far as the next closest person only had two interceptions. Antonio Langham had a great rookie season as he played and started in all sixteen games. He had two interceptions and recorded fifty-five tackles, including one forced fumble. Rob Burnett led the team in sacks with ten. Free agent pick up Carl Banks played well and was worth the money spent on him. He started fifteen games and had fifty-six tackles with 1.5 sacks. Pepper Johnson also played well at middle linebacker, leading the team with ninety-five tackles. It was an all-around great year for the defense.

The special teams also continued to play well as Matt Stover remained clutch. He converted twenty-six of thirty-two field goal attempts, including nine of nine from forty-plus yards. Stover also converted thirty-two of thirty-two extra points. The extra point team itself did great, as they converted three of four two-point conversions. Tom Tupa did his part in his first season with the team, punting the ball eighty times for a 40.1 yard average. Eric Metcalf once again shined on special teams as he took two punts back for touchdowns. Randy Baldwin handled most of the kickoff return duties, and he did it well as he had one touchdown and 753 yards.

Vinny Testaverde played in fourteen games, started in thirteen of them and tossed sixteen touchdowns, but also eighteen interceptions. He really didn't have that great of a season when you look at the stats alone; he only threw for 2,575 yards and only led one game-winning drive.

The difference was, unlike the last couple of years, the Browns finally had a decent running game thanks to Leroy Hoard who finished with 890 yards and five touchdowns. He also caught forty-five balls for 445 yards with four touchdowns. Hoard had a great year and proved how valuable he could be when given the chance to play. Eric Metcalf had 329 yards on the ground with two touchdowns. He also caught forty-seven balls for 436 yards and two touchdowns receiving. The two back combination came through big for the Browns, and they needed to as Vardell was hurt most of the season, and only played in five games. The returning Earnest Byner even chipped in with 219 yards on seventy-five carries.

The wide receiving core improved as well with the addition of rookie wide out Derrick Alexander who completed his first season with a team leading forty-eight catches. He earned 828 yards and scored two touchdowns, including one from eighty-one yards out. The emergence of Alexander was very important and crucial because their normal number one starting receiver Michael Jackson was banged up most of the season, only playing in nine games. Jackson was reduced to twenty-one catches for 304 yards and two touchdowns. Mark Carrier needed to step up in the absence of Jackson, and he did so with twenty-nine for 452 yards and five touchdowns. Brian Kinchen made the most of his starting role and caught twenty-four passes for 232 yards and scored one touchdown. The only down note was Rico Smith continuing to be a draft day bust with only two catches for sixty-one yards during the entire season.

It was clear that their dominant defense was the main reason for winning eleven games, but it didn't matter to the Cleveland Browns fans, they were just happy to be back in the playoffs. The first round game would be at home, featuring a regular season rematch against Bill Parcells, Drew Bledsoe, Ben Coates, and the New England Patriots. It had been an incredible two-year turnaround for the Patriots under Parcells. He took them from a two-win team to finish 10–6 in 1994. He also led them on a courageous seven-game winning streak to close out the season and sneak into the playoffs. In fact, they hadn't lost since week ten against the

Browns in Cleveland. The Patriots were red hot and this match-up was sure to provide a classic rematch of teacher versus student, Bill Parcells versus Bill Belichick.

Drew Bledsoe's second season in the league had been a masterpiece as he threw for an amazing 4,555 yards and a respectable twenty-five touchdowns. His only downfall had been his tendency to turn the ball over with twenty-seven interceptions. The Browns' secondary would have to force Bledsoe to throw into tight windows all game like they did in their earlier match-up if they wanted to win. His number one receiver was his tight end Ben Coates, who had ninety-six catches for 1,174 yards and seven touchdowns. Coates was one of the best tight ends in football. Another key threat for Bledsoe had been Michael Timpson who pulled in seventy-four balls for 941 yards and scored three touchdowns. Vincent Brisby also had one of his best seasons as a pro with fifty-eight receptions for 904 yards and five touchdowns. It was evident that Drew Bledsoe was capable of making everyone around him better.

Similar to the Cleveland Browns, the Patriots did not boast a one thousand yard rusher on the roster. Their top running back was Marion Butts who had 703 yards on 243 carries. Joining Butts in the backfield was Leroy Thompson, who had 102 carries for 312 yards and scored two touchdowns. Thompson was better catching balls out of the backfield than taking handoffs, and the Patriots realized that as he caught sixty-five passes for 465 yards while scoring five touchdowns.

The New England Patriots had an average to below-average defense for a playoff team as they relied mainly on outscoring opponents to win games. In two of their six losses, they scored at least thirty-five points. Their defense did have a couple of All-Pros as Chris Slade had a team high 9.5 sacks. Leading the team in interceptions with seven was Maurice Hurst. The offense had been bailing them out all season as the defense had let up twenty plus points seven times. It would be up to defensive line coach Romeo Crennel to design several different strategies to try and get pressure on Testaverde, and hopefully force him into bad passes to make up for the interceptions that Bledsoe was sure to throw.

The first half of the game was tight as expected, and ended in a 10–10 tie. Both quarterbacks tossed a touchdown pass in the process—Testaverde connected with Mark Carrier from five yards out, and Bledsoe hit Thompson from thirteen yards away. Both field goal kickers, Matt Bahr and Matt Stover, hit field goals as well. Cleveland would break the tie in the third quarter when Leroy Hoard scored on a handoff from ten yards away, giving the Browns a 17–10 lead heading into the fourth quarter.

The Cleveland Browns were clinging to a seven point lead late in the game when Matt Stover gave them a little extra breathing room with a twenty-one yard field goal. New England's Matt Bahr answered with a thirty-three yarder but they never got any closer, despite recovering an on-side kick late in the game to get the ball back.

The Cleveland Browns' game plan worked to perfection as they kept the pressure on Bledsoe and never let him get comfortable despite a whopping fifty pass attempts. The Browns' defense picked off Drew Bledsoe three times en route to their 20–13 victory. The Patriots were never able to establish any running game either as their top rusher Corey Croom had thirty-six yards on nine carries. Like they had done all season, the Cleveland Browns' defense carried them to a victory.

Matt Stover recalls his memories of that playoff season and why things went so well, as well as his fond recollection of the playoff victory over the New England Patriots:

> *"I have a painting of me in my Browns uniform from that playoff game. I made a kick that day prior to halftime and pointed to the sky to thank God. It was the start of a tradition that I started doing after every kick regardless of if I made it or not. That game was very tough because of the tough conditions...the dirt was painted green just to make it seem as though grass was there. It was a feeling of such accomplishment to win that game because of all the changes we had to endure. The prior season was bad with the players leaving, and it was nice to overcome all of that and win the game. This was the team Belichick had built, and it was starting to work as we were starting to become a really good team. Belichick did have the formula even then...it just happened that the next year, the final year, the carpet would be ripped away from underneath us."*

The following week on the road in Pittsburgh, they would get one more chance to beat their hated rivals the Steelers and knock them out of the playoffs. Pittsburgh had boasted a strong running game all season, and the normally vaunted Browns' defense looked old and slow for the first time all year, not being able to stop it in their two regular season match-ups. The Steelers came in with a two back rotation that had been crushing teams all season. Barry Foster had 851 rushing yards on 216 regular season carries with five touchdowns. Bam Morris had 836 regular season rushing yards on 198 carries for seven touchdowns. The strong running game made up for the mediocre quarterback play from Neil O'Donnell who had only thrown for thirteen touchdowns and 2,443 yards.

Sadly for the Cleveland Browns and their fans, it was never close and the Steelers crushed the Browns 29–9. The Steelers led 24–3 at the half and never looked back. Vinny Testaverde was held to 144 yards and was picked off twice in a lackluster effort. Barry Foster ran all over the Browns, rushing for 133 yards on only twenty-four carries. Pittsburgh backup running back Bam Morris rushed for sixty yards on twenty-two carries. Their third string running John Williams even looked good as he went for forty-three yards on just two carries, including a twenty-six yard touchdown run.

It was a disappointing way for the Cleveland Browns to end a great season. Pittsburgh would get knocked off the following week by the San Diego Chargers at home in the AFC Championship Game in a major upset. The Steelers lost on a very late forty-three yard touchdown pass from San Diego quarterback Stan Humphries to Tony Martin. Many NFL pundits assessed that if the match-up would have been Cleveland versus San Diego, the Browns would have won and went to the Super Bowl based on the way both teams were constructed.

It was a great season with tremendous improvement for the Cleveland Browns, despite not being able to get past their hated rivals in the regular season and post-season. Exactly half of their losses came against Pittsburgh. Heading into the off-season, they knew they were only a couple of players away from finally making that jump in front of the Steelers.

The Director of Pro Personnel, Ozzie Newsome, along with the Director of Player Personnel Michael Lombardi knew they had a few moves to make, but most likely didn't want to over-think things because too much tinkering could screw up a really good team. Apparently, they didn't get the memo not to mess or tweak with too many things because they immediately started making moves on draft day. The Cleveland Browns were originally slated to pick 26th in the first round and made a trade with the Atlanta Falcons for their first round pick, which was tenth overall. They traded their 26th pick and Eric Metcalf to Atlanta for their tenth pick. This appeared to be a great first-round swap. They moved ahead sixteen picks in the first round, and only had to give away Eric Metcalf who was now suddenly expendable with the emergence of Leroy Hoard, and a healthy Tommy Vardell set to return to the lineup.

All goodwill and positive feelings towards the Metcalf draft trade quickly turned sour, and made fans angry and local media question it when the Browns promptly turned around and traded the number ten pick to the San Francisco 49ers for their pick, which was 30th overall. San Francisco also sent the Browns their third round, fourth round, and 1996 first round picks. So, basically, it boiled down to the Browns giving away their 26th overall selection, to move down four spots to use San Francisco's 30th pick; in the process, they gained a third round and fourth round pick.

The main reason they swapped was to gain an extra pick in the first round for the following year's draft. Even though the chances were with San Francisco, it would be a low pick in the first round as the 49ers usually finished towards the top of the league every year. Looking ahead, that first round pick obtained from the 49ers the following season ended up being the 26th overall pick and was used on Ray Lewis, one of the greatest defensive players in NFL history. However, Ray Lewis would never play a single NFL game in a Cleveland Browns uniform, but more on that later.

After all the NFL draft day trading was done, they finally stepped up to the podium and made their selection with the 30th overall pick from San Francisco. The Browns took Craig Powell, a linebacker from Ohio State University. There was nothing too special about the pick of Powell, and the moving back from ten to thirty really hurt them when you look at the list of people they passed up by dropping back twenty picks. They passed up on players such as Warren Sapp, Hugh Douglas, James Stewart, Ty

Law, Korey Stringer, and most notably, Derrick Brooks. It was a list of star-studded talent that they could have selected instead of the mediocre Powell.

Perhaps if Nick Saban was still the defensive coordinator of the Browns, the pick would have been used differently. After the incredible 1994 season for the Browns' defense, Saban was suddenly a hot coaching commodity in both the NFL and NCAA, and had numerous job offers waiting for him. He chose to leave the NFL and take the head coaching job at Michigan State University. The move ended up being one of the smartest he could have made. Saban ended up becoming one of the greatest college football coaches in the long rich history of the NCAA.

Saban would spend five seasons with the Michigan State Spartans where they improved from a terrible program to win thirty-four games in his five-year stretch as coach. He left the Spartans to become the new head coach of the Louisiana State Tigers, a decision that would pay off in scores. He spent five seasons at LSU and compiled forty-eight wins, three bowl victories, and led the Tigers to the National Championship in 2003 with a Sugar Bowl victory against the Oklahoma Sooners.

After a brief stint back in the NFL as head coach of the Miami Dolphins, Saban returned to the NCAA and SEC, and took over the Alabama Crimson Tide. Nick Saban once again proved that he was the most successful coach to come from the Belichick coaching tree as his time in Alabama has been incredibly successful. In his eight years at Alabama, Saban has led them to eighty-six wins and three National Championships. To say that the Browns lost a real gem in Saban would be a drastic understatement.

The man called on to replace Nick Saban was Rick Venturi. He got his start in football during high school when he played quarterback at Rockford Auburn High School in Illinois. He attended Northwestern University where he played quarterback and defensive back. After his playing days were done, he would eventually get into the coaching ranks. He had coaching in his blood as his father, Joe Venturi, was a member of the Illinois High School Football Coaches Hall of Fame. His brother, John, is also a member of the Illinois High School Football Coaches Hall of Fame, as he coached at Washington High School. While there, John won the 1985 Class 4A State Championship. John's 1983 Washington team was the 4A Runner-Up.

Sadly for Rick Venturi, he wouldn't encounter the same type of success that his father and brother did as his stint as head coach of the Northwestern Wildcats went down as one of the worst in sports history when looked at purely on wins and losses. He took over as the head coach at Northwestern University in 1978 and went 1–34 in that three-year period. He returned to coaching a few years later, this time in the NFL with the Indianapolis Colts in 1984 as an assistant coach on their defensive. He eventually rose through the ranks in Indianapolis and became their defensive coordinator in 1992.

Venturi arrived in Cleveland in 1994, and was a key member of Nick Saban's staff during the prior season when the Browns had one of the most impressive defenses in the league. Venturi would have the crucial task of keeping one of the league's best defensive units sharp without changing too many things that had worked well for Nick Saban. Rick Venturi wouldn't have to do it alone, however, as he had Eric Mangini and Jim Schwartz to help him. Mangini would one day become head coach of the Browns, while Schwartz would become head coach of the Detroit Lions.

Rick Venturi, Michael Lombardi, and Bill Belichick held high hopes that the addition of Craig Powell would help the line backing unit with a bit of a youthful injection as several of their better players were starting to get a little up there in years. Men such as Carl Banks and Pepper Johnson had been staples of the Bill Belichick defenses in the past, but he knew that Powell was needed to replace them one day soon. Belichick was always thinking one or two steps ahead and knew that Banks and Johnson would not have much left in the tank, thus the biggest reason for bringing Powell onboard.

Speaking of youth injections, the Browns made sure to stay with that theme in the positions they felt would eventually need it; thus their next pick, a third rounder as they did not have a second rounder, they used on University of Georgia quarterback Eric Zeier. As a Georgia Bulldog, Zeier possessed a rocket arm and used it to become one of the greatest quarterbacks in the history of the school. While at the University of Georgia, Zeier set sixty-seven school records and eighteen S.E.C. records. In 1994, he became only the third quarterback in NCAA Division I history to throw for more than eleven thousand yards in his career. He earned All-Academic S.E.C. honors in 1992 and 1993. So beloved was he by his teammates and coaches that Zeier was named team captain in 1993 and 1994. He fell to the Browns in the third round and they were smart to take him. Testaverde was less than brilliant in 1994, and despite leading them to the playoffs, he still wasn't beloved by the Browns fans because he would always be seen as the man who replaced Bernie Kosar.

Eric Zeier came to the Cleveland Browns with a bit of a chip on his shoulder, and with something to prove. He was the fourth quarterback selected behind Steve McNair, Kerry Collins, and Stoney Case. The Browns felt strongly about Zeier despite him dropping into the third round. One season after winning eleven games and one playoff game, Testaverde would already have to look over his shoulder at someone trying to take his position. Sadly for the Browns, the Zeier pick would be their only one of note as the rest of their draft became a colossal flop. They took defensive end Mike Fredrick and defensive tackle Tau Pupua, two men who would never even make a dent in the NFL. They followed those picks up with two wide receivers, Mike Miller from Notre Dame and A. C. Tellison from the University of Miami. Two big name schools, but neither man ever did anything in the NFL. In fact, Tellison never played a single time.

Even with the two draft picks at wide receiver, the Browns still needed to fill a hole at the position. Mark Carrier, who had two great seasons with the Browns, had one year left on his contract. However, when the Cleveland Browns made a huge mistake and did not protect him in the upcoming expansion draft, he was selected by the Carolina Panthers in the 1995 NFL Expansion Draft. The Browns were okay with it because they felt that Michael Jackson and Derrick Alexander would be enough to fill the position. They also had one more trick up their sleeve; it would just require owner Art Modell making a trip to the bank and applying for a loan.

The loan that Art Modell applied for was to obtain funds to sign on high-priced free agent wide receiver Andre Rison. At the risk of sounding too cliché, this move was the official beginning of the end for Art Modell and his financial empire as the Cleveland Browns' owner. Why would an owner of a NFL team need to acquire a loan just to sign a football player? Well, that was the writing on the wall that something may have been seriously wrong.

Andre Rison was a huge gamble that the Cleveland Browns' owner was willing to take based on his prior playing experience as a member of the Atlanta Falcons. Rison was one of the best receivers in the NFL for several years and was viewed as the missing piece to the Browns' offense that could put them over the top. With the strong arm of Testaverde and the speed of Rison, it would sure up their vertical passing attack and provide a triple threat at the position. It was seen as a huge upgrade from the sure-handed Carrier, and had the fans extremely excited at the thought of Rison catching touchdown bombs from Testaverde as the Browns finally had a proven big name threat. It was also seen to help the void that losing Eric Metcalf had created. Rison was sure to make up the yardage lost by the departure of Metcalf and Carrier. He was "Bad Moon Rison" and was sure to electrify the AFC upon arrival.

Andre Rison was a star player in high school and college while attending Flint Northwestern High School and Michigan State University. Rison was coming off of a great senior year at Michigan State where he had thirty receptions for 709 yards and five touchdowns. He was also a giant part of their Rose Bowl victory when they defeated the USC Trojans 20–17. On a crucial third down with only a few minutes left on the clock, Rison caught a crucial pass for a first down that kept the drive alive and allowed the Spartans to obtain the victory.

Andre Rison was drafted by the Indianapolis Colts in the first round of the 1989 NFL Draft and performed very well in his rookie season. Rison caught fifty-two passes for 820 yards with four touchdowns in his rookie campaign. He was viewed as one of the best young receivers in the game after only one season with a ton of promise and potential, which is why it was seen as a shock when he was traded to the Atlanta Falcons as part of a deal for the number one pick in the 1990 NFL Draft, which the Colts used to select Jeff George.

It didn't take either team long to realize that the Atlanta Falcons got the better of that trade as Rison continued to grow into one of the best players in the NFL. In his five seasons with the Falcons, Rison finished near the top of most receiving categories. Most notably, he led the NFL with fifteen receiving touchdowns in 1993. He became only the fifth receiver in NFL history to score sixty touchdowns in his first six seasons. He was at the top of or close to the top of every offensive category for a wide receiver every single year, including leading the NFL in receptions in four of his five seasons with the Atlanta Falcons. The irony being that his quarterback during the final season in Atlanta was Jeff George.

It was a huge coup for the Cleveland Browns to sign Andre Rison, but he did not come without a little baggage and off-field drama. Rison had been dating and living with music recording artist Lisa "Left Eye" Lopes of the hugely popular music group, TLC. One fateful day in 1994, the couple got into a heated physical altercation at Rison's Atlanta mansion. Lopes became irate from the incident and decided it would be a smart idea to throw of all Rison's shoes into the bathtub with the intention of burning them. Her initial thought may have been keeping the blaze contained in the bathroom but sadly for Rison that wasn't the case. The flames soon spread throughout the house, resulting in the loss of all his possessions. This was normal off-field behavior for Rison, and should have been a giant red flag for the Cleveland Browns, but it wasn't! They obviously had game-winning potential on their minds.

Not everyone was sold on the addition of Andre Rison, however, including his new teammate Leroy Hoard who had these comments:

> *"I loved Andre Rison...I believe he was a superstar. But when you think of Cleveland and you think of the way Cleveland was built, they didn't need a superstar. I don't think one superstar was going to get us over the hump. He brought a different attitude to Cleveland, and I just think that it didn't click. If I was able to put myself in Andre Rison's shoes...where he came from Atlanta catching one hundred balls a season...I understand why things didn't work out. He's not even getting the ball thrown to him as much...so he's already put in an unfair situation. It became frustrating for him because of what he was asked to do...and what he was expected to do was so much different than what he thought when he signed the contract.*

> *He was a product of the 'run and shoot offense', and this was more of structured setting. It was built on more structured routes and offenses. That's why he struggled so bad, because we were doing things so radically different than what he was used too. It just didn't work out...not because he wasn't a good player. Fans got mad because he was making all of that money."*

Heading into the 1995 regular season, they were picked by many pundits to be even better in the new season, and many in the national media had them reaching the Super Bowl. The Cleveland Indians baseball team were red hot and playing for the World Series title right down the block from the stadium, so Browns fans hoped that momentum would carry over.

The hype for the Cleveland Browns was at a high. It hadn't been that way since the late 1980s when the Browns were a staple of the NFL playoff scene. The players could feel the fans' excitement coming into the new season, and used it for motivation during some of those long days at training camp that Belichick was notorious for.

Leroy Hoard was one of the players who fed off the fans' passionate emotion and support. He is currently a sports radio host in Miami and explains the difference between Cleveland fans and other fans from around the country, including Miami:

"In Cleveland, you can be a fan and have four tickets to the game...the second you mention it, you have a packed car of people ready to go in minutes. It doesn't matter who they're playing, Cleveland Browns fans are passionate and ready. In Miami, you have to let them know who they're playing, what the weather is going to be like, and still having to pull teeth for fans to want to go."

Michael Jackson gives his thoughts on the hype surrounding the 1995 pre-season:

> *"The excitement of going to the playoffs and then getting picked to do well again in 1995 was awesome. We had just done something that we hadn't done since I had been there and since the '80s. All the players were very excited about the 1995 season heading into it. A lot of the former alumni were behind us...guys like Jim Brown and Doug Dieken giving us the full support really helped. These were legends that we looked up to and wanted to*

impress. It really helped with the overall experience. All the young guys were excited about that."

With the national media behind the Cleveland Browns for the first time in many years, and the hype behind the Andre Rison addition, the Browns' front office and fans were confident that this would be the season to end their long Super Bowl drought. Those dreams and hopes took an instant blow as the Browns looked flat in their season opening loss to the New England Patriots on the road. The Patriots were the same team that the Browns had beaten twice the prior season, including one of those wins coming in the playoffs. So, what was going on?

This game would be different than the two played during the 1994 regular season and playoffs. The Browns looked sluggish all day and could never seem to pull away despite building a 14–6 halftime lead on the strength of two Vinny Testaverde passes to Michael Jackson of seventy yards and thirty yards. The Browns only mustered up sixteen first downs all game, and it allowed Drew Bledsoe and the Patriots to make a good second-half comeback to beat the Browns 17–14. The Browns failed to score in the second half. The final blow came on the legs of Curtis Martin who scored a one yard touchdown late in the fourth quarter to seal the victory for the New England Patriots.

With all the pre-game hype and buildup regarding Andre Rison, it was Michael Jackson who did much of the work for the Browns as he caught seven passes for 157 yards and the two touchdowns. As for Rison, it was not a good debut in the orange and brown as he only caught two balls for fourteen yards. The running game never got off the ground either as Leroy Hoard was held to thirty-nine yards on nine carries. For his credit, Testaverde did play well as he went twenty of twenty-nine for 254 yards and two touchdowns with an interception. The problem for Testaverde was that the lack of a running game greatly hurt the team's ability to do anything in the second half. The presence of Nick Saban running the defense was also promptly felt as the Browns allowed Bledsoe to throw for 302 yards and not be able to sack or intercept him a single time.

The Browns returned home to Cleveland Municipal Stadium the following week for their home opener against the visiting Tampa

Bay Buccaneers. This was a big bounce-back game for the Browns as they were desperate to shake off their week one loss to the New England Patriots. It was also a big game for Vinny Testaverde as it was his first start against his former team, the team that gave up on him and considered him a huge draft-day bust.

After a scoreless first quarter, Testaverde got his revenge against his former team and led the Browns to a 22–6 rout of the Buccaneers. Testaverde looked sharp for the second week in a row with 256 yards and two touchdown passes to fourth string receiver Keenan McCardell. In the first two games, Testaverde had thrown four touchdowns with only one interception. He didn't seem fazed by the young and confident rookie Zeier waiting on the sidelines to take his position.

Leroy Hoard once again received the bulk of the carries, gaining forty-four yards on thirteen carries. The defense dominated the Tampa Bay offense all game long as they sacked quarterback Trent Dilfer seven times and picked him off twice. As for Andre Rison, he was once again held to only two catches, this time for a meager eighteen yards.

The Browns hoped to get on a roll the following week as they traveled to Houston, Texas to take on the Oilers in the Astrodome. It was a game dominated by defense that saw the Browns squeak by with a 14–7 victory. The Browns' offense was held to only fourteen first downs which led to eight Tom Tupa punts, but they made it stand up for the win with the help of some excellent defense once again.

Vinny Testaverde connected on two more touchdown passes to Keenan McCardell and Michael Jackson. Testaverde now had six touchdowns through three games with only one interception. None of the six touchdown tosses came to Andre Rison, however, as he was still struggling. Rison only caught one ball for fifteen yards against the Oilers, down one from his two-catch-a-game average since coming to the Browns. Leroy Hoard picked up the slack left behind from players such as Rison, and had another steady game out of the backfield. Hoard carried the ball twenty times for eighty-eight yards.

The Browns' defense continued to dominate for the second straight week. They intercepted Houston Oilers quarterback Will

Furrer four times. Three of those interceptions came from Stevon Moore. Despite the overall lack of offense, the Browns were now 2-1 and seemed to be headed on the right path.

All worries about the Browns' slow start on offense seemed to be quelled the following week as they beat the Kansas City Chiefs in Cleveland by a score of 35-17 and looked strong on both sides of the ball. Vinny Testaverde looked great, tossing two more touchdown passes and passing for 204 yards. He had now thrown eight touchdown passes and only one interception in the first four games. Through the first quarter of the season, Testaverde was putting up MVP type numbers.

Andre Rison finally showed some very small flashes of the talent that made him a star in Atlanta as he caught four balls for only thirty-five yards, but did have a touchdown in the win. The Browns even pulled off a bit of trickery as Tom Tupa converted a fake punt for a beautiful twenty-five yard pass completion. The Browns' defense continued to shine and be the driving force behind another win as linebackers Gerald Dixon and Mike Caldwell both picked off Kansas City Chiefs quarterback Steve Bono and returned them for touchdowns as part of a twenty-one point fourth-quarter explosion.

At 3-1, the Cleveland Browns looked to be exactly where they needed to be to make another serious run at the division title, and to go deep into the playoffs. They had outscored their three opponents in their victories by a score of 71-30. Testaverde was playing great, the defense seemed to be on track and wreaking havoc on all of their opponents. With the Cleveland Indians baseball team set to start their first round playoff series against the Boston Red Sox, their first playoff appearance in forty-one years, the city was abuzz with excitement over their two favorite sports teams. The excitement would continue to build as the Buffalo Bills were coming to Cleveland in week five to take on the Browns, which would be televised on ABC's *Monday Night Football*. With everything looking great and the goodwill in Cleveland sports at an all-time high for the fans, what could possibly go wrong in Browns town?

Chapter Eight

The Unthinkable Happens

Everything was looking great for the Browns and the city of Cleveland. That is...until things started to change for the worse. The Cleveland Browns lost to the Buffalo Bills on Monday night. Tied 19–19 with a mere five seconds left to go in the game, Browns fans watched in agony as Buffalo place kicker Steve Christie sailed a thirty-three yard field through the uprights to win the game for the Bills. It was sweet redemption for Christie who had missed both an extra point and a field goal earlier in the game.

With no running game to speak off, Testaverde continued to carry the Browns as he threw for 224 yards, but no touchdowns or interceptions. The Browns earned most of their scoring on four Matt Stover field goals, but it wasn't enough and their record fell to 3–2. The lone bright spot was Andre Rison who shined under the lights of national television with six catches for 126 yards.

It seemed quite peculiar that Rison waited until the nationally televised game to show up and play well. A fact that truly stood out the following week as Rison failed to show up in a game against the Detroit Lions in which the Browns were blown out 38–20 in one of their most embarrassing losses in years. Rison didn't catch a single pass that day and did nothing to help Cleveland avoid the embarrassing loss.

Vinny Testaverde was yanked midway through the crushing loss. He had thrown for 154 yards and a touchdown with no interceptions. It wasn't enough. Coach Belichick inserted the rookie Eric Zeier who threw for forty-six yards and a touchdown after the game was well out of reach. The once-stout Browns defense were soundly beaten as Barry Sanders rushed for 157 yards and three touchdowns against them. Scott Mitchell joined in the fun for Detroit with 273 yards and two touchdowns.

The pain continued the following week with their third straight loss, this time with a 23–15 defeat at the hands of the upstart expansion Jacksonville Jaguars. It was yet another lackluster effort from Andre Rison who continued to play terribly and only caught two passes for twenty-seven yards. It was official; the signing of Andre Rison was a giant mistake and epic letdown for the team.

Vinny Testaverde threw for 299 yards and tossed two interceptions in the loss. The Browns defense also continued to struggle as once again they couldn't stop the run. This week, it was Vaughn Dunbar rushing for ninety yards and a touchdown. It was also their rushing quarterback Mark Brunell scrambling for fifty-eight back-breaking yards. When a quarterback is running all over your defense that is a bad sign of things to come.

The once-promising Cleveland Browns were suddenly on the verge of collapse, as they had lost three straight games and were 3–4 on the season. In their next game, it took overtime, but they were finally able to snap loose from their three-game losing streak with a thrilling 29–26 win over the Bengals in Cincinnati. Eric Zeier started his first NFL game and played great. Zeier threw for 310 yards in his starting debut and tossed a seventeen yard touchdown pass to Andre Rison in the fourth quarter.

Andre Rison responded well to the switch at quarterback by having his best game of the season with seven catches for 179 yards. The whole team seemed to play better and benefit well from the switch at quarterback as four Browns running backs combined for 179 yards, and a touchdown on thirty-five carries. The star of the game, however, was place kicker Matt Stover who connected on five field goals, including one in overtime from twenty-eight yards to win the game. It was a crucial win that brought their record to even at 4–4. Hopefully, they could go on a run in the second half of the season and reach their potential and promise that so many people envisioned for them before the season began.

The Cleveland Browns stuck with Eric Zeier the following week at home against the visiting Houston Oilers, but things did not go as planned. The Browns' team came out flat and got crushed by the Oilers 37–10. Zeier threw three interceptions in the loss, and the Browns dropped to 4–5 on the season. Things were looking bleak for the once-promising and Super Bowl-bound Cleveland Browns, but in a matter of hours following their game loss, the worst and most unthinkable thing possible would occur. The culprit of the heinous act was someone who had been closer to the team than anyone for nearly half of a century.

Arthur B. Modell was born on June 23, 1925. He was born into a Jewish family living in Brooklyn, New York. His father George was a once prominent wine salesman, until the fatal stock market crash of 1929, when his business failed miserably as result of the crash. His father passed away when Art was only fourteen years of age. This horrible tragedy forced the young Modell to drop out of school to get a job and support his family. He came from humble beginnings, making ends meet by cleaning the hulls of ship yards. It was also at this young age that Modell learned to do whatever necessary to survive in any situation.

Modell was a true patriot and loved his country; he showed as much when he turned eighteen by joining the United States Army Air Corps. He left the military following the completion of World War II. The young and ambitious Modell decided to enroll in a New York City television school with the help of the GI Bill. This showed his ability to make the most of an opportunity to cash in, and any money thrown his way. He began his first foray into ownership when he went on to form his own production company with a fellow student in 1947. Only two years into the business, Modell was quickly met with success when in 1949, they produced one of the first daytime shows in the country, Market Melodies. It was a show dedicated to cooking and decorating. In 1954, using the lucrative Grand Union account as leverage, he was hired as a senior account executive at the advertising company L.H. Hartman Co. in New York City, eventually becoming a partner. Modell continued to expand and grow his brand, fifty years before these terms were used on as frequent of a basis as today.

His passion for ownership and taking control of business ventures grew even more as he spent the majority of the 1950s working in public relations and television production in New York City. He wanted to get his hands on as many things as possible and see how every aspect of television and marketing worked. He had a bigger plan in mind all along. It was in 1961 that Modell took his love of business and put that same passion into sports. With the accompaniment of a few others, he purchased the Cleveland Browns football team. He borrowed nearly three million dollars, and found partners to cover the rest of the purchase. The Browns were already a very successful franchise at this point with an incredible head coach, and the investment was a sound one for Modell and his associates.

It didn't take Modell long into his time in ownership to anger fans and cause havoc in the organization. Original Coach Paul Brown had already led the Cleveland Browns to eleven straight title games, but that wasn't good enough for Art Modell. In an immediate power play, Modell fired Brown on January 9, 1964. It was done in the middle of a newspaper strike and went down as one of the most cowardly and shocking moments in Cleveland's sports history. After firing Paul Brown, Modell quickly named Brown's assistant, Blanton Collier, as the new coach on January 16, 1964. Paul Brown had lost control of the team because of Jim Brown's horrible antics in the locker room that caused turmoil. Instead of sticking by the legendary coach, Modell sided with the player and fired one of the greatest coaches in the history of sports. Jim Brown may have been one of the best to ever play the game, but his influence on the Cleveland Browns was the biggest reason that they would never again be the dominant franchise they once were.

Fans were irate and players who loved Paul Brown were confused, but Modell was brash and determined to do things his way. In 1964, the Browns finished 10–3–1 and appeared in the 1964 NFL Championship Game against a heavily favored Don Shula-coached Baltimore Colts team. The Browns beat the Colts 27–0 at home in Cleveland Municipal Stadium. This particular Browns' team consisted of many players initially drafted and acquired by Paul Brown. Thus, in actuality, it was Paul Brown's team that won the championship, not the newly appointed owner, Art Modell.

Over the next thirty years in Cleveland, not a single Modell team won the league title. Prior to Modell's arrival, the Browns had dominated the NFL and the AAFC, winning seven championships in seventeen years. They fired a proven winner in Paul Brown, and Modell slowly began to run the team down the tubes after that.

Despite the chaos that Modell was creating in Cleveland, he was doing positives for the NFL as a whole. He carried with him a past talent for promotions and used that skill to start many new innovations in the NFL. He began by scheduling pro football pre-season doubleheaders at Cleveland Municipal Stadium. He was a genius when it came to using his assets to create more money. Modell didn't hesitate to provide his team as an opponent for both the first prime time Thanksgiving game in 1966, and the opening *Monday Night Football* broadcast in 1970. Many historians give Modell full credit for inventing Monday Night Football.

He continued to live the life of glamour and power when he married Patricia Breslin in 1969. Modell took an active role in the Cleveland community life and was a leader in fundraising for numerous charities. He also got behind and financially supported various Republican Party candidates. He made sure to be a man around town and place his mark on many things. Despite all the mistakes he would go on to make in his career, no one can ever dispute his passion for what he did and his true commitment to the community. It was, however, only a matter of time before his love of the almighty dollar took control over most, if not all, of his decisions.

He was also no stranger to controversy. In 1967, five African-American members of the Cleveland Browns team who were involved in a contract dispute refused to report to training camp. Modell eventually traded or released four of those players, with only standout running back Leroy Kelly remaining. It was yet another sign that Modell was slowly starting to anger fans and players alike. Quite frankly, he didn't care who he was going to piss off and he was going to do things his way. The irony was, Modell didn't stand up to Jim Brown and his trouble-making ways because he was afraid of the ongoing Civil Rights Movement at the time; instead, he chose to fire the white coach. This time around, he simply did not care; if he could save a nickel, he was going to do it and the hell with anyone else.

In 1973, Art Modell signed a twenty-five year lease to operate Cleveland Stadium. Modell's newly formed company, Stadium Corporation, assumed the expenses of operations from the City of Cleveland, freeing up tax dollars for other purposes. Modell would pay an annual rent of $150,000 for the first five years and $200,000 afterwards to the city. In exchange, Modell would receive all revenue generated by the stadium. This was a giant steal for Modell when you factor in all the things that generated money for the stadium. Not only did they have a major league baseball team playing there, the Cleveland Indians, but when you factor in the countless concerts and other entertainment events at the stadium, this deal was huge. Stadium Corporation invested in improvements, including new electronic scoreboards and luxury suites. It didn't take Modell long to piss off the Cleveland Indians' ownership as he did not share a portion of revenues earned from baseball games with the Indians. He was very greedy and wanted to keep every dime for himself. However, at the same time, he was the only one paying the yearly rent of $150,000 plus operation expenses; so, I'm not sure how much he was in the wrong, if at all, not to share the revenue.

In 1979, Modell was once again the centerpiece of controversy when Stadium Corporation and himself were implicated in a lawsuit brought by Cleveland Browns minority shareholder Robert Gries of Gries Sports Enterprises, who successfully alleged that Stadium Corporation manipulated the Cleveland Browns' accounting records to help Stadium Corporation and Modell absorb a loss on real estate property that had been purchased in the Cleveland suburb of Strongsville as a potential site for a new stadium. It was becoming quite clear that Art Modell was not an honest human being.

Despite the Cleveland Browns team's recent success in the mid to late 1980s, Modell continued to claim that he was losing money. He allowed the stadium to be rented out for the Belkin Concert Series ran by Jules Belkin. The World Series of Rock was a recurring, day-long and usually multi-act summer rock concert held outdoors at Cleveland Stadium in Cleveland, Ohio from 1974 through 1980. It was popular enough to drive in 88,000 fans at times. This should have helped Modell generate money for the stadium, however, he mainly complained that it tore up his field. Stadium officials allowed fans to congregate near the stage on the playing field, which required fixing the turf before the Cleveland Indians returned home. After the 1975 football season, groundskeepers completely resurfaced the field, and installed a drainage system, to repair damage from the rock concerts. This, too, cost Modell even more money that he wasn't happy to be spending. It seemed at times that he was fine with collecting the money from the revenue the events brought in, but never too happy about having to spend money on the improvements and repairs to the stadium that the events would cause.

By the time Art Modell hired Bill Belichick as coach, he continued to lose money. Despite the solid attendance, the team was losing and he was scrapping to find money to repair the fields and stands. Things went from bad to worse for Modell when in May 1990, the Cuyahoga County voters approved a fifteen year "sin tax" on alcohol and cigarette sales to finance the new Gateway Sports and Entertainment Complex. Construction began eighteen months later, and the new era in Cleveland baseball began on the corner of Carnegie and Ontario in downtown Cleveland. Modell had now lost his biggest tenant and was left to occupy the aging building by himself as most concerts would move into the Gun Arena, and not be held at the stadium. Modell quickly went to the city to complain and try to get the money to repair his stadium or get a brand new stadium.

Stadium Corporation's suite revenues declined sharply when the Cleveland Indians moved from the stadium to Jacobs Field in 1994. Combined with rising player costs and deficits, it contributed to Modell's financial issues. Modell lost twenty-one million dollars between 1993 and 1994. When Modell realized how much revenue he had lost from the Indians moving out of Cleveland Stadium, he requested an issue be placed on the ballot to provide $175 million in tax dollars to refurbish the outmoded and declining Cleveland Stadium. His request was denied, and things just continued to get worse.

This is where the biggest disagreement comes from with many fans and media who were familiar with the situation at the time. The fans and residents of Cleveland, Ohio were not obligated to spend their tax dollars on re-building an aging Cleveland Municipal Stadium, or even having the money spent on a new stadium. The issue with Modell was that he saw all the funding from the tax payers going towards the Cavs and Indians, to both get brand new facilities, and yet, his franchise was being left in the cold. Fans and media alike can argue about this for the next one hundred years, but the bottom line is, Modell was pissed off because he saw the other two teams in town get treated like royalty and his beloved Browns left to scrap for themselves. If the City of Cleveland and its tax payers would have agreed to build him a new home, or fix the current stadium, who knows if what was soon to happen, would have actually occurred.

The City of Cleveland was in a state of resurgence as they gave a total rebirth to the downtown area. They built two beautiful new venues and left out Art Modell and the Cleveland Browns football team. His overall fan rating continued to plummet as well as he allowed Bill Belichick to cut fan favorite quarterback Bernie Kosar from the team. The Browns couldn't seem to do anything right as they missed the playoffs for the fourth straight year after cutting Kosar. Despite finally returning to the playoffs in 1994, Modell was just about tapped out of funds when the City of Baltimore came calling with an offer he couldn't refuse.

Art Modell poses with these little Browns fans.
Photo courtesy of Anna DeLuca

It was then that the unthinkable happened as Modell still had time left on his lease but chose to ignore that and make the decision that no one saw coming, and stunned not only the Cleveland sports fans, but the entire sporting world. The Cleveland Browns were a staple of the NFL and had one of the strongest fan bases in all of sports. However, none of that mattered to Modell as it was time to put his checkbook and own personal financial security in front of all loyalty and common sense.

Modell announced on November 6, 1995 that he had signed a deal to relocate the Browns from Cleveland, Ohio to Baltimore, Maryland in 1996. The very next day, on November 7, 1995, Cleveland voters overwhelmingly approved an issue that had been placed on the ballot at Modell's request, before he made his decision to move the franchise, which would provide $175 million in tax dollars to refurbish the outdated and declining Cleveland Municipal Stadium. The tax bill being passed was not enough to convince Modell to stay. It was too little too late, as Modell had his mind made up. He was pissed that the City of Cleveland had given the Indians and Cavs a new home, and had left him out; this last second show of attention to the Browns was not enough to keep him or the Browns in Cleveland.

Art Modell made the announcement that shocked the sports world. He was moving one of the most beloved sports franchises in the history of sports away from their home city and the most passionate fans on planet earth. Art Modell held a press conference in Baltimore, Maryland to announce that he was leaving the City of Cleveland, and taking the Browns with him to their new home the following season in Baltimore. The sports world stood in shock, and Cleveland Browns' fans both past and present, sorrowed in shocked sadness. It was the bitter end of a reign of terror that began nearly fifty years earlier when Modell originally bought the team.

Ed Sutter, defensive team member for several years at that point, gives his initial reaction to hearing the news:

> *"I thought it was impossible to move the Cleveland Browns, and everyone scoffed at the possibility, until Art Modell came into our team meeting after eight games and announced his decision. I was completely shocked and disappointed. Pro players do not*

expect to stay in the same city for long, but I had been in Cleveland for four years, and grew close to my teammates as well as friends I had met off the field, including my wife. Art asked us at that meeting to do him a favor and go out and win the rest of our games...we promptly went out and lost all but one. I have friends in Cleveland to this day that used be huge fans, Dog Pound season ticket holders, etcetera that now only passively follow the team. I don't think that scar will ever fully heal. It was truly wonderful how the fans of Cleveland would support the players. No matter how down the city was on the owners and coaches, they were always so eager to encourage and support the players. As a player, I took great pride in playing for the Cleveland Browns."

Cleveland Browns alumni and former standout receiver Brian Brennan shares his reaction to hearing the news of his beloved Cleveland Browns moving:

"I was shocked. Most of us had kids and still lived in Cleveland after our playing career was done, and I always thought it would be nice to raise them up as Browns fans. I wanted my son, Brian Jr., to know about the team his father played on. I wanted him to know the history of the team and things of that nature. It was disbelief in a sense that I thought people were joking...there was just no way the NFL could move the Cleveland Browns away from Cleveland. There was no way the Browns could ever leave this fan base and the history of the team. The fabric of the fans that followed the team was so diverse...it didn't matter if they were white collar or blue collar, everyone loved the Browns. From a personal standpoint, it was devastating to hear the news.

From a business standpoint, it was hard to understand why...but I guess when you examine it further you'll find out that Art got a sweetheart deal. I think that Mayor White could have done a better job beforehand taking care of Art Modell and the Cleveland Browns organization when they built Gateway. They focused their efforts on the Indians and Cavaliers, and Art was not too happy about it."

Matt Stover, who had lived in Strongsville, Ohio, just a stone's throw from Fran Morino, made a home for himself in the Cleveland area and was not happy upon hearing about the move:

> *"That move and the announcement of that move came as a surprise. I loved Cleveland and the Cleveland fans, so did my wife. I was able to understand the business side of it and the issues Art Modell was having with cash flow. He had to take out a loan from the bank just to fill the salary commitment he made to Rison for five million dollars. The salary caps and collective bargaining were different, and the amount of money around the NFL hurt him as well. It didn't help matters that Cleveland was making moves to build a new arena and stadium for the Cavs and Indians along with a Rock and Roll Hall of Fame, and new science center and yet they ignored helping Modell with his aging stadium. Art had made some personal decisions that created an issue and chose to do what was best for his family going forward."*

Cleveland Browns alumni George Lilja wasn't shy when giving his thoughts about Modell moving the team out of Cleveland:

> *"My favorite team to play for in the NFL was the Cleveland Browns because I got to play in front of passionate fans in a great city. My kids grew up in Cleveland so all they knew was Cleveland Browns football when it came to the NFL. I felt I had such a special connection to Cleveland and that Cleveland Browns team. It was painful to hear that there would be Sundays in the fall without Browns football. It was devastating. I went to the last game when fans were ripping the seats from out of the stadium; I had brought two of my kids with me as well. You could feel the frustration of the fans as it was a sad day! It was hard to accept and clearly the NFL never anticipated the outcry of the fan base and if it wasn't for that base and the way they reacted to it, we wouldn't have a team today.*
>
> *Los Angeles, where I played with the Rams, still doesn't have a team and that is a huge media base. I will always have passion for the Browns fans and the entire city of Cleveland. They really are my sports family because of just the passion they had and how fun it was to play for people like that."*

If George Lilja's words are true, and the NFL really didn't realize that the backlash coming from the fans would occur, then they were more out of touch with common sense and reality than Art Modell was. How could they not expect the fans reaction to be anything other than irate?

Leroy Hoard discusses the giant letdown of the move:

"The team moved in the middle of the year in true Cleveland fashion...at one point, we were still okay with an above five hundred record. We, as players, were getting hounded by reporters as to why the team was moving...we had no idea...I couldn't explain it. It became a giant distraction and that was unfortunate. The most unfortunate thing about the whole ordeal was Bill Belichick lost his job. Think about that...he went from the playoffs to losing his job. How many four-time Super Bowl winners have gotten fired?

The fans and city officials were in an outrage, as their beloved Cleveland Browns were about to leave town, and leave the city void of football altogether. Virtually, all of the team's sponsors pulled their support, leaving Cleveland Stadium devoid of advertising during the team's final weeks. Cleveland filed an injunction to keep the Browns in the city until at least 1998, while several other lawsuits were filed by fans and ticket holders. Despite all the rallies by protests and city officials, it simply didn't matter as the NFL was not about to block the move.

Current Browns network host Vic Travagliante was just a little boy at the time, but has vivid memories about one of the darkest times of being an avid Browns fan:

"I remember being very confused. I was a die-hard Browns fan and when the move was announced I wasn't even ten years old. I didn't understand what was going on! My family explained to me what 'The Move' meant and the fact that there was going to be no football in Cleveland. That's when I remember crying. As a child you do not comprehend matters as clear as you do as an adult and I was lost. My tears were not just about football, they were about spending time in the front yard with my older brothers before games and going to my grandparents' house for some games. Playing video games with my cousin Phil and learning what it was about to be a true football fan.

I was crushed! My mother could tell you that I called the NFL offices in New York every day or every other day for weeks and ran up a very large long distance phone bill for her. She realized how much I was hurt and what the Browns meant to me and our family. I tried my best, as much as a nine year old can, to voice my opinion. I stayed up some nights making signs and posters to hang on our front windows. Some teachers who saw them when they passed the house told me it looked like I spent more time on those than I did my actual homework. The move is definitely one of the memories I have as a child and it's not pleasant.

Looking back now at the events and being in the media, I do understand why it happened. At the end of the day, each of the men that were involved in 'the move' were businessmen. Art Modell felt cheated by the city in terms of the Gateway project and not wanting to share certain revenue with the Cleveland Indians and he wanted things done to Municipal Stadium. The main reason I believe Modell took the team to Baltimore was because he felt the city would build him a state-of-the-art stadium. With that being said, I know that Cleveland voters approved an issue that had been placed on the ballot at Modell's request, before he made his decision to move the team. I remember the lawsuits that were filed by fans and even the City of Cleveland. It was a very odd time to be a Browns fan."

Cleveland finally caught a break and accepted a settlement that would still allow the team to move to Baltimore, but they were able to keep the rights to the team's name and the colors. On February 9, 1996, the NFL announced that the Cleveland Browns would be 'deactivated' for three years, and that a new stadium would be built for a new Browns team, as either an expansion team or a team relocated from another city, that would begin play in 1999. Modell would in turn then be granted a new franchise for Baltimore, retaining the current contracts of players and personnel. There would be a reactivated team for Cleveland, where the Browns' name, colors, history, records, awards, and archives would remain in Cleveland. This turned out to be an expansion team thrown at Cleveland at almost the last notice, which allowed them to never truly get things off the ground in the way other expansion teams were allowed to. A major reason that the new Browns team would get off to a horrible start, and still have never truly recovered twenty years later.

Tommy Vardell was still with the Cleveland Browns at the time of the announcement and shares his feelings towards all of the drama, including why he thinks it happened:

"This was extraordinarily difficult playing during this time. We effectively had a sixteen game season of away games. In fact, there were fewer boos in Pittsburgh stadium than there were at home. Every game was greeted with a roar of boos when this was announced. And the players knew that the fans weren't booing the players, but it still made for a difficult environment. And this definitely impacted our performance."

Tommy Vardell goes on to explain that NFL owners look at football as strictly a business and that is why the move happened:

"All business...and remember, in business there is often no loyalty."

Michael Jackson gives his take on what happened and the shock of it all:

"Art Modell had made the decision to move the team from Cleveland to Baltimore...and with that, the air went out of our sales because the players were getting held at fault for that decision as opposed to just Art Modell who made the actual decision. The fans were against us...we felt that everyone was against the Browns at that time. It sucked! It was like having another death in the family after it took us long to get over Bernie Kosar being cut two years prior.

What could we do? We wanted to have the support of the fans and all of that, but the fans were about being angry at the big picture...what I call the parent company. We were just the workers within the organization but yet we were going to take the heat for it. So now when the fans are booing the corporate structure of the team, it's us the players that are forced unfairly to take the direct hit. So now us, as players, feel like we're being let down by the fans. They didn't understand that we weren't making the move. We were just the worker bees...we were not the whole hive!

The decision to move the team was on someone else, not us. What can we do? We can't quit. Are we going to be able to get a job that will pay us the kind of money that we make as members of a pro football team? We would have loved to stay in Cleveland, but what were we going to do? It wasn't like we could quit playing football because we were mad at Art Modell, just to stay in

Cleveland and work at McDonald's or Burger King instead of playing for him. We had to make a decision for our families.

The decision was to move with the team and ownership. These are the types of things I tried to tell the fans at the time...we couldn't quit and just not play...we had families to feed and had to move to Baltimore. Now, I can't justify Art Modell's decision to move the company, but it had nothing to do with the players so the fans shouldn't give them any grief for it. The players were there for the fans because the fans were our motivation. The fans started to dislike the entire organization, which effected the players overall morale. The move to Baltimore was a blessing in disguise for people like myself who had the chance to prove themselves once again. I felt like a rookie my first season with the Ravens, it was a chance for a fresh start. We knew we could come right in and make an immediate impact! I jumped in the city feet first and put my own marketing plan together."

As a fan at the time, I truly believe no one blamed the players. If anything, we booed because we were angry at the franchise's ownership. No one with any basic understanding of business or common sense blamed the players. I don't think anyone, who has worked a day in their lives to support their family, would expect professional athletes making millions of dollars playing a game to quit their job. The even slightest thought of that is beyond asinine, and I was blown away to hear Jackson mention that.

Reggie Langhorne, former wide receiver, and beloved Cleveland Brown Alumni shares his reaction to hearing the news:

"Two things happened in Cleveland that I just couldn't believe... the first was Bernie Kosar being cut. The other one was when Eric Metcalf called me and said the Browns were going to be moving. I thought that there was no way the City of Cleveland would be losing a football team...it just didn't even compute to me that it would be possible for this city to lose their football team. That was the biggest disappointment for me as a player who loved this city...I still live in this city. It didn't seem possible or sensible enough to even consider moving the team away.

Langhorne goes on to explain why he believed it happened:

"I have heard it nineteen different ways as there was a lot of blame to go around and numerous people who dropped the ball. All I know is that it was a matter of money. Big business is usually a matter of money and those who had it ended up getting their way. The fans here have been great to us, and a lot of that was because of how Art Modell taught us to act. He made sure we were a part of the community and helped out with charities on our days off. He was a big reason why we were in contact with fans and made us aware of how important it was to sign autographs on the way into games and after games despite winning or losing.

We got involved with hospitals and youth programs...he was teaching young men how to love this city back because the fans were so supportive. Art did a lot of great things for this city. Sadly, he found himself in a position that was beneficiary for his wallet and the gentleman who had the money got what he wanted. That's just business...that's how politics can go. He made a mistake in the eyes of many. The city didn't want to build him a new stadium or so the stories go. I don't know what was going on behind closed doors...I just know this, the guy with the most money won!"

Ex-Cleveland Browns safety Felix Wright shares his thoughts on the move:

"I was disappointed to hear the news because they were the team that brought me into the league. To not have football in Cleveland was just really weird. It was going to be weird for me and all of the fans. I think all the retired guys were just shocked and besides ourselves. We were in shock just like everyone else was. It was very tough and out of our hands. It had to do with Art Modell and the city council. I thought the City of Cleveland kind of dropped the ball.

I was upset at Art Modell for moving the team, but as a business person, I can't say I wouldn't have made the same move. Everyone in the city was getting new stadiums and he wasn't when he needed one, then I can see why he got upset. If people put themselves in Art Modell's situation in business, they would probably see it a little different. But, when you talk about moving a football team everyone grew up with and cherished, you don't

> *really care, you just want your team! I was sad because of the situation, but I wasn't mad at Art Modell...I was disappointed at the City of Cleveland for allowing it. They dropped the ball in not taking care of business to keep their team in town. I think that is the only way a city loses a sports franchise if the city council and the government doesn't take care of the team to keep them there. They would have never left if Modell felt the City of Cleveland officials were being fair about matters. If this city would have just taken care of business, then maybe Art would have stayed. Why did we have to lose a team just to build a stadium? We could have built a stadium and kept the Browns, instead of having to wait for three years. It is what it is I guess. It's kind of sad that we still have to talk about the eighties because we are two decades past it now. We need to start some more history."*

Ex-punter Brian Hansen wasn't with the team at the time, but was still in the league and recalls his reaction to hearing of the news:

> *"I was shocked to hear the news! I wasn't sure what was behind the decision. I was glad that they eventually got to keep their names and colors."*

Tight end Brian Kinchen, who was a member of the team at the time, gives his reflections on the horrible time in Cleveland Browns' history:

> *"It was so unusual. Basically, we had no home once it happened. My most vivid memory of that season is when we were hosting the Pittsburgh Steelers and our fans were cheering the Steelers and booing us. In my mind, that sticks out the most as to how I remember that entire year. It was frustrating and disheartening... just every cliché you can think about it we had to go through. The whole reason I started playing football is because I wanted to prove to people that I was good enough to achieve something and I was always looking for that validation. It was my basic nature to want to be approved and liked by the fans. I wanted the fans to see the hard work that not only I was putting out but also my teammates.*
>
> *There is really nothing that matches that feel on Sundays in the NFL when you're playing at the highest level in the sport. No one*

was cheering for us, and it had nothing to do with you or your team...but it was all because of one man deciding to move the team and make more money for himself. It just made it the most miserable season of my life. I would have to believe that everyone would have to agree with that statement. We were literally looking around and wondering if this was really happening. We just kept telling ourselves 'this can't be really happening'. It was the longest, most miserable, unfulfilling season any player could ever have. I wouldn't wish that on anyone. I had been there for four years and the fan base in Cleveland was the best in the sport! It didn't matter where we played...we would travel anywhere, and Cleveland Browns fans were waiting for us to get off the bus in droves, cheering and screaming our names in approval. We went from that pure love to disaster. The fan base was everywhere; they were large and loved their Browns unlike any team in any other sport. For Art Modell to rip the team away from them seemed so bizarre and wrong. It was almost surreal...it just didn't seem like reality."

Leroy Hoard discusses the passion of the fans:

"Years later, I came in to play the first game at the new Browns stadium as a member of the visiting Minnesota Vikings. I scored a touchdown and you would swear at that moment that I still played for the Browns with the way the fans treated me. It was cool and unexpected. As long as I have been away from Cleveland, I still come back three times a year and don't have a single bad thing to say about the city and the fans. I wish I could take every person from Cleveland and bring them down here into the sun because they would have a blast.

I have been very fortunate to play in the Big Ten, which was a madhouse. I got to play in Cleveland, which was a madhouse. I have been very lucky to have the luxury of playing in front of fans all over the country. I have played in two of the best places as far as fans are concerned. There is no better football than Midwest football...there is not! People in Cleveland are hard working and down to earth; they are a blue collar bunch that gets through the work week by thinking about football on Sunday. They just want to see their football team work as hard as they do. I appreciated how great the fans were. I was real lucky that my style of football was able to go well wherever I went. When I visit Cleveland, I try to say 'hi' to as many people as I can. I still love coming up there and make sure to take my family up there as well. I take my family to games so they can see what real fans look like. I even told my dad, 'You can't experience a Cleveland game until you go to one in December'. So I took him to the last game of the season a few years ago, and it was the coldest game ever in the new stadium. That's Cleveland football! I was very lucky that I had the pleasure of playing in Cleveland with a bunch of other guys who also understood the honor and importance of playing in Cleveland!"

The Cleveland Browns did their best to try and focus on football despite the unfolding horror all around them but it was almost impossible as every game felt like a nightmare. The next game after the move was announced was televised on *Monday Night Football* in Pittsburgh against the Steelers. Many fans from Cleveland even traveled to the game with signs protesting the move with anti-NFL signs, but the ABC network refused to show the crowd on television a single time throughout the game.

The game itself was a dud as the Browns met with defeat yet again; this time not even being able to score a touchdown in the 20–3 loss. Eric Zeier was seven of nineteen passing for only sixty-seven yards and an interception. Any hopes of him being the quarterback of the future were quickly fading. It was also another disappointing game for the gigantic bust known as Andre Rison who was held to only two catches for twenty-two yards total.

The Browns headed back home after the loss to prepare for their first game in front of their hometown fans after the announcement of the move to play against the Green Bay Packers. Lifelong Browns fan Frankie McMasters was only in the eighth grade at the time, but recalls being at the Green Bay game and just how hard it was:

"I remember my last Browns game at the Old Cleveland Municipal Stadium. It was a game in mid-late November 1995 against the upcoming Green Bay Packers. I had gotten the tickets a few days earlier from my parents as an early birthday present. I remember my parents asking me if I still wanted to go, with the impending move on the horizon. I said, 'Yes, I want to go'. I

remember vividly the moment the Browns emerged from the first base dugout and my eyes began to tear up, because I knew this was the last time I would see my Browns in person."

It felt like an away game for the Browns' players as the crowd was angry with Modell and the entire situation, so they decided to boo the entire game no matter who had the ball. The hostility from the crowd didn't help the already struggling Browns team who let Green Bay build a 24-6 lead after three quarters. Despite a Vinny Testaverde-led comeback off the bench in the fourth quarter, the Browns still didn't win, as they dropped to 4-7 with the 31-20 loss to Brett Favre and the Green Bay Packers.

Emotions boiled over in the locker room following the loss to Green Bay, as Andre Rison was booed loudly throughout the game due to his horrid play on the field after signing the giant off-season contract. When asked about the booing caused from the emotion of the fans who were not only heartbroken from the team moving to Baltimore but also Rison's poor play, Andre did not hold back with his comments:

"We didn't make the fucking move. So, for all the booers, fuck you, too. I'll be glad when we get to Baltimore...if that's the case. We don't have any home-field advantage. I've never been booed at home. Baltimore's our home. Baltimore, here we come."

Things went from bad to worse the following week as the Pittsburgh Steelers visited Cleveland and handed the Browns their fourth straight loss, and their seventh loss in eight games by a score of 20-17. The truly sad thing was the fact that the Browns' players were booed all game again, this time even against their hated rivals. It was unthinkable that such a vile act could ever occur, but the Browns fans felt betrayed and made their disgust vocal.

Their season of dreams had turned into a truly nightmarish situation, and that fact was never more evident the following week with another pathetic loss, this time coming in San Diego against the Chargers. With less than five seconds left on the clock, the Browns were getting clobbered 31-10 and everyone involved just wanted to let the last few seconds tick off the clock. Then, Belichick did the unthinkable himself by calling a time out. It made no sense, they were in field goal range, but being down twenty-one points, a three-point field goal would do no good. Bill Belichick didn't care and sent Matt Stover to the field to kick for three.

At the time, it seemed like one of the dumbest moves in the history of organized professional sports, but as Matt Stover explains here, the move was done out of kindness from Belichick for Matt Stover:

> *"The week before that game, we had left Cleveland to go practice in San Diego and get away from it all. We just left town because there was no constructive environment for us in Cleveland. I owe Bill Belichick my NFL career without question because he is a loyal guy if you get to know what is underneath. He is for the players and he is for you. He wants to bless the guys around him and wants to make everyone winners.*
>
> *At the time of the San Diego game, I was having a really good season that year as one of the few shining things that was going on with that team at the time. I had a chance to make the Pro Bowl because of my numbers, and I needed to keep improving on my numbers to get more Pro Bowl votes. We were getting our asses kicked in that game and were not going to win, so he knew that he could do something good for me and let me get that kick so I could pad my numbers even more. He never actually told me...but for him to call a field goal in the final seconds of a twenty-one point deficit shows what kind of great man and coach that he is.*
>
> *That was a 'wow' moment. I'll never forget that Steve Everitt threw a really high snap on that one, and Tom Tupa did a masterful job of getting the ball down and placed perfectly so I could make the kick. I remember I looked at Tom and said, 'Dear God, am I glad I made that kick'. I was taken aback by the gesture of Belichick to allow me to pad my numbers. It shows you that he had enough guts to do it. He got criticized by the media for doing it, but he knew that was all that mattered."*

Even with the act of kindness shown by Belichick, it still couldn't change the emotion of the fans who were still engulfed in a mixture of sadness and anger towards their beloved Browns' impending departure for Baltimore. As bad as the fans felt, the players were performing worse on the field because of the constant booing and feeling as if they no longer had a home. Most of them hoped the season would end quickly so they could just get to Baltimore and away from all of the drama.

The losing continued the following week on the road against the Minnesota Vikings in the Metrodome as the Cleveland Browns were beaten 27-11. The Browns continued to play multiple quarterbacks in the hopes of doing anything to stop their losing streak. Vinny Testaverde went five of six for fifty-four yards while Eric Zeier continued to go from draft day steal to draft day gigantic bust by throwing four more interceptions in the loss. Andre Rison continued to make everyone wonder if his career was over with, and had one catch. He was a shell of his former self and it showed every time Rison took the field. He was one of the few players who couldn't blame the fans booing and the distraction of the move, because he was playing horrible even before all of that happened.

With a 4-10 record, the Browns just wanted the miserable season to end, but not before having one last chance to say good-bye to the fans who actually remained loyal to the players. Their last home game was December 17, 1995 against the Cincinnati Bengals. The box score will tell you that the Cleveland Browns won 26-10 on the strength of four Matt Stover field goals and two Vinny Testaverde touchdown passes, but honestly, none of that even mattered. It was an emotional good-bye for both the fans and players. Despite the craziness of fans ripping their actual seats from the stadium and taking them home, emotions continued to range from anger to sadness as most fans were seen crying throughout the game.

After their game victory, most of the players went into the crowd and shared emotional hugs with the fans. Players like Earnest Byner ran a lap around the parameter of the field, trying to interact with as many fans as possible, giving them a personal good-bye and thank you. All hard feelings towards Byner for the fumble seemed to be forgotten and forgiven. A few weeks later, when the emotions of the final home game simmered down, fans once again released his fumble in the AFC Championship Game in Denver, which will forever outweigh anything he ever does again, in terms of impact. His fumble will forever stand the test of time as one of the biggest mistakes in the history of modern day sports.

Lifelong Browns fan Dr. John Reese was there for that final game and remembers the emotions of the crowd during the final contest:

> *"I remember people tearing out the seats and some were caught on fire...very surly mood as the town was in a fighting mood and people spent the next week jamming the NFL phone lines and clogging their fax machines...that went on for WEEKS until the NFL promised to give us a team back with our colors and history."*

Lifelong Cleveland sports fan Suzy Beatrice was also at the final game, and had these memories to share about that sad day:

> *"We met our usual group of friends at the Pewter Mug inside the stadium. I'm pretty sure it was on the upper level. At the time, my dad owned the season tickets as he had since moving to Cleveland in 1965. The entire mood was festive but muted. We usually had our fair share of beers and other adult beverages. The most memorable thing was what occurred after the game. Many fans brought wrenches and tools to dismantle and take their seats with them. We settled for a photograph of the seats in the upper deck in section thirty, row G. Art Modell effigies were everywhere of course. It was just sad. I had been going to games there since I was in grade school with my dad. We rode the rapid down to every game and it is one of the best memories of my dad."*

The Cleveland Browns would lose the following week, once again to the upstart expansion Jacksonville Jaguars. This time by a score of 24–21 on a last second field goal by Jacksonville kicker Mike Hollis. Despite the loss, in a weird way, many fans and players secretly hoped the kick would go through; no one was excited for a game to possibly go into overtime between one of the worst teams in the league and a team that just wanted their nightmare 1995 season to finally end. It was almost as if the football gods made sure the kick went through, ending the pain. Andre Rison finished the season with another stellar performance, earning every penny of his massive contract by catching exactly one ball that day.

The season of nightmares came to a merciful end that day in Jacksonville, Florida as the Cleveland Browns finished 5–11, in fourth place in the AFC Central Division. It was a far cry from the

Super Bowl aspirations they once held. The offense had the fifth worst overall scoring performance as they only scored 289 points all season. The defense allowed 356 points; it was a season differential of sixty-seven points, their worst in years. Clearly, Defensive Coordinator Steve Venturi was unable to have the success that Nick Saban did.

Despite the Cleveland Browns' overall performance, and not being as good as hoped for, certain players still had a season to be proud of. Vinny Testaverde threw for 2,883 yards and seventeen touchdowns with only ten interceptions. They were actually better numbers than he had in the playoff season. The backup Eric Zeier, who everyone thought would eventually take over the job, had a horrible season in his chances to play. He finished with a putrid 864 yards, four touchdowns and nine interceptions. Leroy Hoard once again led the team in rushing yards, this time with 547 yards despite not scoring a single rushing touchdown all year. Hoard did his best though, all things considered. Tommy Vardell battled injuries, and only played in five games, getting four carries for nine yards.

Michael Jackson led the team in receiving yards with 714 yards on forty-four catches as well as scoring a team high of nine touchdowns. Previously unknown Keenan McCardell stepped it up to have a big year with 709 yards on a team high of fifty-six catches with four touchdowns. As for Andre Rison—the guy who was supposed to lead the Browns into the promise land—well, things didn't go exactly as planned as he only caught forty-seven balls and found the end zone just three times. The person who felt the biggest backlash from Andre Rison joining the team was second year starter Derrick Alexander. After a great rookie season, there seemed to be no room for Alexander with Rison in the lineup, and Alexander had a huge drop-off in his second year, being held to fifteen catches for 216 yards and zero receiving touchdowns. He did have a punt return for a touchdown for his one and only highlight.

As mentioned earlier, Matt Stover had one of the best seasons of his career as he made twenty-nine of thirty-three field goals. Eight of his field goal conversions came from forty plus yards, including one of those from fifty plus. Anthony Pleasant led the team in sacks with eight while Rob Burnett was right behind him with 7.5 sacks. Eric Turner, who led the team the prior season in interceptions, failed to get a single one this season as he only played in exactly half of the games because of injury. Stevon Moore led the team with five interceptions, although three of them came in one game.

The 1995 season wasn't about stats or wins and losses. The season was about lost hope, failed dreams and aspirations and in the end, pure heartbreak for players, fans, and generations of human beings who counted on the Cleveland Browns every Sunday for three months in the fall and winter season to provide a positive distraction from their stressful and sometimes not so happy existence. The Cleveland Browns were more than just a local team in town; they were a part of life for so many that was suddenly taken from them by Modell. Those who were lucky enough to watch the Cleveland Browns during that magical ten year stretch from 1985 to 1995 will never forget the rollercoaster of emotions that they had experienced. The thrill of watching a young man named Bernie Kosar take the team on his shoulders and lead them to the playoffs in five consecutive seasons. The fans experienced the excitement of getting to the AFC Championship game three times in four seasons, only to have the agony of defeat in three heart-breaking losses. Despite their losses in big games, it didn't matter, because the fans and players still got to experience it. Now, suddenly and harshly, all of that was gone.

It was a small victory for the City of Cleveland and the fans, but they would have to live without a professional football team in their hometown for three more seasons. The Cleveland Browns became the Baltimore Ravens, and relocated to their new city packed with fans waiting to cheer them on. The cheers would not last long as they went 4–12 in their inaugural season, despite Vinny Testaverde playing well enough to make the Pro Bowl. Things didn't get much better the next season as the Baltimore Ravens finished 6–9–1. They did show promise, however, as linebacker Peter Boulware was named AFC Defensive Rookie Player of the Year after he finished with 11.5 sacks. The newly-formed Baltimore Ravens finished with a 6–10 record the following season, which led to the firing of head coach Ted Marchibroda. He was succeeded by Brian Billick, who had served as the offensive coordinator for the record-setting offense of the Minnesota Vikings the season before.

It was another bitter blow that owner Art Modell dealt Cleveland because the new ownership led by Al Lerner, coveted Brian Billick as their prime candidate to be their first head coach of the expansion team. They had to settle for the little known quarterbacks coach Chris Palmer instead. As the Browns struggled through their first season and finished with a 2–14 record, Billick led the Ravens to an improved 8–8 record.

In 2001, the Browns continued to struggle through their rebirth and finished with a 3–13 record. Meanwhile, Baltimore took off with one of the best defenses in NFL history. Ray Lewis was named Defensive Player of the Year. Two of his defensive teammates, Sam Adams and Rod Woodson, made the Pro Bowl. The Ravens' defense broke two notable NFL records as they held opposing teams to 165 total points, surpassing the 1985 Chicago Bears' mark of 198 points for a sixteen game season as well as surpassing the 1986 Chicago Bears' mark of 187 points for a sixteen game season, which at that time was the current NFL record. It also helped matters that rookie Jamal Lewis had a 1,364 yard rushing season. Despite the inconsistent quarterback play of both Tony Banks and Trent Dilfer, many media experts picked the Baltimore Ravens to be a real threat to make it far in the playoffs because of the strong defense they possessed. They carried a 12–4 record with them into the playoffs and were ready to shut down any offense they faced. The Baltimore Ravens dominated the Denver Broncos 21–3 in the divisional playoff to reach the second round against the high-powered Tennessee Titans. They beat the Titans 24–10 on the strength of two defensive touchdowns in the fourth quarter. An Al Del Greco field goal attempt was blocked and returned for a touchdown by Anthony Mitchell, followed by a Ray Lewis interception return for a touchdown. The Ravens' vaunted defense was willing the team on to victory after victory. The defense again flexed their muscle by crushing the Oakland Raiders in the AFC Championship game the following week, holding them without a single touchdown and winning 16–3.

The worst fears of Cleveland fans were coming true; the hated Art Modell had reached the Super Bowl while the new Browns had only won five games in two seasons. It was a nightmare for Browns fans as the man who cheated them was only one win away from becoming a Super Bowl champion owner. Once again, the Baltimore defense single-handedly took over a game and shut down the NFC Champion New York Giants during Super Bowl XXXV in Tampa Bay, Florida. They recorded four sacks and forced five turnovers, one of which was a Kerry Collins interception returned for a touchdown by Duane Starks. The Giants' only score was a Ron Dixon kickoff return for another touchdown. The Baltimore Ravens–the once Cleveland Browns–were now Super Bowl champions with a 34–7 win. The nightmare was complete as the worst had happened.

It was a dark time in Cleveland, Ohio for the fans as the team they had been loyal to and loved for fifty plus years had left them, and then within five years had won a Super Bowl championship. It was as if the evil Art Modell had been rewarded by the football gods for his treachery.

Epilogue

Growing up in the mid to late 1980s I quickly learned the Cleveland Browns ran the city of Cleveland. Browns fever was a fever that didn't have a cure. Everyone was a Browns fan and we lived and breathed the orange and brown. The Dog Pound was a religious cathedral like no others on Sunday, and most weekends Bernie Kosar was a preacher at the altar of Cleveland Municipal Stadium.

The first football game I ever watched was the double overtime game against the Jets in the 1986-1987 playoffs. I fondly recall, being only five years old but realizing that something extraordinary was going on in front of me on the TV. All of my uncles and even my Dad were screaming at the TV in disbelief as the high flying Browns were down ten in the late moments of the fourth quarter. Their jeers turned to cheers after a bone headed Mark Gastineau roughing the passer penalty, breathed new life into the Browns and the entire city by the shore. That one play led to a miraculous comeback only minutes later.

As the years went on, my love of Cleveland Browns football only grew as the team reached three AFC Championship games in four years. Despite not reaching the Super Bowl, they still owned the city and everyone continued to bleed orange and brown. Such was the hope that in the fall of 1995, after a solid 1994 season, the Browns were picked by many to win it all. Who really knew the nightmare the fans and city were soon in for instead?

Nearly twenty years later after the shocking move of the Browns, I decided to write this book. Not just to write it, but to relive it through the eyes, ears, and memories of the men who lived it. As I spoke with men such as Tommy Vardell, Felix Wright, Reggie Langhorne, Leroy Hoard, Michael Jackson, Brian Brennan, and many others, it was easy to see why the fans, myself included, gravitated towards these men the way we did. They loved the city, they loved the game, and they loved being a Cleveland Brown.

As I wrote the book, I sought two coveted interviews, Bernie Kosar and Bill Belichick. My quest for Bernie almost stalled numerous times despite constant efforts. I called everyone from his mailman to his milkman in search of a connection to Bernie. Finally after over a year, I had the chance to meet him. He was signing autographs at Summit Mall in Akron. I had already interviewed over eleven of his teammates and just wanted a few words with the popular quarterback. After paying twenty-five dollars for the twenty-five second encounter with old number 19, I was informed that anything longer in private with him would cost me ten thousand dollars. I quickly declined and went about my way.

Here was this man that Clevelanders still lined up in hour long lines just to get a glimpse at. A quarterback who never led the Browns to a championship, yet was still idolized more than the great Otto Graham. He was the only athlete in over five years of writing sports book to ever ask for money to do an interview. I told myself there was a reason it didn't happen for me with him, I didn't know it at the time, but this book was meant for something more.

That "something more" was on August 12, 2015 when I received a call from one of the greatest coaches in the history of the NFL, the one and only Mr. Bill Belichick. He took time out of his busy schedule in the middle of training camp, to place a call to me. He didn't want a dime, but he just wanted to help a young sports writer. People in Cleveland tend to speak of Belichick as some evil demon, when he was really a genius. The man built a great team in the Browns, it wasn't his fault that Modell took the money and the easy way out. Belichick was a visionary well before his time.

Speaking with him was one of the greatest thrills as a sportswriter, and always one of the best teaching moments I could have. For a man who has won four Super Bowls as a head coach and two as an assistant, he treated me as an equal and answered each question I had. I learned that he had tremendous respect for Paul Brown, and the history of the Browns. He had nothing but good things to say about his time in Cleveland and the fans. He was candid about Bernie and his diminishing skills that led to his departure. He didn't pull punches when it came to Modell, but he wasn't bitter. He was honest and giving. Born from a military background, he knew the importance of respect and discipline from a young age and has carried it with him the rest of his life.

Epilogue

Looking back on all of it now, twenty years after the fact, I ask you, who was really the hero and who was the villain? Clearly Modell will always be the villain and the players the heroes – still beloved to this day by some of the most passionate and loyal fans on earth. But when you dig deeper, it becomes clear, Kosar was done, and Belichick was a genius in breeding. It just took time for everything to shake out but the fact remains at the end of the day, the city and the fans are the most loyal in sports and deserve a winner. It was a decade of greatness, great plays, near misses and a heartbreaking betrayal. It truly has proven to be, the last great era in Cleveland Browns football.

GARY PUBLIC
3 9222 03163 9607